Go Programming Cookbook
Second Edition

Over 85 recipes to build modular, readable, and testable
Golang applications across various domains

Aaron Torres

BIRMINGHAM - MUMBAI

Go Programming Cookbook
Second Edition

Commissioning Editor: Amey Varangaonkar
Acquisition Editor: Shahnish Khan
Content Development Editor: Rohit Kumar Singh
Technical Editor: Romy Dias
Copy Editor: Safis Editing
Project Coordinator: Vaidehi Sawant
Proofreader: Safis Editing
Indexer: Tejal Daruwale Soni
Production Designer: Aparna Bhagat
Graphic Coordinator: Alishon Mendonsa

First published: June 2017
Second edition: July 2019

Production reference: 1190719

Published by Packt Publishing Ltd.
Livery Place
35 Livery Street
Birmingham
B3 2PB, UK.

ISBN 978-1-78980-098-2

www.packtpub.com

To my wife, Kaylee, and my daughters, Hazel, Oleander, and Aranea. Thank you for your patience, love, and support. This book would not be possible without you.

Packt.com

Subscribe to our online digital library for full access to over 7,000 books and videos, as well as industry leading tools to help you plan your personal development and advance your career. For more information, please visit our website.

Why subscribe?

- Spend less time learning and more time coding with practical eBooks and Videos from over 4,000 industry professionals

- Improve your learning with Skill Plans built especially for you

- Get a free eBook or video every month

- Fully searchable for easy access to vital information

- Copy and paste, print, and bookmark content

Did you know that Packt offers eBook versions of every book published, with PDF and ePub files available? You can upgrade to the eBook version at www.packt.com and as a print book customer, you are entitled to a discount on the eBook copy. Get in touch with us at customercare@packtpub.com for more details.

At www.packt.com, you can also read a collection of free technical articles, sign up for a range of free newsletters, and receive exclusive discounts and offers on Packt books and eBooks.

Contributors

About the author

Aaron Torres received his master's degree in computer science from the New Mexico Institute of Mining and Technology. He has worked on distributed systems in high-performance computing and in large-scale web and microservices applications. He currently leads a team of Go developers that refines and focuses on Go best practices with an emphasis on continuous delivery and automated testing.

Aaron has published a number of papers and has several patents in the area of storage and I/O. He is passionate about sharing his knowledge and ideas with others. He is also a huge fan of the Go language and open source for backend systems and development.

About the reviewer

Eduard Bondarenko is a software developer living in Kyiv, Ukraine. He started programming using BASIC on ZXSpectrum a long time ago. Later, he worked in the web development domain. He has used Ruby on Rails for over 8 years. Having used Ruby for a long time, he discovered Clojure in early 2009, and liked the simplicity of language. Besides Ruby and Clojure, he is interested in Go and ReasonML development.

> *I want to thank my wonderful wife, kids, and parents for all the love, support, and help they are giving to me.*

Packt is searching for authors like you

If you're interested in becoming an author for Packt, please visit `authors.packtpub.com` and apply today. We have worked with thousands of developers and tech professionals, just like you, to help them share their insight with the global tech community. You can make a general application, apply for a specific hot topic that we are recruiting an author for, or submit your own idea.

Table of Contents

Preface

Thank you for choosing this book! I hope it will be a handy reference for developers to quickly look up Go development patterns. It is meant to be a companion to other resources and a reference that will hopefully be useful long after reading it once. Each recipe in this book includes working, simple, and tested code that can be used as a reference or foundation for your own applications. The book covers a range of content from basic to advanced topics.

Who this book is for

This book is aimed for web developers, programmers, and enterprise developers. Basic knowledge of the Go language is assumed. Experience with backend application development is not necessary, but may help understand the motivation behind some of the recipes.

This book serves as a good reference for Go developers who are already proficient but need a quick reminder, example, or reference. With the open source repository, it should be possible to share these examples quickly with a team as well. If you are looking for quick solutions to common and not-so-common problems in Go programming, this book is for you.

What this book covers

Chapter 1, *I/O and Filesystems*, covers common Go I/O interfaces and explores working with filesystems. This includes temporary files, templates, and CSV files.

Chapter 2, *Command-Line Tools*, looks at taking in user input via the command line and explores processing common datatypes such as TOML, YAML, and JSON.

Chapter 3, *Data Conversion and Composition*, demonstrates methods for casting and converting between Go interfaces and data types. It also showcases encoding strategies and some functional design patterns for Go.

Chapter 4, *Error Handling in Go*, showcases strategies to handle errors in Go. It explores how to pass errors, handle them, and log them.

Chapter 5, *Network Programming*, demonstrates usage of various networking primitives such as UDP and TCP/IP. It also explores **Domain Name System** (**DNS**), working with raw email messages, and basic **Remote Procedure Call** (**RPC**).

Chapter 6, *All about Databases and Storage*, deals with various storage libraries for accessing data storage systems such as MySQL. It also demonstrates the use of interfaces to decouple your library from your application logic.

Chapter 7, *Web Clients and APIs*, implements Go HTTP client interfaces, REST clients, OAuth2 clients, decorating and extending clients, and gRPC.

Chapter 8, *Microservices for Applications in Go*, explores web handlers, passing in a state to a handler, validation of user input, and middleware.

Chapter 9, *Testing Go Code*, focuses on mocking, test coverage, fuzzing, behavior testing, and helpful testing tools.

Chapter 10, *Parallelism and Concurrency*, provides a reference for channels and async operations, atomic values, Go context objects, and channel state management.

Chapter 11, *Distributed Systems*, implements service discovery, Docker containerization, metrics and monitoring, and orchestration. It mostly deals with deployment and productionization of Go applications.

Chapter 12, *Reactive Programming and Data Streams*, explores reactive and dataflow applications, Kafka and distributed message queues, and GraphQL servers.

Chapter 13, *Serverless Programming*, deals with deploying Go applications without maintaining a server. This includes using Google App Engine, Firebase, Lambda, and logging in a serverless environment.

Chapter 14, *Performance Improvements, Tips, and Tricks*, deals with benchmarking, identifying bottlenecks, optimizing, and improving the HTTP performance for Go applications.

To get the most out of this book

To use this book, you'll need the following:

- A Unix programming environment.
- The latest version of the Go 1.x series.
- An internet connection.
- Permission to install additional packages as described in each chapter.
- Prerequisites and other installation requirements for each recipe are mentioned in the *Technical requirements* section of the respective chapters.

Download the example code files

You can download the example code files for this book from your account at www.packtpub.com. If you purchased this book elsewhere, you can visit www.packtpub.com/support and register to have the files emailed directly to you.

You can download the code files by following these steps:

1. Log in or register at www.packtpub.com.
2. Select the **SUPPORT** tab.
3. Click on **Code Downloads & Errata**.
4. Enter the name of the book in the **Search** box and follow the onscreen instructions.

Once the file is downloaded, please make sure that you unzip or extract the folder using the latest version of:

- WinRAR/7-Zip for Windows
- Zipeg/iZip/UnRarX for Mac
- 7-Zip/PeaZip for Linux

The code bundle for the book is also hosted on GitHub at https://github.com/PacktPublishing/Go-Programming-Cookbook-Second-Edition. We also have other code bundles from our rich catalog of books and videos available at https://github.com/PacktPublishing/. Check them out!

Code in Action

Visit the following link to check out videos of the code being run: `http://bit.ly/2J2uqQ3`

Conventions used

There are a number of text conventions used throughout this book.

`CodeInText`: Indicates code words in text, database table names, folder names, filenames, file extensions, pathnames, dummy URLs, user input, and Twitter handles. Here is an example: "The `bytes` library provides a number of convenient functions when working with data."

A block of code is set as follows:

```
b, err := ioutil.ReadAll(r)
if err != nil {
    return "", err
}
return string(b), nil
}
```

When we wish to draw your attention to a particular part of a code block, the relevant lines or items are set in bold:

```
package bytestrings
import (
        "bytes"
        "io"
        "io/ioutil"
)
```

Any command-line input or output is written as follows:

```
$ go mod init github.com/PacktPublishing/Go-Programming-Cookbook-Second-
Edition/Chapter01/interfaces
```

Bold: Indicates a new term, an important word, or words that you see onscreen. For example, words in menus or dialog boxes appear in the text like this. Here is an example: "Select **System info** from the **Administration** panel."

Warnings or important notes appear like this.

 Tips and tricks appear like this.

Sections

In this book, you will find several headings that appear frequently (*Getting ready, How to do it..., How it works..., There's more...,* and *See also*).

To give clear instructions on how to complete a recipe, use these sections as follows:

Getting ready

This section tells you what to expect in the recipe and describes how to set up any software or any preliminary settings required for the recipe.

How to do it...

This section contains the steps required to follow the recipe.

How it works...

This section usually consists of a detailed explanation of what happened in the previous section.

There's more...

This section consists of additional information about the recipe in order to make you more knowledgeable about the recipe.

See also

This section provides helpful links to other useful information for the recipe.

Get in touch

Feedback from our readers is always welcome.

General feedback: Email `feedback@packtpub.com` and mention the book title in the subject of your message. If you have questions about any aspect of this book, please email us at `questions@packtpub.com`.

Errata: Although we have taken every care to ensure the accuracy of our content, mistakes do happen. If you have found a mistake in this book, we would be grateful if you would report this to us. Please visit `www.packtpub.com/submit-errata`, selecting your book, clicking on the Errata Submission Form link, and entering the details.

Piracy: If you come across any illegal copies of our works in any form on the internet, we would be grateful if you would provide us with the location address or website name. Please contact us at `copyright@packtpub.com` with a link to the material.

If you are interested in becoming an author: If there is a topic that you have expertise in and you are interested in either writing or contributing to a book, please visit `authors.packtpub.com`.

Reviews

Please leave a review. Once you have read and used this book, why not leave a review on the site that you purchased it from? Potential readers can then see and use your unbiased opinion to make purchase decisions, we at Packt can understand what you think about our products, and our authors can see your feedback on their book. Thank you!

For more information about Packt, please visit `packtpub.com`.

1
I/O and Filesystems

Go provides excellent support for both basic and complex I/O. The recipes in this chapter will explore common Go interfaces that are used to deal with I/O and show you how to make use of them. The Go standard library frequently uses these interfaces, and they will be used by recipes throughout the book.

You'll learn how to work with data in memory and in the form of streams. You'll see examples of working with files, directories, and the CSV format. The temporary files recipe looks at a mechanism to work with files without the overhead of dealing with name collision and more. Lastly, we'll explore Go standard templates for both plain text and HTML.

These recipes should lay the foundation for the use of interfaces to represent and modify data, and should help you think about data in an abstract and flexible way.

In this chapter, the following recipes will be covered:

- Using the common I/O interfaces
- Using the bytes and strings packages
- Working with directories and files
- Working with the CSV format
- Working with temporary files
- Working with text/template and html/template

Technical requirements

In order to proceed with all the recipes in this chapter, configure your environment according to these steps:

1. Download and install Go 1.12.6 or greater on your operating system at `https://golang.org/doc/install`.

2. Open a Terminal or console application and create and navigate to a project directory, such as `~/projects/go-programming-cookbook`. All code will be run and modified from this directory.

3. Clone the latest code into `~/projects/go-programming-cookbook-original`, as shown in the following code. It is recommended that you work from that directory rather than typing the examples manually:

```
$ git clone git@github.com:PacktPublishing/Go-Programming-Cookbook-
Second-Edition.git go-programming-cookbook-original
```

Using the common I/O interfaces

The Go language provides a number of I/O interfaces that are used throughout the standard library. It is best practice to make use of these interfaces wherever possible rather than passing structures or other types directly. Two powerful interfaces we will explore in this recipe are the `io.Reader` and `io.Writer` interfaces. These interfaces are used throughout the standard library, and understanding how to use them will make you a better Go developer.

The `Reader` and `Writer` interfaces look like this:

```
type Reader interface {
        Read(p []byte) (n int, err error)
}

type Writer interface {
        Write(p []byte) (n int, err error)
}
```

Go also makes it easy to combine interfaces. For example, take a look at the following code:

```
type Seeker interface {
        Seek(offset int64, whence int) (int64, error)
}

type ReadSeeker interface {
        Reader
        Seeker
}
```

This recipe will also explore an `io` function called `Pipe()`, as shown in the following code:

```
func Pipe() (*PipeReader, *PipeWriter)
```

The remainder of this book will make use of these interfaces.

How to do it...

The following steps cover how to write and run your application:

1. From your Terminal or console application, create a new directory called `~/projects/go-programming-cookbook/chapter1/interfaces`.
2. Navigate to this directory.
3. Run the following command:

   $ go mod init github.com/PacktPublishing/Go-Programming-Cookbook-Second-Edition/chapter1/interfaces

   You should see a file called `go.mod` that contains the following:

   ```
   module github.com/PacktPublishing/Go-Programming-Cookbook-Second-
   Edition/chapter1/interfaces
   ```

4. Copy tests from `~/projects/go-programming-cookbook-original/chapter1/interfaces` or use this as an exercise to write some of your own code!

5. Create a file called `interfaces.go` with the following contents:

```go
package interfaces

import (
        "fmt"
        "io"
        "os"
)


// Copy copies data from in to out first directly,
// then using a buffer. It also writes to stdout
func Copy(in io.ReadSeeker, out io.Writer) error {
        // we write to out, but also Stdout
        w := io.MultiWriter(out, os.Stdout)
        // a standard copy, this can be dangerous if there's a
        // lot of data in in
        if _, err := io.Copy(w, in); err != nil {
            return err
        }
        in.Seek(0, 0)

        // buffered write using 64 byte chunks
        buf := make([]byte, 64)
        if _, err := io.CopyBuffer(w, in, buf); err != nil {
            return err
        }

        // lets print a new line
        fmt.Println()
        return nil
}
```

6. Create a file called `pipes.go` with the following contents:

```go
package interfaces

import (
        "io"
        "os"
)
// PipeExample helps give some more examples of using io
//interfaces
func PipeExample() error {
        // the pipe reader and pipe writer implement
        // io.Reader and io.Writer
        r, w := io.Pipe()
```

```
        // this needs to be run in a separate go routine
        // as it will block waiting for the reader
        // close at the end for cleanup
        go func() {
            // for now we'll write something basic,
            // this could also be used to encode json
            // base64 encode, etc.
            w.Write([]byte("test\n"))
            w.Close()
        }()
        if _, err := io.Copy(os.Stdout, r); err != nil {
            return err
        }
        return nil
    }
```

7. Create a new directory named `example` and navigate to it.

8. Create a `main.go` file with the following contents:

```
package main

import (
    "bytes"
    "fmt"
    "github.com/PacktPublishing/
    Go-Programming-Cookbook-Second-Edition/
    chapter1/bytestrings"
)
func main() {
        in := bytes.NewReader([]byte("example"))
        out := &bytes.Buffer{}
        fmt.Print("stdout on Copy = ")
        if err := interfaces.Copy(in, out); err != nil {
                panic(err)
        }
        fmt.Println("out bytes buffer =", out.String())
        fmt.Print("stdout on PipeExample = ")
        if err := interfaces.PipeExample(); err != nil {
                panic(err)
        }
    }
```

9. Run `go run ..`

10. You may also run the following:

```
$ go build
$ ./example
```

You should see the following output:

```
$ go run .
stdout on Copy = exampleexample
out bytes buffer = exampleexample
stdout on PipeExample = test
```

11. If you copied or wrote your own tests, go up one directory and run `go test`, and ensure that all tests pass.

How it works...

The `Copy()` function copies bytes between interfaces and treats that data like a stream. Thinking of data as streams has a lot of practical uses, especially when working with network traffic or filesystems. The `Copy()` function also creates a `MultiWriter` interface that combines two writer streams and writes to them twice using `ReadSeeker`. If a `Reader` interface was used instead, rather than seeing `exampleexample`, you would only see `example` despite copying to the `MultiWriter` interface twice. You can also use a buffered write if your stream is not fitted into the memory.

The `PipeReader` and `PipeWriter` structures implement the `io.Reader` and `io.Writer` interfaces. They're connected, creating an in-memory pipe. The primary purpose of a pipe is to read from a stream while simultaneously writing from the same stream to a different source. In essence, it combines the two streams into a pipe.

Go interfaces are a clean abstraction to wrap data that performs common operations. This is made apparent when doing I/O operations, and so the `io` package is a great resource for learning about interface composition. The `pipe` package is often underused, but provides great flexibility with thread safety when linking input and output streams.

Using the bytes and strings packages

The `bytes` and `strings` packages have a number of useful helpers to work with and convert the data from string to byte types, and vice versa. They allow the creation of buffers that work with a number of common I/O interfaces.

How to do it...

The following steps cover how to write and run your application:

1. From your Terminal or console application, create a new directory called
    `~/projects/go-programming-cookbook/chapter1/bytestrings`.
2. Navigate to this directory.
3. Run the following command:

    ```
    $ go mod init github.com/PacktPublishing/Go-Programming-Cookbook-
    Second-Edition/chapter1/bytestrings
    ```

    You should see a file called `go.mod` that contains the following content:

    ```
    module github.com/PacktPublishing/Go-Programming-Cookbook-Second-
    Edition/chapter1/bytestrings
    ```

4. Copy the tests from `~/projects/go-programming-cookbook-
    original/chapter1/bytestrings` or use this as an exercise to write some of
    your own code!
5. Create a file called `buffer.go` with the following contents:

    ```go
    package bytestrings
    import (
            "bytes"
            "io"
            "io/ioutil"
    )
    // Buffer demonstrates some tricks for initializing bytes
    //Buffers
    // These buffers implement an io.Reader interface
    func Buffer(rawString string) *bytes.Buffer {
            // we'll start with a string encoded into raw bytes
            rawBytes := []byte(rawString)
            // there are a number of ways to create a buffer from
            // the raw bytes or from the original string
            var b = new(bytes.Buffer)
            b.Write(rawBytes)
            // alternatively
            b = bytes.NewBuffer(rawBytes)
            // and avoiding the initial byte array altogether
            b = bytes.NewBufferString(rawString)
            return b
    }
    // ToString is an example of taking an io.Reader and consuming
    // it all, then returning a string
    ```

```
func toString(r io.Reader) (string, error) {
    b, err := ioutil.ReadAll(r)
    if err != nil {
        return "", err
    }
    return string(b), nil
}
```

6. Create a file called `bytes.go` with the following contents:

```
package bytestrings
import (
    "bufio"
    "bytes"
    "fmt"
)
// WorkWithBuffer will make use of the buffer created by the
// Buffer function
func WorkWithBuffer() error {
    rawString := "it's easy to encode unicode into a byte
                  array"

    b := Buffer(rawString)

    // we can quickly convert a buffer back into byes with
    // b.Bytes() or a string with b.String()
    fmt.Println(b.String())
    // because this is an io Reader we can make use of
    // generic io reader functions such as
    s, err := toString(b)
    if err != nil {
        return err
    }
    fmt.Println(s)

    // we can also take our bytes and create a bytes reader
    // these readers implement io.Reader, io.ReaderAt,
    // io.WriterTo, io.Seeker, io.ByteScanner, and
    // io.RuneScanner interfaces
    reader := bytes.NewReader([]byte(rawString))
    // we can also plug it into a scanner that allows
    // buffered reading and tokenzation
    scanner := bufio.NewScanner(reader)
    scanner.Split(bufio.ScanWords)
    // iterate over all of the scan events
    for scanner.Scan() {
        fmt.Print(scanner.Text())
    }
```

```
        return nil
}
```

7. Create a file called `string.go` with the following contents:

```go
package bytestrings
import (
        "fmt"
        "io"
        "os"
        "strings"
)
// SearchString shows a number of methods
// for searching a string
func SearchString() {
        s := "this is a test"
        // returns true because s contains
        // the word this
        fmt.Println(strings.Contains(s, "this"))
        // returns true because s contains the letter a
        // would also match if it contained b or c
        fmt.Println(strings.ContainsAny(s, "abc"))
        // returns true because s starts with this
        fmt.Println(strings.HasPrefix(s, "this"))
        // returns true because s ends with this
        fmt.Println(strings.HasSuffix(s, "test"))
        }
// ModifyString modifies a string in a number of ways
func ModifyString() {
        s := "simple string"
        // prints [simple string]
        fmt.Println(strings.Split(s, " "))
        // prints "Simple String"
        fmt.Println(strings.Title(s))
        // prints "simple string"; all trailing and
        // leading white space is removed
        s = " simple string "
        fmt.Println(strings.TrimSpace(s))
}
// StringReader demonstrates how to create
// an io.Reader interface quickly with a string
func StringReader() {
        s := "simple stringn"
        r := strings.NewReader(s)
        // prints s on Stdout
        io.Copy(os.Stdout, r)
}
```

8. Create a new directory named `example` and navigate to it.

9. Create a `main.go` file with the following contents:

```
package main
import "github.com/PacktPublishing/
        Go-Programming-Cookbook-Second-Edition/
        chapter1/bytestrings"
func main() {
        err := bytestrings.WorkWithBuffer()
        if err != nil {
                panic(err)
        }
        // each of these print to stdout
        bytestrings.SearchString()
        bytestrings.ModifyString()
        bytestrings.StringReader()
}
```

10. Run `go run ..`

11. You may also run the following:

```
$ go build
$ ./example
```

You should see the following output:

```
$ go run .
it's easy to encode unicode into a byte array ??
it's easy to encode unicode into a byte array ??
it'seasytoencodeunicodeintoabytearray??true
true
true
true
[simple string]
Simple String
simple string
simple string
```

12. If you copied or wrote your own tests, go up one directory and run `go test`, and ensure that all tests pass.

How it works...

The `bytes` library provides a number of convenience functions when working with data. A buffer, for example, is far more flexible than an array of bytes when working with stream-processing libraries or methods. Once you've created a buffer, it can be used to satisfy an `io.Reader` interface so that you can take advantage of `ioutil` functions to manipulate the data. For streaming applications, you'd probably want to use a buffer and a scanner. The `bufio` package comes in handy for these cases. Sometimes, using an array or slice is more appropriate for smaller datasets or when you have a lot of memory on your machine.

Go provides a lot of flexibility in converting data between interfaces when using these basic types—it's relatively simple to convert between strings and bytes. When working with strings, the `strings` package provides a number of convenience functions to work with, search, and manipulate strings. In some cases, a good regular expression may be appropriate, but most of the time, the `strings` and `strconv` packages are sufficient. The `strings` package allows you to make a string look like a title, split it into an array, or trim whitespace. It also provides a `Reader` interface of its own that can be used instead of the `bytes` package reader type.

Working with directories and files

Working with directories and files can be difficult when you switch between platforms (Windows and Linux, for example). Go provides cross-platform support to work with files and directories in the `os` and `ioutils` packages. We've already seen examples of `ioutils`, but now we'll explore how to use them in another way!

How to do it...

The following steps cover how to write and run your application:

1. From your Terminal or console application, create a new directory called `~/projects/go-programming-cookbook/chapter1/filedirs`.
2. Navigate to this directory.

3. Run the following command:

```
$ go mod init github.com/PacktPublishing/Go-Programming-Cookbook-
Second-Edition/chapter1/filedirs
```

You should see a file called `go.mod` that contains the following contents:

```
module github.com/PacktPublishing/Go-Programming-Cookbook-Second-
Edition/chapter1/filedirs
```

4. Copy tests from `~/projects/go-programming-cookbook-original/chapter1/filedirs` or use this as an exercise to write some of your own code!

5. Create a file called `dirs.go` with the following contents:

```go
package filedirs
import (
        "errors"
        "io"
        "os"
)
// Operate manipulates files and directories
func Operate() error {
        // this 0755 is similar to what you'd see with Chown
        // on a command line this will create a director
        // /tmp/example, you may also use an absolute path
        // instead of a relative one
        if err := os.Mkdir("example_dir", os.FileMode(0755));
        err != nil {
                return err
        }

        // go to the /tmp directory
        if err := os.Chdir("example_dir"); err != nil {
                return err
        }

        // f is a generic file object
        // it also implements multiple interfaces
        // and can be used as a reader or writer
        // if the correct bits are set when opening
        f, err := os.Create("test.txt")
        if err != nil {
                return err
        }

        // we write a known-length value to the file and
```

```
        // validate that it wrote correctly
        value := []byte("hellon")
        count, err := f.Write(value)
        if err != nil {
                return err
        }
        if count != len(value) {
                return errors.New("incorrect length returned
                from write")
        }

        if err := f.Close(); err != nil {
                return err
        }

        // read the file
        f, err = os.Open("test.txt")
        if err != nil {
                return err
        }
        io.Copy(os.Stdout, f)
        if err := f.Close(); err != nil {
                return err
        }
        // go to the /tmp directory
        if err := os.Chdir(".."); err != nil {
                return err
        }
        // cleanup, os.RemoveAll can be dangerous if you
        // point at the wrong directory, use user input,
        // and especially if you run as root
        if err := os.RemoveAll("example_dir"); err != nil {
                return err
        }
        return nil
}
```

6. Create a file called `files.go` with the following contents:

```
package filedirs
import (
        "bytes"
        "io"
        "os"
        "strings"
)
// Capitalizer opens a file, reads the contents,
// then writes those contents to a second file
```

```go
func Capitalizer(f1 *os.File, f2 *os.File) error {
    if _, err := f1.Seek(0, io.SeekStart); err != nil {
        return err
    }
    var tmp = new(bytes.Buffer)
    if _, err := io.Copy(tmp, f1); err != nil {
        return err
    }

    s := strings.ToUpper(tmp.String())
    if _, err := io.Copy(f2, strings.NewReader(s)); err !=
nil {
        return err
    }
    return nil
}
// CapitalizerExample creates two files, writes to one
//then calls Capitalizer() on both
func CapitalizerExample() error {
    f1, err := os.Create("file1.txt")
    if err != nil {
        return err
    }
    if _, err := f1.Write([]byte(`this file contains a
number of words and new lines`)); err != nil {
        return err
    }
    f2, err := os.Create("file2.txt")
    if err != nil {
        return err
    }
    if err := Capitalizer(f1, f2); err != nil {
        return err
    }
    if err := os.Remove("file1.txt"); err != nil {
        return err
    }
    if err := os.Remove("file2.txt"); err != nil {
        return err
    }
    return nil
}
```

7. Create a new directory named `example` and navigate to it.

8. Create a `main.go` file with the following contents:

```
package main
import "github.com/PacktPublishing/
        Go-Programming-Cookbook-Second-Edition/
        chapter1/filedirs"
func main() {
        if err := filedirs.Operate(); err != nil {
                panic(err)
        }
        if err := filedirs.CapitalizerExample(); err != nil {
                panic(err)
        }
}
```

9. Run `go run ..`

10. You may also run the following:

```
$ go build
$ ./example
```

You should see the following output:

```
$ go run .
hello
```

11. If you copied or wrote your own tests, go up one directory and run `go test`, and ensure that all tests pass.

How it works...

If you're familiar with files in Unix, the Go `os` library should feel very familiar. You can perform basically all common operations—`Stat` a file to collect attributes, collect a file with different permissions, and create and modify directories and files. In this recipe, we performed a number of manipulations to directories and files and then cleaned up after ourselves.

Working with file objects is very similar to working with in-memory streams. Files also provide a number of convenience functions directly, such as `Chown`, `Stat`, and `Truncate`. The easiest way to get comfortable with files is to make use of them. In all the previous recipes, we have to be careful to clean up after our programs.

Working with files is a very common operation when building backend applications. Files can be used for configuration, secret keys, as temporary storage, and more. Go wraps OS system calls using the `os` package and allows the same functions to operate regardless of whether you're using Windows or Unix.

Once your file is opened and stored in a `File` structure, it can easily be passed into a number of interfaces (we discussed these interfaces earlier). All the earlier examples can use `os.File` structures directly instead of buffers and in-memory data streams in order to operate on data stored on the disk . This may be useful for certain techniques, such as writing all logs to `stderr` and the file at the same time with a single write call.

Working with the CSV format

CSV is a common format that is used to manipulate data. It's common, for example, to import or export a CSV file into Excel. The Go `csv` package operates on data interfaces, and as a result, it's easy to write data to a buffer, `stdout`, a file, or a socket. The examples in this section will show some common ways to get data into and out of the CSV format.

How to do it...

These steps cover how to write and run your application:

1. From your Terminal or console application, create a new directory called `~/projects/go-programming-cookbook/chapter1/csvformat`.
2. Navigate to this directory.
3. Run the following command:

```
$ go mod init github.com/PacktPublishing/Go-Programming-Cookbook-
Second-Edition/chapter1/csvformat
```

You should see a file called `go.mod` that contains the following contents:

```
module github.com/PacktPublishing/Go-Programming-Cookbook-Second-
Edition/chapter1/csvformat
```

4. Copy the tests from ~/projects/go-programming-cookbook-
   original/chapter1/csvformat or use this as an exercise to write some of
   your own code!
5. Create a file called read_csv.go with the following contents:

```go
package csvformat
import (
        "bytes"
        "encoding/csv"
        "fmt"
        "io"
        "strconv"
)
// Movie will hold our parsed CSV
type Movie struct {
        Title string
        Director string
        Year int
}
// ReadCSV gives shows some examples of processing CSV
// that is passed in as an io.Reader
func ReadCSV(b io.Reader) ([]Movie, error) {
        r := csv.NewReader(b)
        // These are some optional configuration options
        r.Comma = ';'
        r.Comment = '-'
        var movies []Movie
        // grab and ignore the header for now
        // we may also want to use this for a dictionary key or
        // some other form of lookup
        _, err := r.Read()
        if err != nil && err != io.EOF {
                return nil, err
        }
        // loop until it's all processed
        for {
                record, err := r.Read()
                if err == io.EOF {
                        break
                } else if err != nil {
                        return nil, err
                }
                year, err := strconv.ParseInt(record[2], 10,
                64)
                if err != nil {
                        return nil, err
                }
```

```
                    m := Movie{record[0], record[1], int(year)}
                    movies = append(movies, m)
            }
            return movies, nil
    }
```

6. Add this additional function to `read_csv.go`, as follows:

```
    // AddMoviesFromText uses the CSV parser with a string
    func AddMoviesFromText() error {
            // this is an example of us taking a string, converting
            // it into a buffer, and reading it
            // with the csv package
            in := `
            - first our headers
            movie title;director;year released
            - then some data
            Guardians of the Galaxy Vol. 2;James Gunn;2017
            Star Wars: Episode VIII;Rian Johnson;2017
            `

            b := bytes.NewBufferString(in)
            m, err := ReadCSV(b)
            if err != nil {
                    return err
            }
            fmt.Printf("%#vn", m)
            return nil
    }
```

7. Create a file called `write_csv.go` with the following contents:

```
    package csvformat
    import (
            "bytes"
            "encoding/csv"
            "io"
            "os"
    )
    // A Book has an Author and Title
    type Book struct {
            Author string
            Title string
    }
    // Books is a named type for an array of books
    type Books []Book
    // ToCSV takes a set of Books and writes to an io.Writer
    // it returns any errors
    func (books *Books) ToCSV(w io.Writer) error {
```

```go
n := csv.NewWriter(w)
err := n.Write([]string{"Author", "Title"})
if err != nil {
        return err
}
for _, book := range *books {
        err := n.Write([]string{book.Author,
        book.Title})
        if err != nil {
                return err
        }
}
n.Flush()
return n.Error()
}
```

8. Add these additional functions to `write_csv.go`, as follows:

```go
// WriteCSVOutput initializes a set of books
// and writes the to os.Stdout
func WriteCSVOutput() error {
        b := Books{
                Book{
                        Author: "F Scott Fitzgerald",
                        Title: "The Great Gatsby",
                },
                Book{
                        Author: "J D Salinger",
                        Title: "The Catcher in the Rye",
                },
        }
        return b.ToCSV(os.Stdout)
}

// WriteCSVBuffer returns a buffer csv for
// a set of books
func WriteCSVBuffer() (*bytes.Buffer, error) {
        b := Books{
                Book{
                        Author: "F Scott Fitzgerald",
                        Title: "The Great Gatsby",
                },
                Book{
                        Author: "J D Salinger",
                        Title: "The Catcher in the Rye",
                },
        }
        w := &bytes.Buffer{}
```

```
            err := b.ToCSV(w)
            return w, err
    }
```

9. Create a new directory named `example` and navigate to it.

10. Create a `main.go` file with the following contents:

```
package main
import (
        "fmt"
        "github.com/PacktPublishing/
        Go-Programming-Cookbook-Second-Edition/
        chapter1/csvformat"
)
func main() {
        if err := csvformat.AddMoviesFromText(); err != nil {
                panic(err)
        }
        if err := csvformat.WriteCSVOutput(); err != nil {
                panic(err)
        }
        buffer, err := csvformat.WriteCSVBuffer()
        if err != nil {
                panic(err)
        }
        fmt.Println("Buffer = ", buffer.String())
}
```

11. Run `go run ..`

12. You may also run the following:

```
$ go build
$ ./example
```

You should see the following output:

```
$ go run .
[]csvformat.Movie{csvformat.Movie{Title:"Guardians of the
Galaxy Vol. 2", Director:"James Gunn", Year:2017},
csvformat.Movie{Title:"Star Wars: Episode VIII", Director:"Rian
Johnson", Year:2017}}
Author,Title
F Scott Fitzgerald,The Great Gatsby
J D Salinger,The Catcher in the Rye
Buffer = Author,Title
F Scott Fitzgerald,The Great Gatsby
J D Salinger,The Catcher in the Rye
```

13. If you copied or wrote your own tests, go up one directory and run `go test`, and ensure that all tests pass.

How it works...

In order to learn how to read a CSV format, we first represent our data as a structure. In Go, it's very useful to format data as a structure, as it makes things such as marshaling and encoding relatively simple. Our read example uses movies as our data type. The function takes an `io.Reader` interface that holds our CSV data as an input. This could be a file or a buffer. We then use that data to create and populate a `Movie` structure, including converting the year into an integer. We also add options to the CSV parser to use ; (semi-colon) as the separator and – (hyphen) as a comment line.

Next, we explore the same idea, but in reverse. Novels are represented with a title and an author. We initialize an array of novels and then write specific novels in the CSV format to an `io.Writer` interface. Once again, this can be a file, `stdout`, or a buffer.

The `CSV` package is an excellent example of why you'd want to think of data flows in Go as implementing common interfaces. It's easy to change the source and destination of our data with small one-line tweaks, and we can easily manipulate CSV data without using an excessive amount of memory or time. For example, it would be possible to read from a stream of data one record at a time and write to a separate stream in a modified format one record at a time. Doing this would not incur significant memory or processor usage.

Later, when we explore data pipelines and worker pools, you'll see how these ideas can be combined and how to handle these streams in parallel.

Working with temporary files

We've created and made use of files for a number of examples so far. We've also had to manually deal with cleanup, name collision, and more. Temporary files and directories are a quicker, simpler way to handle these cases.

How to do it...

The following steps cover how to write and run your application:

1. From your Terminal or console application, create a new directory called `~/projects/go-programming-cookbook/chapter1/tempfiles`.

2. Navigate to this directory.

3. Run the following command:

   ```
   $ go mod init github.com/PacktPublishing/Go-Programming-Cookbook-
   Second-Edition/chapter1/tempfiles
   ```

   You should see a file called `go.mod` that contains the following contents:

   ```
   module github.com/PacktPublishing/Go-Programming-Cookbook-Second-
   Edition/chapter1/tempfiles
   ```

4. Copy the tests from `~/projects/go-programming-cookbook-original/chapter1/tempfiles` or use this as an exercise to write some of your own code!

5. Create a file called `temp_files.go` with the following contents:

   ```go
   package tempfiles
   import (
           "fmt"
           "io/ioutil"
           "os"
   )
   // WorkWithTemp will give some basic patterns for working
   // with temporary files and directories
   func WorkWithTemp() error {
           // If you need a temporary place to store files with
           // the same name ie. template1-10.html a temp directory
           //  is a good way to approach it, the first argument
           // being blank means it will use create the directory
           // in the location returned by
           // os.TempDir()
           t, err := ioutil.TempDir("", "tmp")
           if err != nil {
                   return err
           }
           // This will delete everything inside the temp file
           // when this function exits if you want to do this
           //  later, be sure to return the directory name to the
           // calling function
           defer os.RemoveAll(t)
   ```

```
// the directory must exist to create the tempfile
// created. t is an *os.File object.
tf, err := ioutil.TempFile(t, "tmp")
if err != nil {
        return err
}
fmt.Println(tf.Name())
// normally we'd delete the temporary file here, but
// because we're placing it in a temp directory, it
// gets cleaned up by the earlier defer

return nil
}
```

6. Create a new directory named `example` and navigate to it.

7. Create a `main.go` file with the following contents:

```
package main
import "github.com/PacktPublishing/
        Go-Programming-Cookbook-Second-Edition/
        chapter1/tempfiles"
func main() {
        if err := tempfiles.WorkWithTemp(); err != nil {
                panic(err)
        }
}
```

8. Run `go run ..`

9. You may also run the following:

```
$ go build
$ ./example
```

You should see the following output (with a different path):

```
$ go run .
/var/folders/kd/ygq51_0d1xq11zk_c7htft900000gn/T
/tmp764135258/tmp588787953
```

10. If you copied or wrote your own tests, go up one directory and run `go test`, and ensure that all tests pass.

How it works...

Creating temporary files and directories can be done using the `ioutil` package. Although you must still delete the files yourself, using `RemoveAll` is the convention, and it will do this for you with only one extra line of code.

When writing tests, the use of temporary files is highly recommended. It's also useful for things such as build artifacts and more. The Go `ioutil` package will try and honor the OS preferences by default, but it allows you to fall back to other directories if required.

Working with text/template and html/template

Go provides rich support for templates. It is simple to nest templates, import functions, represent variables, iterate over data, and so on. If you need something more sophisticated than a CSV writer, templates may be a great solution.

Another application for templates is for websites. When we want to render server-side data to the client, templates fit the bill nicely. At first, Go templates can appear confusing. This section will explore working with templates, collecting templates inside of a directory, and working with HTML templates.

How to do it...

These steps cover how to write and run your application:

1. From your Terminal or console application, create a new directory called `~/projects/go-programming-cookbook/chapter1/templates`.
2. Navigate to this directory.

3. Run the following command:

```
$ go mod init github.com/PacktPublishing/Go-Programming-Cookbook-
Second-Edition/chapter1/templates
```

You should see a file called `go.mod` that contains the following content:

```
module github.com/PacktPublishing/Go-Programming-Cookbook-Second-
Edition/chapter1/templates
```

4. Copy the tests from `~/projects/go-programming-cookbook-original/chapter1/templates` or use this as an exercise to write some of your own code!

5. Create a file called `templates.go` with the following contents:

```go
package templates
import (
        "os"
        "strings"
        "text/template"
)
const sampleTemplate = `
        This template demonstrates printing a {{ .Variable |
        printf "%#v" }}.
        {{if .Condition}}
        If condition is set, we'll print this
        {{else}}
        Otherwise, we'll print this instead
        {{end}}
        Next we'll iterate over an array of strings:
        {{range $index, $item := .Items}}
        {{$index}}: {{$item}}
        {{end}}

        We can also easily import other functions like
        strings.Split
        then immediately used the array created as a result:
        {{ range $index, $item := split .Words ","}}
        {{$index}}: {{$item}}
        {{end}}
        Blocks are a way to embed templates into one another
        {{ block "block_example" .}}
        No Block defined!
        {{end}}
        {{/*
        This is a way
        to insert a multi-line comment
```

```
        */}}

const secondTemplate = `
        {{ define "block_example" }}
        {{.OtherVariable}}
        {{end}}
```

6. Add a function to the end of `templates.go`, as follows:

```go
// RunTemplate initializes a template and demonstrates a
// variety of template helper functions
func RunTemplate() error {
        data := struct {
                Condition bool
                Variable string
                Items []string
                Words string
                OtherVariable string
        }{
                Condition: true,
                Variable: "variable",
                Items: []string{"item1", "item2", "item3"},
                Words:
                "another_item1,another_item2,another_item3",
                OtherVariable: "I'm defined in a second
                template!",
        }
        funcmap := template.FuncMap{
                "split": strings.Split,
        }
        // these can also be chained
        t := template.New("example")
        t = t.Funcs(funcmap)
        // We could use Must instead to panic on error
        // template.Must(t.Parse(sampleTemplate))
        t, err := t.Parse(sampleTemplate)
        if err != nil {
                return err
        }
        // to demonstrate blocks we'll create another template
        // by cloning the first template, then parsing a second
        t2, err := t.Clone()
        if err != nil {
                return err
        }
        t2, err = t2.Parse(secondTemplate)
        if err != nil {
```

```
                return err
        }
        // write the template to stdout and populate it
        // with data
        err = t2.Execute(os.Stdout, &data)
        if err != nil {
                return err
        }
        return nil
}
```

7. Create a file called `template_files.go` with the following contents:

```go
package templates
import (
        "io/ioutil"
        "os"
        "path/filepath"
        "text/template"
)
//CreateTemplate will create a template file that contains data
func CreateTemplate(path string, data string) error {
        return ioutil.WriteFile(path, []byte(data),
        os.FileMode(0755))
}

// InitTemplates sets up templates from a directory
func InitTemplates() error {
        tempdir, err := ioutil.TempDir("", "temp")
        if err != nil {
                return err
        }
        defer os.RemoveAll(tempdir)
        err = CreateTemplate(filepath.Join(tempdir, "t1.tmpl"),
        `Template 1! {{ .Var1 }}
{{ block "template2" .}} {{end}}
{{ block "template3" .}} {{end}}
`)
        if err != nil {
                return err
        }
        err = CreateTemplate(filepath.Join(tempdir, "t2.tmpl"),
        `{{ define "template2"}}Template 2! {{ .Var2 }}{{end}}
`)
        if err != nil {
                return err
        }
```

```
        err = CreateTemplate(filepath.Join(tempdir, "t3.tmpl"),
        `{{ define "template3"}}Template 3! {{ .Var3 }}{{end}}
        `)
        if err != nil {
                return err
        }
        pattern := filepath.Join(tempdir, "*.tmpl")

        // Parse glob will combine all the files that match
        // glob and combine them into a single template
        tmpl, err := template.ParseGlob(pattern)
        if err != nil {
                return err
        }
        // Execute can also work with a map instead
        // of a struct
        tmpl.Execute(os.Stdout, map[string]string{
                "Var1": "Var1!!",
                "Var2": "Var2!!",
                "Var3": "Var3!!",
         })

         return nil
}
```

8. Create a file called `html_templates.go` with the following contents:

```
package templates
import (
        "fmt"
        "html/template"
        "os"
)
// HTMLDifferences highlights some of the differences
// between html/template and text/template
func HTMLDifferences() error {
        t := template.New("html")
        t, err := t.Parse("<h1>Hello! {{.Name}}</h1>n")
        if err != nil {
                return err
        }

        // html/template auto-escapes unsafe operations like
        // javascript injection this is contextually aware and
        // will behave differently
        // depending on where a variable is rendered
        err = t.Execute(os.Stdout, map[string]string{"Name": "
                <script>alert('Can you see me?')</script>"})
        if err != nil {
```

```
            return err
    }
    // you can also manually call the escapers
    fmt.Println(template.JSEscaper(`example
    <example@example.com>`))
    fmt.Println(template.HTMLEscaper(`example
    <example@example.com>`))
    fmt.Println(template.URLQueryEscaper(`example
    <example@example.com>`))
    return nil
}
```

9. Create a new directory named `example` and navigate to it.

10. Create a `main.go` file with the following contents:

```
package main
import "github.com/PacktPublishing/
        Go-Programming-Cookbook-Second-Edition/
        chapter1/templates"
func main() {
        if err := templates.RunTemplate(); err != nil {
                panic(err)
        }
        if err := templates.InitTemplates(); err != nil {
                panic(err)
        }
        if err := templates.HTMLDifferences(); err != nil {
                panic(err)
        }
}
```

11. Run `go run .`.

12. You may also run the following:

```
$ go build
$ ./example
```

You should see the following output (with a different path):

```
This template demonstrates printing a "variable".

If condition is set, we'll print this

Next we'll iterate over an array of strings:

    0: item1

    1: item2

    2: item3


We can also easily import other functions like strings.Split
then immediately used the array created as a result:

    0: another_item1

    1: another_item2

    2: another_item3


Blocks are a way to embed templates into one another

    I'm defined in a second template!




    Template 1! Var1!!
    Template 2! Var2!!
    Template 3! Var3!!
 <h1>Hello! &lt;script&gt;alert(&#39;Can you see me?&#39;)&lt;/script&gt;</h1>
example \x3Cexample@example.com\x3E
example &lt;example@example.com&gt;
example+%3Cexample%40example.com%3E
```

13. If you copied or wrote your own tests, go up one directory and run `go test`, and ensure that all tests pass.

How it works...

Go has two template packages: `text/template` and `html/template`. They share functionality and a variety of functions. In general, you should use `html/template` to render websites and `text/template` for everything else. Templates are plain text, but variables and functions can be used inside of curly brace blocks.

The template packages also provide convenience methods to work with files. The example that we used here creates a number of templates in a temporary directory and then reads them all with a single line of code.

The `html/template` package is a wrapper around the `text/template` package. All of the template examples work with the `html/template` package directly, using no modification and only changing the import statement. HTML templates provide the added benefit of context-aware safety; this prevents security breaches such as JavaScript injection.

The template packages provide what you'd expect from a modern template library. It's easy to combine templates, add application logic, and ensure safety when emitting results to HTML and JavaScript.

2
Command-Line Tools

Command-line applications are among the easiest ways to handle user input and output. This chapter will focus on command-line-based interactions, such as command-line arguments, configuration, and environment variables. We will conclude with a library for coloring text output in Unix and Bash for Windows.

With the recipes in this chapter, you should be equipped to handle expected and unexpected user input. The *Catching and handling signals* recipe is an example of cases where users may send unexpected signals to your application, and the pipes recipe is a good alternative to taking user inputs compared to flags or command-line arguments.

The ANSI color recipe will hopefully provide some examples of cleaning up output to users. For example, in logging, being able to color text based on its purpose can sometimes make large blocks of text significantly clearer.

In this chapter, we will cover the following recipes:

- Using command-line flags
- Using command-line arguments
- Reading and setting environment variables
- Configuration using TOML, YAML, and JSON
- Working with Unix pipes
- Catching and handling signals
- An ANSI coloring application

Technical requirements

In order to proceed with all the recipes in this chapter, configure your environment according to these steps:

1. Download and install Go 1.12.6 or greater on your operating system at `https://golang.org/doc/install`.

2. Open a Terminal or console application and create and navigate to a project directory such as `~/projects/go-programming-cookbook`. All of our code will be run and modified from this directory.

3. Clone the latest code into `~/projects/go-programming-cookbook-original` and work from that directory rather than typing the examples manually:

```
$ git clone git@github.com:PacktPublishing/Go-Programming-Cookbook-
Second-Edition.git go-programming-cookbook-original
```

Using command-line flags

The `flag` package makes it simple to add command-line flag arguments to a Go application. It has a few shortcomings—you tend to duplicate a lot of code in order to add shorthand versions of flags, and they're ordered alphabetically from the help prompt. There are a number of third-party libraries that attempt to address these shortcomings, but this chapter will focus on the standard library version and not on those libraries.

How to do it...

These steps cover writing and running your application:

1. From your Terminal or console application, create a new directory called `~/projects/go-programming-cookbook/chapter2/flags`.

2. Navigate to this directory.

3. Run the following command:

```
$ go mod init github.com/PacktPublishing/Go-Programming-Cookbook-
Second-Edition/chapter2/flags
```

You should see a file called `go.mod` that contains the following:

```
module github.com/PacktPublishing/Go-Programming-Cookbook-Second-
Edition/chapter2/flags
```

4. Copy tests from `~/projects/go-programming-cookbook-original/chapter2/flags`, or use this as an opportunity to write some of your own code!

5. Create a file called `flags.go` with the following contents:

```go
package main

import (
    "flag"
    "fmt"
)

// Config will be the holder for our flags
type Config struct {
    subject string
    isAwesome bool
    howAwesome int
    countTheWays CountTheWays
}

// Setup initializes a config from flags that
// are passed in
func (c *Config) Setup() {
    // you can set a flag directly like so:
    // var someVar = flag.String("flag_name", "default_val",
    // "description")
    // but in practice putting it in a struct is generally
    // better longhand
    flag.StringVar(&c.subject, "subject", "", "subject is a
    string, it defaults to empty")
    // shorthand
    flag.StringVar(&c.subject, "s", "", "subject is a string,
    it defaults to empty (shorthand)")

    flag.BoolVar(&c.isAwesome, "isawesome", false, "is it
    awesome or what?")
    flag.IntVar(&c.howAwesome, "howawesome", 10, "how awesome
    out of 10?")

    // custom variable type
    flag.Var(&c.countTheWays, "c", "comma separated list of
    integers")
```

```
}

// GetMessage uses all of the internal
// config vars and returns a sentence
func (c *Config) GetMessage() string {
    msg := c.subject
    if c.isAwesome {
        msg += " is awesome"
    } else {
        msg += " is NOT awesome"
    }

    msg = fmt.Sprintf("%s with a certainty of %d out of 10. Let
    me count the ways %s", msg, c.howAwesome,
    c.countTheWays.String())
    return msg
}
```

6. Create a file called `custom.go` with the following contents:

```
package main

import (
    "fmt"
    "strconv"
    "strings"
)

// CountTheWays is a custom type that
// we'll read a flag into
type CountTheWays []int

func (c *CountTheWays) String() string {
    result := ""
    for _, v := range *c {
        if len(result) > 0 {
            result += " ... "
        }
        result += fmt.Sprint(v)
    }
    return result
}

// Set will be used by the flag package
func (c *CountTheWays) Set(value string) error {
    values := strings.Split(value, ",")

    for _, v := range values {
```

```
            i, err := strconv.Atoi(v)
            if err != nil {
                return err
            }
            *c = append(*c, i)
        }

        return nil
    }
```

7. Run the following command:

```
$ go mod tidy
```

8. Create a file called main.go with the following contents:

```
package main

import (
    "flag"
    "fmt"
)

func main() {
    // initialize our setup
    c := Config{}
    c.Setup()

    // generally call this from main
    flag.Parse()

    fmt.Println(c.GetMessage())
}
```

9. Run the following commands on the command line:

```
$ go build
$ ./flags -h
```

10. Try these and some other arguments; you should see the following output:

```
$ go build
$ ./flags -h
Usage of ./flags:
-c value
comma separated list of integers
-howawesome int
how awesome out of 10? (default 10)
```

```
-isawesome
is it awesome or what? (default false)
-s string
subject is a string, it defaults to empty (shorthand)
-subject string
subject is a string, it defaults to empty
$ ./flags -s Go -isawesome -howawesome 10 -c 1,2,3
Go is awesome with a certainty of 10 out of 10. Let me count
the ways 1 ... 2 ... 3
```

11. If you copied or wrote your own tests, go up one directory and run `go test`, and ensure that all the tests pass.

How it works...

This recipe attempts to demonstrate most of the common usages of the `flag` package. It shows custom variable types, a variety of built-in variables, shorthand flags, and writing all flags to a common structure. This is the first recipe to require a main function, as the main usage of flag (`flag.Parse()`) should be called from main. As a result, the normal example directory is omitted.

The example usage of this application shows that you get `-h` automatically to get a list of flags that are included. Some other things to note are Boolean flags that are invoked without arguments, and that the flag order doesn't matter.

The `flag` package is a quick way to structure input for command-line applications and provide a flexible means of specifying upfront user input for things such as setting up log levels or the verbosity of an application. In the *Using command-line arguments* recipe, we'll explore flag sets and switch between them using arguments.

Using command-line arguments

The flags from the previous recipe are a type of command-line argument. This chapter will expand on other uses for these arguments by constructing a command that supports nested subcommands. This will demonstrate flagsets and also use positional arguments that are passed into your application.

Like the previous recipe, this one requires a main function to run. There are a number of third-party packages that deal with complex nested arguments and flags, but we'll investigate how to do this using only the standard library.

How to do it...

These steps cover writing and running your application:

1. From your Terminal or console application, create a new directory called `~/projects/go-programming-cookbook/chapter2/cmdargs`.
2. Navigate to this directory.
3. Run the following command:

   $ go mod init github.com/PacktPublishing/Go-Programming-Cookbook-Second-Edition/chapter2/cmdargs

   You should see a file called `go.mod` that contains the following:

   ```
   module github.com/PacktPublishing/Go-Programming-Cookbook-Second-
   Edition/chapter2/cmdargs
   ```

4. Copy tests from `~/projects/go-programming-cookbook-original/chapter2/cmdargs`, or use this as an opportunity to write some of your own code!
5. Create a file called `cmdargs.go` with the following contents:

   ```
   package main
   import (
       "flag"
       "fmt"
       "os"
   )
   const version = "1.0.0"
   const usage = `Usage:
   %s [command]
   Commands:
       Greet
       Version
   `
   const greetUsage = `Usage:
   %s greet name [flag]
   Positional Arguments:
       name
           the name to greet
   Flags:
   `
   // MenuConf holds all the levels
   // for a nested cmd line argument
   type MenuConf struct {
   ```

```
        Goodbye bool
}
// SetupMenu initializes the base flags
func (m *MenuConf) SetupMenu() *flag.FlagSet {
    menu := flag.NewFlagSet("menu", flag.ExitOnError)
    menu.Usage = func() {
        fmt.Printf(usage, os.Args[0])
        menu.PrintDefaults()
    }
    return menu
}
// GetSubMenu return a flag set for a submenu
func (m *MenuConf) GetSubMenu() *flag.FlagSet {
    submenu := flag.NewFlagSet("submenu", flag.ExitOnError)
    submenu.BoolVar(&m.Goodbye, "goodbye", false, "Say goodbye
    instead of hello")
    submenu.Usage = func() {
        fmt.Printf(greetUsage, os.Args[0])
        submenu.PrintDefaults()
    }
    return submenu
}
// Greet will be invoked by the greet command
func (m *MenuConf) Greet(name string) {
    if m.Goodbye {
        fmt.Println("Goodbye " + name + "!")
    } else {
        fmt.Println("Hello " + name + "!")
    }
}
// Version prints the current version that is
// stored as a const
func (m *MenuConf) Version() {
    fmt.Println("Version: " + version)
}
```

6. Create a file called `main.go` with the following contents:

```
package main

import (
  "fmt"
  "os"
  "strings"
)

func main() {
  c := MenuConf{}
```

```go
    menu := c.SetupMenu()

  if err := menu.Parse(os.Args[1:]); err != nil {
    fmt.Printf("Error parsing params %s, error: %v",
os.Args[1:], err)
    return
  }

  // we use arguments to switch between commands
  // flags are also an argument
  if len(os.Args) > 1 {
    // we don't care about case
    switch strings.ToLower(os.Args[1]) {
    case "version":
      c.Version()
    case "greet":
      f := c.GetSubMenu()
      if len(os.Args) < 3 {
        f.Usage()
        return
      }
      if len(os.Args) > 3 {
        if err := f.Parse(os.Args[3:]); err != nil {
          fmt.Fprintf(os.Stderr, "Error parsing params %s,
error: %v", os.Args[3:], err)
          return
        }

      }
      c.Greet(os.Args[2])

    default:
      fmt.Println("Invalid command")
      menu.Usage()
      return
    }
  } else {
    menu.Usage()
    return
  }
}
```

7. Run `go build`.

8. Run the following commands and try a few other combinations of arguments:

```
$ ./cmdargs -h
Usage:

./cmdargs [command]

Commands:
Greet
Version

$./cmdargs version
Version: 1.0.0

$./cmdargs greet
Usage:

./cmdargs greet name [flag]

Positional Arguments:
 name
 the name to greet

Flags:
 -goodbye
 Say goodbye instead of hello

$./cmdargs greet reader
Hello reader!

$./cmdargs greet reader -goodbye
Goodbye reader!
```

9. If you copied or wrote your own tests, go up one directory and run `go test`, and ensure that all the tests pass.

How it works...

Flagsets can be used to set up independent lists of expected arguments, usage strings, and more. The developer is required to perform validation on a number of arguments, parsing in the right subset of arguments to commands and defining usage strings. This can be error-prone and requires a lot of iteration to get completely right.

The `flag` package makes parsing arguments much easier and includes convenience methods to get the number of flags, arguments, and more. This recipe demonstrates basic ways to construct a complex command-line application using arguments, including a package-level configuration, required positional arguments, multi-level command usage, and how to split these things into multiple files or packages if required.

Reading and setting environment variables

Environment variables are another way that you can pass state into an application beyond reading data in from a file or passing it explicitly over the command line. This recipe will explore some very basic getting and setting of environment variables and then work with the highly useful third-party library `envconfig` (`https://github.com/kelseyhightower/envconfig`).

We'll build an application that can read a `config` file via JSON or through environment variables. The next recipe will explore alternative formats, including TOML and YAML.

How to do it...

These steps cover writing and running your application:

1. From your Terminal or console application, create a new directory called `~/projects/go-programming-cookbook/chapter2/envvar`.
2. Navigate to this directory.
3. Run the following command:

    ```
    $ go mod init github.com/PacktPublishing/Go-Programming-Cookbook-
    Second-Edition/chapter2/envvar
    ```

    You should see a file called `go.mod` that contains the following:

    ```
    module github.com/PacktPublishing/Go-Programming-Cookbook-Second-
    Edition/chapter2/envvar
    ```

4. Copy tests from ~/projects/go-programming-cookbook-original/chapter2/envvar, or use this as an opportunity to write some of your own code!

5. Create a file called config.go with the following contents:

```go
package envvar

import (
    "encoding/json"
    "os"

    "github.com/kelseyhightower/envconfig"
    "github.com/pkg/errors"
)

// LoadConfig will load files optionally from the json file
// stored at path, then will override those values based on the
// envconfig struct tags. The envPrefix is how we prefix our
// environment variables.
func LoadConfig(path, envPrefix string, config interface{})
error {
    if path != "" {
        err := LoadFile(path, config)
        if err != nil {
            return errors.Wrap(err, "error loading config from
            file")
        }
    }
    err := envconfig.Process(envPrefix, config)
    return errors.Wrap(err, "error loading config from env")
}

// LoadFile unmarshalls a json file into a config struct
func LoadFile(path string, config interface{}) error {
    configFile, err := os.Open(path)
    if err != nil {
        return errors.Wrap(err, "failed to read config file")
    }
    defer configFile.Close()

    decoder := json.NewDecoder(configFile)
    if err = decoder.Decode(config); err != nil {
        return errors.Wrap(err, "failed to decode config file")
    }
    return nil
}
```

6. Create a new directory named `example` and navigate to it.

7. Create a `main.go` file with the following contents:

```go
package main

import (
    "bytes"
    "fmt"
    "io/ioutil"
    "os"

    "github.com/PacktPublishing/
    Go-Programming-Cookbook-Second-Edition/
    chapter2/envvar"
)

// Config will hold the config we
// capture from a json file and env vars
type Config struct {
    Version string `json:"version" required:"true"`
    IsSafe bool `json:"is_safe" default:"true"`
    Secret string `json:"secret"`
}

func main() {
    var err error

    // create a temporary file to hold
    // an example json file
    tf, err := ioutil.TempFile("", "tmp")
    if err != nil {
        panic(err)
    }
    defer tf.Close()
    defer os.Remove(tf.Name())

    // create a json file to hold
    // our secrets
    secrets := `{
        "secret": "so so secret"
    }`

    if _, err =
    tf.Write(bytes.NewBufferString(secrets).Bytes());
    err != nil {
        panic(err)
    }
```

```
        // We can easily set environment variables
        // as needed
        if err = os.Setenv("EXAMPLE_VERSION", "1.0.0"); err != nil
        {
            panic(err)
        }
        if err = os.Setenv("EXAMPLE_ISSAFE", "false"); err != nil {
            panic(err)
        }

        c := Config{}
        if err = envvar.LoadConfig(tf.Name(), "EXAMPLE", &c);
        err != nil {
            panic(err)
        }

        fmt.Println("secrets file contains =", secrets)

        // We can also read them
        fmt.Println("EXAMPLE_VERSION =",
        os.Getenv("EXAMPLE_VERSION"))
        fmt.Println("EXAMPLE_ISSAFE =",
        os.Getenv("EXAMPLE_ISSAFE"))

        // The final config is a mix of json and environment
        // variables
        fmt.Printf("Final Config: %#v\n", c)
    }
```

8. Run `go run main.go`.

9. You may also run the following commands:

   ```
   go build
   ./example
   ```

10. You should see the following output:

    ```
    $ go run main.go
    secrets file contains = {
    "secret": "so so secret"
    }
    EXAMPLE_VERSION = 1.0.0
    EXAMPLE_ISSAFE = false
    Final Config: main.Config{Version:"1.0.0", IsSafe:false,
    Secret:"so so secret"}
    ```

11. The `go.mod` file may be updated, and the `go.sum` file should now be present in the top-level recipe directory.

12. If you copied or wrote your own tests, go up one directory and run `go test`, and ensure that all the tests pass.

How it works...

Reading and writing environment variables is pretty simple with the `os` package. The `envconfig` third-party library this recipe uses is a clever way to capture environment variables and specify certain requirements using `struct` tags.

The `LoadConfig` function is a flexible way to pull in configuration information from a variety of sources without a lot of overhead or too many extra dependencies. It would be simple to convert the primary `config` into another format aside from JSON or just always use environment variables as well.

Also, note the use of errors. We wrapped errors throughout the code in this recipe so that we can annotate errors without losing the original error's information. There will be more details on this in `Chapter 4`, *Error Handling in Go*.

Configuration using TOML, YAML, and JSON

There are many configuration formats that Go, with the use of third-party libraries, supports. Three of the most popular data formats are TOML, YAML, and JSON. Go can support JSON out of the box, and the others have clues on how to marshal/unmarshal or encode/decode data for these formats. These formats have many benefits beyond configuration, but this chapter will largely focus on converting a Go structure in the form of a configuration structure. This recipe will explore basic input and output using these formats.

These formats also provide an interface by which Go and applications written in other languages can share the same configuration. There are also a number of tools that deal with these formats and simplify working with them.

How to do it...

These steps cover writing and running your application:

1. From your Terminal or console application, create a new directory
   called `~/projects/go-programming-cookbook/chapter2/confformat`.
2. Navigate to this directory.
3. Run the following command:

   ```
   $ go mod init github.com/PacktPublishing/Go-Programming-Cookbook-
   Second-Edition/chapter2/confformat
   ```

   You should see a file called `go.mod` that contains the following:

   ```
   module github.com/PacktPublishing/Go-Programming-Cookbook-Second-
   Edition/chapter2/confformat
   ```

4. Copy tests from `~/projects/go-programming-cookbook-
   original/chapter2/confformat`, or use this as an opportunity to write some
   of your own code!
5. Create a file called `toml.go` with the following contents:

   ```go
   package confformat

   import (
       "bytes"

       "github.com/BurntSushi/toml"
   )

   // TOMLData is our common data struct
   // with TOML struct tags
   type TOMLData struct {
       Name string `toml:"name"`
       Age int `toml:"age"`
   }

   // ToTOML dumps the TOMLData struct to
   // a TOML format bytes.Buffer
   func (t *TOMLData) ToTOML() (*bytes.Buffer, error) {
       b := &bytes.Buffer{}
       encoder := toml.NewEncoder(b)
       if err := encoder.Encode(t); err != nil {
           return nil, err
       }
       return b, nil
   ```

```
}

// Decode will decode into TOMLData
func (t *TOMLData) Decode(data []byte) (toml.MetaData, error) {
    return toml.Decode(string(data), t)
}
```

6. Create a file called `yaml.go` with the following contents:

```
package confformat

import (
    "bytes"

    "github.com/go-yaml/yaml"
)

// YAMLData is our common data struct
// with YAML struct tags
type YAMLData struct {
    Name string `yaml:"name"`
    Age int `yaml:"age"`
}

// ToYAML dumps the YAMLData struct to
// a YAML format bytes.Buffer
func (t *YAMLData) ToYAML() (*bytes.Buffer, error) {
    d, err := yaml.Marshal(t)
    if err != nil {
        return nil, err
    }

    b := bytes.NewBuffer(d)

    return b, nil
}

// Decode will decode into TOMLData
func (t *YAMLData) Decode(data []byte) error {
    return yaml.Unmarshal(data, t)
}
```

7. Create a file called `json.go` with the following contents:

```go
package confformat

import (
    "bytes"
    "encoding/json"
    "fmt"
)

// JSONData is our common data struct
// with JSON struct tags
type JSONData struct {
    Name string `json:"name"`
    Age int `json:"age"`
}

// ToJSON dumps the JSONData struct to
// a JSON format bytes.Buffer
func (t *JSONData) ToJSON() (*bytes.Buffer, error) {
    d, err := json.Marshal(t)
    if err != nil {
        return nil, err
    }

    b := bytes.NewBuffer(d)

    return b, nil
}

// Decode will decode into JSONData
func (t *JSONData) Decode(data []byte) error {
    return json.Unmarshal(data, t)
}

// OtherJSONExamples shows ways to use types
// beyond structs and other useful functions
func OtherJSONExamples() error {
    res := make(map[string]string)
    err := json.Unmarshal([]byte(`{"key": "value"}`), &res)
    if err != nil {
        return err
    }

    fmt.Println("We can unmarshal into a map instead of a
    struct:", res)

    b := bytes.NewReader([]byte(`{"key2": "value2"}`))
```

```
decoder := json.NewDecoder(b)

if err := decoder.Decode(&res); err != nil {
    return err
}

fmt.Println("we can also use decoders/encoders to work with
streams:", res)

return nil
}
```

8. Create a file called `marshal.go` with the following contents:

```
package confformat

import "fmt"

// MarshalAll takes some data stored in structs
// and converts them to the various data formats
func MarshalAll() error {
    t := TOMLData{
        Name: "Name1",
        Age: 20,
    }

    j := JSONData{
        Name: "Name2",
        Age: 30,
    }

    y := YAMLData{
        Name: "Name3",
        Age: 40,
    }

    tomlRes, err := t.ToTOML()
    if err != nil {
        return err
    }

    fmt.Println("TOML Marshal =", tomlRes.String())

    jsonRes, err := j.ToJSON()
    if err != nil {
        return err
    }
```

```
    fmt.Println("JSON Marshal=", jsonRes.String())

    yamlRes, err := y.ToYAML()
    if err != nil {
        return err
    }

    fmt.Println("YAML Marshal =", yamlRes.String())
        return nil
}
```

9. Create a file called `unmarshal.go` with the following contents:

```
package confformat
import "fmt"
const (
    exampleTOML = `name="Example1"
age=99
    `
    exampleJSON = `{"name":"Example2","age":98}`
    exampleYAML = `name: Example3
age: 97
    `
)
// UnmarshalAll takes data in various formats
// and converts them into structs
func UnmarshalAll() error {
    t := TOMLData{}
    j := JSONData{}
    y := YAMLData{}
    if _, err := t.Decode([]byte(exampleTOML)); err != nil {
        return err
    }
    fmt.Println("TOML Unmarshal =", t)

    if err := j.Decode([]byte(exampleJSON)); err != nil {
        return err
    }
    fmt.Println("JSON Unmarshal =", j)

    if err := y.Decode([]byte(exampleYAML)); err != nil {
        return err
    }
    fmt.Println("Yaml Unmarshal =", y)
        return nil
}
```

10. Create a new directory named `example` and navigate to it.

11. Create a `main.go` file with the following contents:

```
package main

import "github.com/PacktPublishing/
        Go-Programming-Cookbook-Second-Edition/
        chapter2/confformat"

func main() {
    if err := confformat.MarshalAll(); err != nil {
        panic(err)
    }

    if err := confformat.UnmarshalAll(); err != nil {
        panic(err)
    }

    if err := confformat.OtherJSONExamples(); err != nil {
        panic(err)
    }
}
```

12. Run `go run main.go`.

13. You may also run the following commands:

```
$ go build
$ ./example
```

14. You should see the following output:

```
$ go run main.go
TOML Marshal = name = "Name1"
age = 20

JSON Marshal= {"name":"Name2","age":30}
YAML Marshal = name: Name3
age: 40

TOML Unmarshal = {Example1 99}
JSON Unmarshal = {Example2 98}
Yaml Unmarshal = {Example3 97}
We can unmarshal into a map instead of a struct: map[key:value]
we can also use decoders/encoders to work with streams:
map[key:value key2:value2]
```

15. The `go.mod` file may be updated and the `go.sum` file should now be present in the top-level recipe directory.

16. If you copied or wrote your own tests, go up one directory and run `go test`. Ensure that all the tests pass.

How it works...

This recipe provided us with examples of how to use the TOML, YAML, and JSON parsers to both write raw data to a go structure and read data out of it and into the corresponding format. Like the recipes in `Chapter 1`, *I/O and Filesystems*, we saw how common it is to quickly switch between `[]byte`, `string`, `bytes.Buffer`, and other I/O interfaces.

The `encoding/json` package is the most comprehensive in providing encoding, marshaling, and other methods to work with the JSON format. We abstracted these away with our `ToFormat` functions, and it would be very simple to attach multiple methods such as this so that we could use a single structure that can quickly be converted into or from any of these types.

This recipe also touched upon structure tags and their use. The previous chapter also made use of these, and they're a common way to give hints to packages and libraries about how to treat data contained within a structure.

Working with Unix pipes

Unix pipes are useful when we are passing the output of one program to the input of another. For example, take a look at the following code:

```
$ echo "test case" | wc -l
    1
```

In a Go application, the left-hand side of the pipe can be read in using `os.Stdin`, which acts like a file descriptor. To demonstrate this, this recipe will take an input on the left-hand side of a pipe and return a list of words and their number of occurrences. These words will be tokenized on white space.

How to do it...

These steps cover writing and running your application:

1. From your Terminal or console application, create a new directory called `~/projects/go-programming-cookbook/chapter2/pipes`.
2. Navigate to this directory.
3. Run the following command:

   ```
   $ go mod init github.com/PacktPublishing/Go-Programming-Cookbook-Second-Edition/chapter2/pipes
   ```

   You should see a file called `go.mod` that contains the following:

   ```
   module github.com/PacktPublishing/Go-Programming-Cookbook-Second-Edition/chapter2/pipes
   ```

4. Copy tests from `~/projects/go-programming-cookbook-original/chapter2/pipes`, or use this as an opportunity to write some of your own code!
5. Create a file called `pipes.go` with the following contents:

   ```go
   package main

   import (
       "bufio"
       "fmt"
       "io"
       "os"
   )

   // WordCount takes a file and returns a map
   // with each word as a key and it's number of
   // appearances as a value
   func WordCount(f io.Reader) map[string]int {
       result := make(map[string]int)

       // make a scanner to work on the file
       // io.Reader interface
       scanner := bufio.NewScanner(f)
       scanner.Split(bufio.ScanWords)

       for scanner.Scan() {
           result[scanner.Text()]++
       }
   ```

```
        if err := scanner.Err(); err != nil {
            fmt.Fprintln(os.Stderr, "reading input:", err)
        }

        return result
    }

func main() {
    fmt.Printf("string: number_of_occurrences\n\n")
    for key, value := range WordCount(os.Stdin) {
        fmt.Printf("%s: %d\n", key, value)
    }
}
```

6. Run `echo "some string" | go run pipes.go`.

7. You may also run the following commands:

```
$ go build
echo "some string" | ./pipes
```

You should see the following output:

```
$ echo "test case" | go run pipes.go
string: number_of_occurrences

test: 1
case: 1

$ echo "test case test" | go run pipes.go
string: number_of_occurrences

test: 2
case: 1
```

8. If you copied or wrote your own tests, go up one directory and run `go test`. Ensure that all the tests pass.

How it works...

Working with pipes in Go is pretty simple, especially if you're familiar with working with files. For example, you could use the pipe recipe from Chapter 1, *I/O and Filesystems*, to create a **tee** application (https://en.wikipedia.org/wiki/Tee_(command)) where everything piped in is immediately written to stdout and to a file.

This recipe uses a scanner to tokenize the io.Reader interface of the os.Stdin file object. You can see how you must check for errors after completing all of the reads.

Catching and handling signals

Signals are a useful way for the user or the OS to kill your running application. Sometimes, it makes sense to handle these signals in a more graceful way than the default behavior. Go provides a mechanism to catch and handle signals. In this recipe, we'll explore the handling of signals through the use of a signal that handles the Go routine.

How to do it...

These steps cover writing and running your application:

1. From your Terminal or console application, create a new directory called ~/projects/go-programming-cookbook/chapter2/signals.
2. Navigate to this directory.
3. Run the following command:

```
$ go mod init github.com/PacktPublishing/Go-Programming-Cookbook-
Second-Edition/chapter2/signals
```

You should see a file called go.mod that contains the following:

```
module github.com/PacktPublishing/Go-Programming-Cookbook-Second-
Edition/chapter2/signals
```

4. Copy tests from `~/projects/go-programming-cookbook-original/chapter2/signals`, or use this as an opportunity to write some of your own code!

5. Create a file called `signals.go` with the following contents:

```go
package main

import (
    "fmt"
    "os"
    "os/signal"
    "syscall"
)

// CatchSig sets up a listener for
// SIGINT interrupts
func CatchSig(ch chan os.Signal, done chan bool) {
    // block on waiting for a signal
    sig := <-ch
    // print it when it's received
    fmt.Println("nsig received:", sig)

    // we can set up handlers for all types of
    // sigs here
    switch sig {
    case syscall.SIGINT:
        fmt.Println("handling a SIGINT now!")
    case syscall.SIGTERM:
        fmt.Println("handling a SIGTERM in an entirely
        different way!")
    default:
        fmt.Println("unexpected signal received")
    }

    // terminate
    done <- true
}

func main() {
    // initialize our channels
    signals := make(chan os.Signal)
    done := make(chan bool)

    // hook them up to the signals lib
    signal.Notify(signals, syscall.SIGINT, syscall.SIGTERM)

    // if a signal is caught by this go routine
```

```
    // it will write to done
    go CatchSig(signals, done)

    fmt.Println("Press ctrl-c to terminate...")
    // the program blocks until someone writes to done
    <-done
    fmt.Println("Done!")


}
```

6. Run the following commands:

```
$ go build
$ ./signals
```

7. Try running the code and then press *Ctrl* + *C*. You should see the following:

```
$./signals
Press ctrl-c to terminate...
^C
sig received: interrupt
handling a SIGINT now!
Done!
```

8. Try running it again. Then, from a separate Terminal, determine the PID and kill the application:

```
$./signals
Press ctrl-c to terminate...

# in a separate terminal
$ ps -ef | grep signals
501 30777 26360 0 5:00PM ttys000 0:00.00 ./signals

$ kill -SIGTERM 30777

# in the original terminal

sig received: terminated
handling a SIGTERM in an entirely different way!
Done!
```

9. If you copied or wrote your own tests, go up one directory and run `go test`. Ensure that all the tests pass.

How it works...

This recipe makes use of channels, which are covered more extensively in `Chapter 9`, *Parallelism and Concurrency*. The `signal.Notify` function requires a channel to send signal notifications to and also the types of signal we care about. Then, we set up a function in a Go routine to handle any activity on the channel we passed to that function. Once we receive the signal, we can handle it however we want. We can terminate the application, respond with a message, and have different behaviors for different signals. The `kill` command is a good way to test passing signals to the applications.

We also use a `done` channel to block the application from terminating until a signal is received. Otherwise, the program would terminate immediately. This is unnecessary for long-running applications such as web applications. It can be very useful to create appropriate signal handling routines to perform cleanup, especially in applications with large amounts of Go routines that are holding a significant amount of state. A practical example of a graceful shutdown might be to allow current handlers to complete their HTTP requests without terminating them midway.

An ANSI coloring application

Coloring an ANSI terminal application is handled by a variety of code before and after a section of text you want colored. This recipe will explore a basic coloring mechanism that colors text red or plain. For a complete application, take a look at `https://github.com/agtorre/gocolorize`, which supports many more colors and text types, and also implements the `fmt.Formatter` interface for ease of printing.

How to do it...

These steps cover writing and running your application:

1. From your Terminal or console application, create a new directory called `~/projects/go-programming-cookbook/chapter2/ansicolor`.
2. Navigate to this directory.

3. Run the following command:

```
$ go mod init github.com/PacktPublishing/Go-Programming-Cookbook-
Second-Edition/chapter2/ansicolor
```

You should see a file called go.mod that contains the following:

```
module github.com/PacktPublishing/Go-Programming-Cookbook-Second-
Edition/chapter2/ansicolor
```

4. Copy tests from ~/projects/go-programming-cookbook-
original/chapter2/ansicolor, or use this as an opportunity to write some of
your own code!

5. Create a file called color.go with the following contents:

```go
package ansicolor

import "fmt"

//Color of text
type Color int

const (
    // ColorNone is default
    ColorNone = iota
    // Red colored text
    Red
    // Green colored text
    Green
    // Yellow colored text
    Yellow
    // Blue colored text
    Blue
    // Magenta colored text
    Magenta
    // Cyan colored text
    Cyan
    // White colored text
    White
    // Black colored text
    Black Color = -1
)

// ColorText holds a string and its color
type ColorText struct {
    TextColor Color
    Text      string
```

```
    }

    func (r *ColorText) String() string {
        if r.TextColor == ColorNone {
            return r.Text
        }

        value := 30
        if r.TextColor != Black {
            value += int(r.TextColor)
        }
        return fmt.Sprintf("33[0;%dm%s33[0m", value, r.Text)
    }
```

6. Create a new directory named `example` and navigate to it.

7. Create a `main.go` file with the following contents:

```
    package main

    import (
        "fmt"

        "github.com/PacktPublishing/
         Go-Programming-Cookbook-Second-Edition/
         chapter2/ansicolor"
    )

    func main() {
        r := ansicolor.ColorText{
            TextColor: ansicolor.Red,
            Text:      "I'm red!",
        }

        fmt.Println(r.String())

        r.TextColor = ansicolor.Green
        r.Text = "Now I'm green!"

        fmt.Println(r.String())

        r.TextColor = ansicolor.ColorNone
        r.Text = "Back to normal..."

        fmt.Println(r.String())
    }
```

8. Run `go run main.go`.

9. You may also run the following commands:

```
$ go build
$ ./example
```

10. You should see the following output with the text colored if your Terminal supports the ANSI coloring format:

```
$ go run main.go
I'm red!
Now I'm green!
Back to normal...
```

11. If you copied or wrote your own tests, go up one directory and run `go test`. Ensure that all the tests pass.

How it works...

This application makes use of a structure to maintain the state of the colored text. In this case, it stores the color of the text and the value of the text. The final string is rendered when you call the `String()` method, which will return either the colored text or plain text, depending on the values stored in the structure. By default, the text will be plain.

3
Data Conversion and Composition

Understanding Go's typing system is a critical step to mastering all levels of Go development. This chapter will show some examples of converting between data types, working with very big numbers, working with currency, using different types of encoding and decoding, including Base64 and `gob`, and creating custom collections using closures. In this chapter, the following recipes will be covered:

- Converting data types and interface casting
- Working with numeric data types using math and math/big
- Currency conversions and float64 considerations
- Using pointers and SQL NullTypes for encoding and decoding
- Encoding and decoding Go data
- Structure tags and basic reflection in Go
- Implementing collections using closures

Technical requirements

In order to proceed with all the recipes in this chapter, configure your environment according to these steps:

1. Download and install Go 1.12.6, or later, on your operating system at `https:// golang.org/doc/install`.
2. Open a Terminal/console application and create and navigate to a project directory, such as `~/projects/go-programming-cookbook`. All code will be run and modified from this directory.

3. Clone the latest code into `~/projects/go-programming-cookbook-original`. If you wish, you can work from this directory rather than type the examples manually:

```
$ git clone git@github.com:PacktPublishing/Go-Programming-Cookbook-Second-Edition.git go-programming-cookbook-original
```

Converting data types and interface casting

Go is typically very flexible when used to convert data from one type to another. A type may inherit another type, as follows:

```
type A int
```

We can always cast back to the type we inherited, as follows:

```
var a A = 1
fmt.Println(int(a))
```

There are also convenience functions for converting between numbers using casting, between strings and other types using `fmt.Sprint` and `strconv`, and between interfaces and types using reflection. This recipe will explore some of these basic conversions, which will be used throughout this book.

How to do it...

The following steps cover how to write and run your application:

1. From your Terminal/console application, create a new directory called `~/projects/go-programming-cookbook/chapter3/dataconv`.
2. Navigate to this directory.
3. Run the following command:

```
$ go mod init github.com/PacktPublishing/Go-Programming-Cookbook-Second-Edition/chapter3/dataconv
```

You should see a file called `go.mod` that contains the following content:

```
module github.com/PacktPublishing/Go-Programming-Cookbook-Second-Edition/chapter3/dataconv
```

4. Copy tests from ~/projects/go-programming-cookbook-original/chapter3/dataconv or use this as an exercise to write some of your own code!

5. Create a file called dataconv.go with the following content:

```go
package dataconv

import "fmt"

// ShowConv demonstrates some type conversion
func ShowConv() {
    // int
    var a = 24

    // float 64
    var b = 2.0

    // convert the int to a float64 for this calculation
    c := float64(a) * b
    fmt.Println(c)
    // fmt.Sprintf is a good way to convert to strings
    precision := fmt.Sprintf("%.2f", b)

    // print the value and the type
    fmt.Printf("%s - %T\n", precision, precision)
}
```

6. Create a file called strconv.go with the following content:

```go
package dataconv

import (
    "fmt"
    "strconv"
)

// Strconv demonstrates some strconv
// functions
func Strconv() error {
    //strconv is a good way to convert to and from strings
    s := "1234"
    // we can specify the base (10) and precision
    // 64 bit
    res, err := strconv.ParseInt(s, 10, 64)
    if err != nil {
        return err
    }
```

```
    fmt.Println(res)

    // lets try hex
    res, err = strconv.ParseInt("FF", 16, 64)
    if err != nil {
        return err
    }

    fmt.Println(res)

    // we can do other useful things like:
    val, err := strconv.ParseBool("true")
    if err != nil {
        return err
    }

    fmt.Println(val)

    return nil
}
```

7. Create a file called `interfaces.go` with the following content:

```
package dataconv

import "fmt"

// CheckType will print based on the
// interface type
func CheckType(s interface{}) {
    switch s.(type) {
    case string:
        fmt.Println("It's a string!")
    case int:
        fmt.Println("It's an int!")
    default:
        fmt.Println("not sure what it is...")
    }
}

// Interfaces demonstrates casting
// from anonymous interfaces to types
func Interfaces() {
    CheckType("test")
    CheckType(1)
    CheckType(false)

    var i interface{}
```

```
        i = "test"

        // manually check an interface
        if val, ok := i.(string); ok {
            fmt.Println("val is", val)
        }

        // this one should fail
        if _, ok := i.(int); !ok {
            fmt.Println("uh oh! glad we handled this")
        }
    }
}
```

8. Create a new directory named example and navigate to it.
9. Create a file named main.go with the following content:

```
package main

import "github.com/PacktPublishing/
        Go-Programming-Cookbook-Second-Edition/
        chapter3/dataconv"

func main() {
    dataconv.ShowConv()
    if err := dataconv.Strconv(); err != nil {
        panic(err)
    }
    dataconv.Interfaces()
}
```

10. Run go run main.go. You could also run the following commands:

```
$ go build
$ ./example
```

You should see the following output:

```
$ go run main.go
48
2.00 - string
1234
255
true
It's a string!
It's an int!
not sure what it is...
val is test
uh oh! glad we handled this
```

11. If you copied or wrote your own tests, go up one directory and run `go test`. Ensure that all tests pass.

How it works...

This recipe demonstrates how to cast between types by wrapping them in a new type by using the `strconv` package and interface reflection. These methods allow Go developers to quickly convert between various abstract Go types. These first two methods will return errors during compilation, but the errors in interface reflection may not be found until runtime. If you reflect incorrectly to an unsupported type, your program will panic. Switching between types is a way to generalize, and is also demonstrated in this recipe.

Conversion becomes important for packages such as `math`, which operate on `float64` exclusively.

Working with numeric data types using math and math/big

The `math` and `math/big` packages focus on exposing more complex mathematical operations to the Go language, such as `Pow`, `Sqrt`, and `Cos`. The `math` package itself operates predominately on `float64` unless a function says otherwise. The `math/big` package is for numbers that are too large to represent in a 64-bit value. This recipe will show some basic usage of the `math` package and demonstrate how to use `math/big` for Fibonacci sequence.

How to do it...

The following steps cover how to write and run your application:

1. From your Terminal/console application, create a new directory called `~/projects/go-programming-cookbook/chapter3/math`.
2. Navigate to this directory.

---

3. Run the following command:

```
$ go mod init github.com/PacktPublishing/Go-Programming-Cookbook-
Second-Edition/chapter3/math
```

You should see a file called `go.mod` that contains the following:

```
module github.com/PacktPublishing/Go-Programming-Cookbook-Second-
Edition/chapter3/math
```

4. Copy tests from `~/projects/go-programming-cookbook-original/chapter3/math` or use this as an exercise to write some of your own code!

5. Create a file called `fib.go` with the following content:

```go
package math

import "math/big"

// global to memoize fib
var memoize map[int]*big.Int

func init() {
    // initialize the map
    memoize = make(map[int]*big.Int)
}

// Fib prints the nth digit of the fibonacci sequence
// it will return 1 for anything < 0 as well...
// it's calculated recursively and use big.Int since
// int64 will quickly overflow
func Fib(n int) *big.Int {
    if n < 0 {
        return big.NewInt(1)
    }

    // base case
    if n < 2 {
        memoize[n] = big.NewInt(1)
    }

    // check if we stored it before
    // if so return with no calculation
    if val, ok := memoize[n]; ok {
        return val
    }
```

```
// initialize map then add previous 2 fib values
memoize[n] = big.NewInt(0)
memoize[n].Add(memoize[n], Fib(n-1))
memoize[n].Add(memoize[n], Fib(n-2))

// return result
return memoize[n]
}
```

6. Create a file called `math.go` with the following content:

```
package math

import (
  "fmt"
  "math"
)

// Examples demonstrates some of the functions
// in the math package
func Examples() {
  //sqrt Examples
  i := 25

  // i is an int, so convert
  result := math.Sqrt(float64(i))

  // sqrt of 25 == 5
  fmt.Println(result)

  // ceil rounds up
  result = math.Ceil(9.5)
  fmt.Println(result)

  // floor rounds down
  result = math.Floor(9.5)
  fmt.Println(result)

  // math also stores some consts:
  fmt.Println("Pi:", math.Pi, "E:", math.E)
}
```

7. Create a new directory named `example` and navigate to it.

8. Create a file named `main.go` with the following content:

```
package main

import (
    "fmt"

    "github.com/PacktPublishing/
    Go-Programming-Cookbook-Second-Edition/
    chapter3/math"
)

func main() {
    math.Examples()

    for i := 0; i < 10; i++ {
        fmt.Printf("%v ", math.Fib(i))
    }
    fmt.Println()
}
```

9. Run `go run main.go`. You could also run the following:

```
$ go build
$ ./example
```

You should see the following output:

```
$ go run main.go
5
10
9
Pi: 3.141592653589793 E: 2.718281828459045
1 1 2 3 5 8 13 21 34 55
```

10. If you copied or wrote your own tests, go up one directory and run `go test`. Ensure that all tests pass.

How it works...

The `math` package makes it possible to perform complex mathematical operations in Go. This recipe should be used in conjunction with this package for performing complex floating-point operations and converting between types as needed. It's worth noting that even with `float64`, there may still be rounding errors for certain floating-point numbers; the following recipe demonstrates some techniques for dealing with this.

The `math/big` section showcases a recursive Fibonacci sequence. If you modify `main.go` to loop well beyond 10, you'll quickly overflow `int64` if it was used instead of `big.Int`. The `big.Int` package also has helper methods to convert between the big types to other types.

Currency conversions and float64 considerations

Working with currency is always a tricky process. It can be tempting to represent money as a `float64`, but this can result in some pretty tricky (and wrong) rounding errors when doing calculations. For this reason, it's preferable to think of money in terms of cents and store the figure as an `int64` instance.

When collecting user input from forms, the command line, or other sources, money is usually represented in dollar form. For this reason, it's best to treat it as a string and convert that string directly to cents without floating-point conversions. This recipe will present ways to convert a string representation of currency into an `int64` (cents) instance and back again.

How to do it...

The following steps cover how to write and run your application:

1. From your Terminal/console application, create a new directory called `~/projects/go-programming-cookbook/chapter3/currency`.
2. Navigate to this directory.

3. Run the following command:

```
$ go mod init github.com/PacktPublishing/Go-Programming-Cookbook-
Second-Edition/chapter3/currency
```

You should see a file called go.mod that contains the following:

```
module github.com/PacktPublishing/Go-Programming-Cookbook-Second-
Edition/chapter3/currency
```

4. Copy tests from ~/projects/go-programming-cookbook-original/chapter3/currency or use this as an exercise to write some of your own code!

5. Create a file called dollars.go with the following content:

```go
package currency

import (
    "errors"
    "strconv"
    "strings"
)

// ConvertStringDollarsToPennies takes a dollar amount
// as a string, i.e. 1.00, 55.12 etc and converts it
// into an int64
func ConvertStringDollarsToPennies(amount string) (int64,
error) {
    // check if amount can convert to a valid float
    _, err := strconv.ParseFloat(amount, 64)
    if err != nil {
        return 0, err
    }

    // split the value on "."
    groups := strings.Split(amount, ".")

    // if there is no . result will still be
    // captured here
    result := groups[0]

    // base string
    r := ""

    // handle the data after the "."
    if len(groups) == 2 {
        if len(groups[1]) != 2 {
```

```
            return 0, errors.New("invalid cents")
        }
        r = groups[1]
    }

    // pad with 0, this will be
    // 2 0's if there was no .
    for len(r) < 2 {
        r += "0"
    }

    result += r

    // convert it to an int
    return strconv.ParseInt(result, 10, 64)
}
```

6. Create a file called `pennies.go` with the following content:

```go
package currency

import (
    "strconv"
)

// ConvertPenniesToDollarString takes a penny amount as
// an int64 and returns a dollar string representation
func ConvertPenniesToDollarString(amount int64) string {
    // parse the pennies as a base 10 int
    result := strconv.FormatInt(amount, 10)

    // check if negative, will set it back later
    negative := false
    if result[0] == '-' {
        result = result[1:]
        negative = true
    }

    // left pad with 0 if we're passed in value < 100
    for len(result) < 3 {
        result = "0" + result
    }
    length := len(result)

    // add in the decimal
    result = result[0:length-2] + "." + result[length-2:]

    // from the negative we stored earlier!
```

```
    if negative {
        result = "-" + result
    }

    return result
}
```

7. Create a new directory named `example` and navigate to it.

8. Create a file called `main.go` with the following content:

```go
package main

import (
    "fmt"

    "github.com/PacktPublishing/
     Go-Programming-Cookbook-Second-Edition/
     chapter3/currency"
)

func main() {
    // start with our user input
    // of fifteen dollars and 93 cents
    userInput := "15.93"

    pennies, err :=
    currency.ConvertStringDollarsToPennies(userInput)
    if err != nil {
        panic(err)
    }

    fmt.Printf("User input converted to %d pennies\n", pennies)

    // adding 15 cents
    pennies += 15

    dollars := currency.ConvertPenniesToDollarString(pennies)

    fmt.Printf("Added 15 cents, new values is %s dollars\n",
    dollars)
}
```

9. Run `go run main.go`. You could also run the following:

```
$ go build
$ ./example
```

You should see the following output:

```
$ go run main.go
User input converted to 1593 pennies
Added 15 cents, new values is 16.08 dollars
```

10. If you copied or wrote your own tests, go up one directory and run `go test`. Ensure that all tests pass.

How it works...

This recipe makes use of the `strconv` and `strings` packages to convert currency between dollars in string format and pennies in `int64`. It does this without converting to a `float64` type, which can result in rounding error, and only does so for validation.

The `strconv.ParseInt` and `strconv.FormatInt` functions are very useful for converting to and from `int64` and strings. We also made use of the fact that Go strings can easily be appended and sliced as needed.

Using pointers and SQL NullTypes for encoding and decoding

When you encode or decode into an object in Go, types that are not explicitly set will be set to their default values. Strings will default to empty string (`""`) and integers will default to `0`, as an example. Normally, this is fine, unless `0` means something for your API or service that is consuming the user input or returning it.

In addition, if you use `struct` tags such as `json omitempty`, the `0` value will be ignored even if they're valid. Another example of this is `Null`, which returns from SQL. What value best represents `Null` for an `Int`? This recipe will explore some of the ways Go developers deal with this issue.

How to do it...

The following steps cover how to write and run your application:

1. From your Terminal/console application, create a new directory called `~/projects/go-programming-cookbook/chapter3/nulls`.
2. Navigate to this directory.
3. Run the following command:

   $ go mod init github.com/PacktPublishing/Go-Programming-Cookbook-Second-Edition/chapter3/nulls

   You should see a file called `go.mod` that contains the following:

   ```
   module github.com/PacktPublishing/Go-Programming-Cookbook-Second-
   Edition/chapter3/nulls
   ```

4. Copy tests from `~/projects/go-programming-cookbook-original/chapter3/nulls` or use this as an exercise to write some of your own code!
5. Create a file called `base.go` with the following content:

   ```go
   package nulls

   import (
       "encoding/json"
       "fmt"
   )

   // json that has name but not age
   const (
       jsonBlob = `{"name": "Aaron"}`
       fulljsonBlob = `{"name":"Aaron", "age":0}`
   )

   // Example is a basic struct with age
   // and name fields
   type Example struct {
       Age int `json:"age,omitempty"`
       Name string `json:"name"`
   }

   // BaseEncoding shows encoding and
   // decoding with normal types
   func BaseEncoding() error {
       e := Example{}
   ```

```
// note that no age = 0 age
if err := json.Unmarshal([]byte(jsonBlob), &e); err != nil
{
    return err
}
fmt.Printf("Regular Unmarshal, no age: %+v\n", e)
value, err := json.Marshal(&e)
if err != nil {
    return err
}
fmt.Println("Regular Marshal, with no age:", string(value))

if err := json.Unmarshal([]byte(fulljsonBlob), &e);
err != nil {
    return err
}
fmt.Printf("Regular Unmarshal, with age = 0: %+v\n", e)

value, err = json.Marshal(&e)
if err != nil {
    return err
}
fmt.Println("Regular Marshal, with age = 0:",
string(value))

return nil
}
```

6. Create a file called `pointer.go` with the following content:

```
package nulls

import (
    "encoding/json"
    "fmt"
)

// ExamplePointer is the same, but
// uses a *Int
type ExamplePointer struct {
    Age *int `json:"age,omitempty"`
    Name string `json:"name"`
}

// PointerEncoding shows methods for
// dealing with nil/omitted values
func PointerEncoding() error {
```

```
    // note that no age = nil age
    e := ExamplePointer{}
    if err := json.Unmarshal([]byte(jsonBlob), &e); err != nil
    {
        return err
    }
    fmt.Printf("Pointer Unmarshal, no age: %+v\n", e)

    value, err := json.Marshal(&e)
    if err != nil {
        return err
    }
    fmt.Println("Pointer Marshal, with no age:", string(value))

    if err := json.Unmarshal([]byte(fulljsonBlob), &e);
    err != nil {
        return err
    }
    fmt.Printf("Pointer Unmarshal, with age = 0: %+v\n", e)

    value, err = json.Marshal(&e)
    if err != nil {
        return err
    }
    fmt.Println("Pointer Marshal, with age = 0:",
    string(value))

    return nil
}
```

7. Create a file called `nullencoding.go` with the following content:

```
package nulls

import (
    "database/sql"
    "encoding/json"
    "fmt"
)

type nullInt64 sql.NullInt64

// ExampleNullInt is the same, but
// uses a sql.NullInt64
type ExampleNullInt struct {
    Age *nullInt64 `json:"age,omitempty"`
    Name string `json:"name"`
}
```

```
func (v *nullInt64) MarshalJSON() ([]byte, error) {
    if v.Valid {
        return json.Marshal(v.Int64)
    }
    return json.Marshal(nil)
}

func (v *nullInt64) UnmarshalJSON(b []byte) error {
    v.Valid = false
    if b != nil {
        v.Valid = true
        return json.Unmarshal(b, &v.Int64)
    }
    return nil
}

// NullEncoding shows an alternative method
// for dealing with nil/omitted values
func NullEncoding() error {
    e := ExampleNullInt{}

    // note that no means an invalid value
    if err := json.Unmarshal([]byte(jsonBlob), &e); err != nil
    {
        return err
    }
    fmt.Printf("nullInt64 Unmarshal, no age: %+v\n", e)

    value, err := json.Marshal(&e)
    if err != nil {
        return err
    }
    fmt.Println("nullInt64 Marshal, with no age:",
    string(value))

    if err := json.Unmarshal([]byte(fulljsonBlob), &e);
    err != nil {
        return err
    }
    fmt.Printf("nullInt64 Unmarshal, with age = 0: %+v\n", e)

    value, err = json.Marshal(&e)
    if err != nil {
        return err
    }
    fmt.Println("nullInt64 Marshal, with age = 0:",
    string(value))
```

```
        return nil
    }
```

8. Create a new directory named `example` and navigate to it.

9. Create a file called `main.go` with the following content:

```go
package main

import (
    "fmt"

    "github.com/PacktPublishing/
     Go-Programming-Cookbook-Second-Edition/
     chapter3/nulls"
)

func main() {
    if err := nulls.BaseEncoding(); err != nil {
        panic(err)
    }
    fmt.Println()

    if err := nulls.PointerEncoding(); err != nil {
        panic(err)
    }
    fmt.Println()

    if err := nulls.NullEncoding(); err != nil {
        panic(err)
    }
}
```

10. Run `go run main.go`. You could also run the following:

```
$ go build
$ ./example
```

You should see the following output:

```
$ go run main.go
Regular Unmarshal, no age: {Age:0 Name:Aaron}
Regular Marshal, with no age: {"name":"Aaron"}
Regular Unmarshal, with age = 0: {Age:0 Name:Aaron}
Regular Marshal, with age = 0: {"name":"Aaron"}

Pointer Unmarshal, no age: {Age:<nil> Name:Aaron}
Pointer Marshal, with no age: {"name":"Aaron"}
Pointer Unmarshal, with age = 0: {Age:0xc42000a610 Name:Aaron}
```

```
Pointer Marshal, with age = 0: {"age":0,"name":"Aaron"}

nullInt64 Unmarshal, no age: {Age:<nil> Name:Aaron}
nullInt64 Marshal, with no age: {"name":"Aaron"}
nullInt64 Unmarshal, with age = 0: {Age:0xc42000a750
Name:Aaron}
nullInt64 Marshal, with age = 0: {"age":0,"name":"Aaron"}
```

11. If you copied or wrote your own tests, go up one directory and run `go test`. Ensure that all tests pass.

How it works...

Switching from a value to a pointer is a quick way to express null values when marshaling and unmarshaling. Setting these values can be a bit tricky, as you can't assign them directly to a pointer, -- `*a := 1`, but, otherwise, it's a flexible way of dealing with it.

This recipe also demonstrated an alternative method using the `sql.NullInt64` type. This is normally used with SQL and `valid` is set if anything other than `Null` is returned; otherwise, it sets `Null`. We added a `MarshalJSON` method and an `UnmarshallJSON` method to allow this type to interact with the `JSON` package and we chose to use a pointer so that `omitempty` would continue to work as expected.

Encoding and decoding Go data

Go features a number of alternative encoding types other than JSON, TOML, and YAML. These are largely meant for transporting data between Go processes with things such as wire protocols and RPC, or in cases where some character formats are restricted.

This recipe will explore how to encode and decode the `gob` format and `base64`. The later chapters will explore protocols such as GRPC.

How to do it...

The following steps cover how to write and run your application:

1. From your Terminal/console application, create a new directory called `~/projects/go-programming-cookbook/chapter3/encoding`.
2. Navigate to this directory.

3. Run the following command:

```
$ go mod init github.com/PacktPublishing/Go-Programming-Cookbook-
Second-Edition/chapter3/encoding
```

You should see a file called `go.mod` that contains the following:

```
module github.com/PacktPublishing/Go-Programming-Cookbook-Second-
Edition/chapter3/encoding
```

4. Copy tests from `~/projects/go-programming-cookbook-original/chapter3/encoding` or use this as an exercise to write some of your own code!

5. Create a file called `gob.go` with the following content:

```go
package encoding

import (
    "bytes"
    "encoding/gob"
    "fmt"
)

// pos stores the x, y position
// for Object
type pos struct {
    X       int
    Y       int
    Object string
}

// GobExample demonstrates using
// the gob package
func GobExample() error {
    buffer := bytes.Buffer{}

    p := pos{
        X:      10,
        Y:      15,
        Object: "wrench",
    }

    // note that if p was an interface
    // we'd have to call gob.Register first

    e := gob.NewEncoder(&buffer)
    if err := e.Encode(&p); err != nil {
```

```
            return err
        }

        // note this is a binary format so it wont print well
        fmt.Println("Gob Encoded valued length: ",
        len(buffer.Bytes()))

        p2 := pos{}
        d := gob.NewDecoder(&buffer)
        if err := d.Decode(&p2); err != nil {
            return err
        }

        fmt.Println("Gob Decode value: ", p2)
        return nil
    }
```

6. Create a file called `base64.go` with the following content:

```go
package encoding

import (
    "bytes"
    "encoding/base64"
    "fmt"
    "io/ioutil"
)

// Base64Example demonstrates using
// the base64 package
func Base64Example() error {
    // base64 is useful for cases where
    // you can't support binary formats
    // it operates on bytes/strings

    // using helper functions and URL encoding
    value := base64.URLEncoding.EncodeToString([]byte("encoding
    some data!"))
    fmt.Println("With EncodeToString and URLEncoding: ", value)

    // decode the first value
    decoded, err := base64.URLEncoding.DecodeString(value)
    if err != nil {
        return err
    }
    fmt.Println("With DecodeToString and URLEncoding: ",
    string(decoded))
```

```
        return nil
    }

    // Base64ExampleEncoder shows similar examples
    // with encoders/decoders
    func Base64ExampleEncoder() error {
        // using encoder/ decoder
        buffer := bytes.Buffer{}

        // encode into the buffer
        encoder := base64.NewEncoder(base64.StdEncoding, &buffer)

        if _, err := encoder.Write([]byte("encoding some other
        data")); err != nil {
            return err
        }

        // be sure to close
        if err := encoder.Close(); err != nil {
            return err
        }

        fmt.Println("Using encoder and StdEncoding: ",
        buffer.String())

        decoder := base64.NewDecoder(base64.StdEncoding, &buffer)
        results, err := ioutil.ReadAll(decoder)
        if err != nil {
            return err
        }

        fmt.Println("Using decoder and StdEncoding: ",
        string(results))

        return nil
    }
```

7. Create a new directory named `example` and navigate to it.
8. Create a file called `main.go` with the following content:

```
package main

import (
    "github.com/PacktPublishing/
    Go-Programming-Cookbook-Second-Edition/
    chapter3/encoding"
)
```

```
func main() {
    if err := encoding.Base64Example(); err != nil {
        panic(err)
    }

    if err := encoding.Base64ExampleEncoder(); err != nil {
        panic(err)
    }

    if err := encoding.GobExample(); err != nil {
        panic(err)
    }
}
```

9. Run `go run main.go`. You could also run the following:

   ```
   $ go build
   $ ./example
   ```

   You should see the following output:

   ```
   $ go run main.go
   With EncodeToString and URLEncoding:
   ZW5jb2Rpbmcgc29tZSBkYXRhIQ==
   With DecodeToString and URLEncoding: encoding some data!
   Using encoder and StdEncoding: ZW5jb2Rpbmcgc29tZSBvdGhlciBkYXRh
   Using decoder and StdEncoding: encoding some other data
   Gob Encoded valued length: 57
   Gob Decode value: {10 15 wrench}
   ```

10. If you copied or wrote your own tests, go up one directory and run `go test`. Ensure that all tests pass.

How it works...

Gob encoding is a streaming format built with Go data types in mind. It is most efficient when sending and encoding many consecutive items. For a single item, other encoding formats, such as JSON, are potentially more efficient and portable. Despite this, `gob` encoding makes it simple to marshal large, complex structures and reconstruct them in a separate process. Although it wasn't shown here, `gob` can also operate on custom types or unexported types with custom `MarshalBinary` and `UnmarshalBinary` methods.

Base64 encoding is useful for communicating via URLs in GET requests or for generating a string representation encoding of binary data. Most languages can support this format and unmarshal the data on the other end. As a result, it's common to encode things such as JSON payloads in cases where the JSON format is not supported.

Structure tags and basic reflection in Go

Reflection is a complicated topic that can't really be covered in a single recipe; however, a practical application of reflection is dealing with structure tags. At their core, struct tags are just key–value strings: you look up the key, then deal with the value. As you can imagine, for something like JSON marshaling and unmarshaling, there's a lot of complexity for dealing with these values.

The reflect package is designed for interrogating and understanding interface objects. It has helper methods to look at the different kinds of structures, values, struct tags, and more. If you need something beyond the basic interface conversion, such as the one at the beginning of this chapter, this is the package you should look at.

How to do it...

The following steps cover how to write and run your application:

1. From your Terminal/console application, create a new directory called ~/projects/go-programming-cookbook/chapter3/tags.

2. Navigate to this directory.

3. Run the following command:

   ```
   $ go mod init github.com/PacktPublishing/Go-Programming-Cookbook-
   Second-Edition/chapter3/tags
   ```

   You should see a file called go.mod that contains the following:

   ```
   module github.com/PacktPublishing/Go-Programming-Cookbook-Second-
   Edition/chapter3/tags
   ```

4. Copy tests from ~/projects/go-programming-cookbook-original/chapter3/tags or use this as an exercise to write some of your own code!

5. Create a file called `serialize.go` with the following content:

```go
package tags

import "reflect"

// SerializeStructStrings converts a struct
// to our custom serialization format
// it honors serialize struct tags for string types
func SerializeStructStrings(s interface{}) (string, error) {
    result := ""

    // reflect the interface into
    // a type
    r := reflect.TypeOf(s)
    value := reflect.ValueOf(s)
    // if a pointer to a struct is passed
    // in, handle it appropriately
    if r.Kind() == reflect.Ptr {
        r = r.Elem()
        value = value.Elem()
    }

    // loop over all of the fields
    for i := 0; i < r.NumField(); i++ {
        field := r.Field(i)
        // struct tag found
        key := field.Name
        if serialize, ok := field.Tag.Lookup("serialize"); ok {
            // ignore "-" otherwise that whole value
            // becomes the serialize 'key'
            if serialize == "-" {
                continue
            }
            key = serialize
        }

        switch value.Field(i).Kind() {
        // this recipe only supports strings!
        case reflect.String:
            result += key + ":" + value.Field(i).String() + ";"
            // by default skip it
        default:
            continue
        }
    }
    return result, nil
}
```

6. Create a file called `deserialize.go` with the following content:

```go
package tags

import (
    "errors"
    "reflect"
    "strings"
)

// DeSerializeStructStrings converts a serialized
// string using our custom serialization format
// to a struct
func DeSerializeStructStrings(s string, res interface{}) error
{
    r := reflect.TypeOf(res)

    // we're setting using a pointer so
    // it must always be a pointer passed
    // in
    if r.Kind() != reflect.Ptr {
        return errors.New("res must be a pointer")
    }

    // dereference the pointer
    r = r.Elem()
    value := reflect.ValueOf(res).Elem()

    // split our serialization string into
    // a map
    vals := strings.Split(s, ";")
    valMap := make(map[string]string)
    for _, v := range vals {
        keyval := strings.Split(v, ":")
        if len(keyval) != 2 {
            continue
        }
        valMap[keyval[0]] = keyval[1]
    }

    // iterate over fields
    for i := 0; i < r.NumField(); i++ {
        field := r.Field(i)

        // check if in the serialize set
        if serialize, ok := field.Tag.Lookup("serialize"); ok {
            // ignore "-" otherwise that whole value
            // becomes the serialize 'key'
```

```
                        if serialize == "-" {
                            continue
                        }
                        // is it in the map
                        if val, ok := valMap[serialize]; ok {
                            value.Field(i).SetString(val)
                        }
                } else if val, ok := valMap[field.Name]; ok {
                        // is our field name in the map instead?
                        value.Field(i).SetString(val)
                }
        }
        return nil
}
```

7. Create a file called `tags.go` with the following content:

```go
package tags

import "fmt"

// Person is a struct that stores a persons
// name, city, state, and a misc attribute
type Person struct {
    Name string `serialize:"name"`
    City string `serialize:"city"`
    State string
     Misc string `serialize:"-"`
     Year int `serialize:"year"`
}

// EmptyStruct demonstrates serialize
// and deserialize for an Empty struct
// with tags
func EmptyStruct() error {
    p := Person{}

    res, err := SerializeStructStrings(&p)
    if err != nil {
        return err
    }
    fmt.Printf("Empty struct: %#v\n", p)
    fmt.Println("Serialize Results:", res)

    newP := Person{}
    if err := DeSerializeStructStrings(res, &newP); err != nil
    {
        return err
```

```
    }
    fmt.Printf("Deserialize results: %#v\n", newP)
        return nil
    }

// FullStruct demonstrates serialize
// and deserialize for an Full struct
// with tags
func FullStruct() error {
    p := Person{
        Name: "Aaron",
        City: "Seattle",
        State: "WA",
        Misc: "some fact",
        Year: 2017,
    }
    res, err := SerializeStructStrings(&p)
    if err != nil {
        return err
    }
    fmt.Printf("Full struct: %#v\n", p)
    fmt.Println("Serialize Results:", res)

    newP := Person{}
    if err := DeSerializeStructStrings(res, &newP);
    err != nil {
        return err
    }
    fmt.Printf("Deserialize results: %#v\n", newP)
    return nil
}
```

8. Create a new directory named example and navigate to it.

9. Create a file called main.go with the following content:

```
package main

import (
    "fmt"

    "github.com/PacktPublishing/
    Go-Programming-Cookbook-Second-Edition/
    chapter3/tags"
)

func main() {

    if err := tags.EmptyStruct(); err != nil {
```

```
            panic(err)
        }

        fmt.Println()

        if err := tags.FullStruct(); err != nil {
            panic(err)
        }
    }
```

10. Run `go run main.go`. You could also run the following:

    ```
    $ go build
    $ ./example
    ```

    You should see the following output:

    ```
    $ go run main.go
    Empty struct: tags.Person{Name:"", City:"", State:"", Misc:"",
    Year:0}
    Serialize Results: name:;city:;State:;
    Deserialize results: tags.Person{Name:"", City:"", State:"",
    Misc:"", Year:0}

    Full struct: tags.Person{Name:"Aaron", City:"Seattle",
    State:"WA", Misc:"some fact", Year:2017}
    Serialize Results: name:Aaron;city:Seattle;State:WA;
    Deserialize results: tags.Person{Name:"Aaron", City:"Seattle",
    State:"WA", Misc:"", Year:0}
    ```

11. If you copied or wrote your own tests, go up one directory and run `go test`. Ensure that all tests pass.

How it works...

This recipe makes a string serialization format that takes a `struct` value and serializes all the string fields into a parseable format. This recipe doesn't deal with certain edge cases; in particular, strings must not contain a colon (:) or semicolon ; characters. Here is a summary of its behavior:

- If a field is a string, it will be serialized/deserialized.
- If a field is not a string, it will be ignored.

- If the `struct` tag of the field contains the serialize "key", then the key will be the returned serialized/deserialized environment.
- Duplicates are not handled.
- If a `struct` tag is not specified, the field name is used instead.
- If the `struct` tag value is a hyphen (–), the field is ignored, even if it's a string.

Some other things to note are that reflection does not entirely work with nonexported values.

Implementing collections via closures

If you've been working with functional or dynamic programming languages, you may feel that `for` loops and `if` statements produce verbose code. Using functional constructs such as `map` and `filter` for processing lists can be useful and make code appear more readable; however, in Go, these types are not in the standard library, and can be difficult to generalize without generics or very complex reflection and the use of empty interfaces. This recipe will provide you with some basic examples of implementing collections using Go closures.

How to do it...

The following steps cover how to write and run your application:

1. From your Terminal/console application, create a new directory called `~/projects/go-programming-cookbook/chapter3/collections`.
2. Navigate to this directory.
3. Run the following command:

   ```
   $ go mod init github.com/PacktPublishing/Go-Programming-Cookbook-
   Second-Edition/chapter3/collections
   ```

   You should see a file called `go.mod` that contains the following:

   ```
   module github.com/PacktPublishing/Go-Programming-Cookbook-Second-
   Edition/chapter3/collections
   ```

4. Copy tests from `~/projects/go-programming-cookbook-original/chapter3/collections`, or use this as an exercise to write some of your own code!

5. Create a file called `collections.go` with the following content:

```
package collections

// WorkWith is the struct we'll
// be implementing collections for
type WorkWith struct {
    Data    string
    Version int
}

// Filter is a functional filter. It takes a list of
// WorkWith and a WorkWith Function that returns a bool
// for each "true" element we return it to the resultant
// list
func Filter(ws []WorkWith, f func(w WorkWith) bool) []WorkWith
{
    // depending on results, smalles size for result
    // is len == 0
    result := make([]WorkWith, 0)
    for _, w := range ws {
        if f(w) {
            result = append(result, w)
        }
    }
    return result
}

// Map is a functional map. It takes a list of
// WorkWith and a WorkWith Function that takes a WorkWith
// and returns a modified WorkWith. The end result is
// a list of modified WorkWiths
func Map(ws []WorkWith, f func(w WorkWith) WorkWith) []WorkWith
{
    // the result should always be the same
    // length
    result := make([]WorkWith, len(ws))

    for pos, w := range ws {
        newW := f(w)
        result[pos] = newW
    }
    return result
}
```

6. Create a file called `functions.go` with the following content:

```go
package collections

import "strings"

// LowerCaseData does a ToLower to the
// Data string of a WorkWith
func LowerCaseData(w WorkWith) WorkWith {
    w.Data = strings.ToLower(w.Data)
    return w
}

// IncrementVersion increments a WorkWiths
// Version
func IncrementVersion(w WorkWith) WorkWith {
    w.Version++
    return w
}

// OldVersion returns a closures
// that validates the version is greater than
// the specified amount
func OldVersion(v int) func(w WorkWith) bool {
    return func(w WorkWith) bool {
        return w.Version >= v
    }
}
```

7. Create a new directory named `example` and navigate to it.
8. Create a file called `main.go` with the following content:

```go
package main

import (
    "fmt"

    "github.com/PacktPublishing/
    Go-Programming-Cookbook-Second-Edition/
    chapter3/collections"
)

func main() {
    ws := []collections.WorkWith{
        collections.WorkWith{"Example", 1},
        collections.WorkWith{"Example 2", 2},
    }
```

```
        fmt.Printf("Initial list: %#v\n", ws)

        // first lower case the list
        ws = collections.Map(ws, collections.LowerCaseData)
        fmt.Printf("After LowerCaseData Map: %#v\n", ws)

        // next increment all versions
        ws = collections.Map(ws, collections.IncrementVersion)
        fmt.Printf("After IncrementVersion Map: %#v\n", ws)

        // lastly remove all versions older than 3
        ws = collections.Filter(ws, collections.OldVersion(3))
        fmt.Printf("After OldVersion Filter: %#v\n", ws)
    }
```

9. Run `go run main.go`. You could also run the following:

```
$ go build
$ ./example
```

You should see the following output:

```
$ go run main.go
Initial list:
[]collections.WorkWith{collections.WorkWith{Data:"Example",
Version:1}, collections.WorkWith{Data:"Example 2", Version:2}}
After LowerCaseData Map:
[]collections.WorkWith{collections.WorkWith{Data:"example",
Version:1}, collections.WorkWith{Data:"example 2", Version:2}}
After IncrementVersion Map:
[]collections.WorkWith{collections.WorkWith{Data:"example",
Version:2}, collections.WorkWith{Data:"example 2", Version:3}}
After OldVersion Filter:
[]collections.WorkWith{collections.WorkWith{Data:"example 2",
Version:3}}
```

10. If you copied or wrote your own tests, go up one directory and run `go test`. Ensure that all tests pass.

How it works...

Closures in Go are very powerful. Although our `collections` functions are not generic, they're relatively small and can be easily applied to our `WorkWith` structure with minimal added code using a variety of functions. You may notice from looking at this that we're not returning errors anywhere. The idea of these functions is that they're pure: there are no side effects to the original list, except that we choose to write over it after each call.

If you need to apply layers of modification to a list or structure of lists, then this pattern can save you a lot of confusion and make testing very straightforward. It is also possible to chain maps and filters together for a very expressive coding style.

Error Handling in Go

4

Error handling is important for even the most basic Go program. Errors in Go implement the `Error` interface and must be dealt with at every layer of the code. Go errors do not work like exceptions, and unhandled errors can cause enormous problems. You should strive to handle and consider errors whenever they occur.

This chapter also covers logging since it's common to log whenever an actual error occurs. We'll also investigate wrapping errors, so that the given error should provide an additional context as it's returned up the function stack, so that it's easier to determine the actual cause of certain errors.

In this chapter, the following recipes will be covered:

- Handling errors and the Error interface
- Using the pkg/errors package and wrapping errors
- Using the log package and understanding when to log errors
- Structured logging with the apex and logrus packages
- Logging with the context package
- Using package-level global variables
- Catching panics for long-running processes

Technical requirements

In order to proceed with all the recipes in this chapter, configure your environment according to these steps:

1. Download and install Go 1.12.6, or later, on your operating system at `https://golang.org/doc/install`.
2. Open a Terminal/console application; create and navigate to a project directory such as `~/projects/go-programming-cookbook`. All code will be run and modified from this directory.

3. Clone the latest code into `~/projects/go-programming-cookbook-original` and, optionally, work from that directory, rather than typing in the examples manually:

```
$ git clone git@github.com:PacktPublishing/Go-Programming-Cookbook-
Second-Edition.git go-programming-cookbook-original
```

Handling errors and the Error interface

The `Error` interface is a pretty small and simple interface:

```
type Error interface{
  Error() string
}
```

This interface is elegant because it's simple to make anything in order to satisfy it. Unfortunately, this also creates confusion for packages that need to take certain actions depending on the error received.

There are a number of ways to create errors in Go; this recipe will explore the creation of basic errors, errors that have assigned values or types, and a custom error using a structure.

How to do it...

These steps cover the writing and running of your application:

1. From your Terminal/console application, create a new directory called `~/projects/go-programming-cookbook/chapter4/basicerrors` and navigate to this directory.
2. Run the following command:

```
$ go mod init github.com/PacktPublishing/Go-Programming-Cookbook-
Second-Edition/chapter4/basicerrors
```

You should see a file called `go.mod` that contains the following:

```
module github.com/PacktPublishing/Go-Programming-Cookbook-Second-
Edition/chapter4/basicerrors
```

3. Copy tests from ~/projects/go-programming-cookbook-original/chapter4/basicerrors, or use this as an exercise to write some of your own code!

4. Create a file called basicerrors.go with the following content:

```go
package basicerrors

import (
  "errors"
  "fmt"
)

// ErrorValue is a way to make a package level
// error to check against. I.e. if err == ErrorValue
var ErrorValue = errors.New("this is a typed error")

// TypedError is a way to make an error type
// you can do err.(type) == ErrorValue
type TypedError struct {
  error
}

//BasicErrors demonstrates some ways to create errors
func BasicErrors() {
  err := errors.New("this is a quick and easy way to create an error")
  fmt.Println("errors.New: ", err)

  err = fmt.Errorf("an error occurred: %s", "something")
  fmt.Println("fmt.Errorf: ", err)

  err = ErrorValue
  fmt.Println("value error: ", err)

  err = TypedError{errors.New("typed error")}
  fmt.Println("typed error: ", err)

}
```

5. Create a file called custom.go with the following content:

```go
package basicerrors

import (
  "fmt"
)
```

```
// CustomError is a struct that will implement
// the Error() interface
type CustomError struct {
  Result string
}

func (c CustomError) Error() string {
  return fmt.Sprintf("there was an error; %s was the result",
c.Result)
}

// SomeFunc returns an error
func SomeFunc() error {
  c := CustomError{Result: "this"}
  return c
}
```

6. Create a new directory named `example` and navigate to it.

7. Create a `main.go` file with the following content:

```
package main

import (
    "fmt"

    "github.com/PacktPublishing/
    Go-Programming-Cookbook-Second-Edition/
    chapter4/basicerrors"
)

func main() {
    basicerrors.BasicErrors()

    err := basicerrors.SomeFunc()
    fmt.Println("custom error: ", err)
}
```

8. Run `go run main.go`.

9. You may also run the following commands:

```
$ go build
$ ./example
```

You should now see the following output:

```
$ go run main.go
errors.New: this is a quick and easy way to create an error
fmt.Errorf: an error occurred: something
typed error: this is a typed error
custom error: there was an error; this was the result
```

10. If you copied or wrote your own tests, then go up one directory and run `go test`. Ensure that all the tests pass.

How it works...

Whether you use `errors.New`, `fmt.Errorf`, or a custom error, the most important thing to remember is that you should never leave errors unhandled in your code. These different methods of defining errors give a lot of flexibility. You can, for example, put extra functions in your structure to further interrogate an error and cast the interface to your error type in the calling function to get some added functionality.

The interface itself is very simple and the only requirement is that you return a valid string. Connecting this to a structure can be useful for some high-level applications that have consistent error handling throughout, but want to work nicely with other applications.

Using the pkg/errors package and wrapping errors

The `errors` package located in `github.com/pkg/errors` is a drop-in replacement for the standard Go `errors` package. Additionally, it provides some very useful functionality for wrapping and handling errors. The typed and declared errors in the preceding recipe are a good example—they can be useful to add additional information to an error, but wrapping it in the standard way will change its type and break the type assertion:

```
// this wont work if you wrapped it
// in a standard way. that is,
// fmt.Errorf("custom error: %s", err.Error())
if err == Package.ErrorNamed{
  //handle this error in a specific way
}
```

This recipe will demonstrate how to use the `pkg/errors` package to add annotation to errors throughout your code.

How to do it...

These steps cover the writing and running of your application:

1. From your Terminal/console application, create a new directory called `~/projects/go-programming-cookbook/chapter4/errwrap` and navigate to this directory.

2. Run the following command:

   ```
   $ go mod init github.com/PacktPublishing/Go-Programming-Cookbook-
   Second-Edition/chapter4/errwrap
   ```

   You should see a file called `go.mod` that contains the following:

   ```
   module github.com/PacktPublishing/Go-Programming-Cookbook-Second-
   Edition/chapter4/errwrap
   ```

3. Copy tests from `~/projects/go-programming-cookbook-original/chapter4/errwrap`, or use this as an exercise to write some of your own code!

4. Create a file called `errwrap.go` with the following content:

   ```go
   package errwrap

   import (
       "fmt"

       "github.com/pkg/errors"
   )
   // WrappedError demonstrates error wrapping and
   // annotating an error
   func WrappedError(e error) error {
       return errors.Wrap(e, "An error occurred in WrappedError")
   }

   // ErrorTyped is a error we can check against
   type ErrorTyped struct{
       error
   }

   // Wrap shows what happens when we wrap an error
   func Wrap() {
       e := errors.New("standard error")

       fmt.Println("Regular Error - ", WrappedError(e))
   ```

```
    fmt.Println("Typed Error - ",
    WrappedError(ErrorTyped{errors.New("typed error")}))

    fmt.Println("Nil -", WrappedError(nil))

}
```

5. Create a file called `unwrap.go` with the following content:

```
package errwrap

import (
    "fmt"

    "github.com/pkg/errors"
)

// Unwrap will unwrap an error and do
// type assertion to it
func Unwrap() {

    err := error(ErrorTyped{errors.New("an error occurred")})
    err = errors.Wrap(err, "wrapped")
    fmt.Println("wrapped error: ", err)

    // we can handle many error types
    switch errors.Cause(err).(type) {
    case ErrorTyped:
        fmt.Println("a typed error occurred: ", err)
    default:
        fmt.Println("an unknown error occurred")
    }
}

// StackTrace will print all the stack for
// the error
func StackTrace() {
    err := error(ErrorTyped{errors.New("an error occurred")})
    err = errors.Wrap(err, "wrapped")

    fmt.Printf("%+v\n", err)
}
```

6. Create a new directory named `example` and navigate to it.

7. Create a `main.go` file with the following content:

```
package main

import (
    "fmt"

    "github.com/PacktPublishing/
    Go-Programming-Cookbook-Second-Edition/
    chapter4/errwrap"
)

func main() {
    errwrap.Wrap()
    fmt.Println()
    errwrap.Unwrap()
    fmt.Println()
    errwrap.StackTrace()
}
```

8. Run `go run main.go`.

9. You may also run the following commands:

```
$ go build
$ ./example
```

You should now see the following output:

```
$ go run main.go
Regular Error - An error occurred in WrappedError: standard
error
Typed Error - An error occurred in WrappedError: typed error
Nil - <nil>

wrapped error: wrapped: an error occurred
a typed error occurred: wrapped: an error occurred

an error occurred
github.com/PacktPublishing/Go-Programming-Cookbook-Second-
Edition/chapter4/errwrap.StackTrace
/Users/lothamer/go/src/github.com/agtorre/go-
cookbook/chapter4/errwrap/unwrap.go:30
main.main
/tmp/go/src/github.com/agtorre/go-
cookbook/chapter4/errwrap/example/main.go:14
```

10. The `go.mod` file should be updated and the `go.sum` file should now be present in the top-level recipe directory.
11. If you copied or wrote your own tests, then go up one directory and run `go test`. Ensure that all the tests pass.

How it works...

The `pkg/errors` package is a very useful tool. It makes sense to wrap every returned error using this package to provide extra context in logging and error debugging. It's flexible enough to print the entire stack traces when an error occurs or to just add a prefix to your errors when printing them. It can also clean up code, since a wrapped nil returns a `nil` value; for example, consider the following code:

```
func RetError() error{
 err := ThisReturnsAnError()
 return errors.Wrap(err, "This only does something if err != nil")
}
```

In some cases, this can save you from having to check whether an error is `nil` first, before simply returning it. This recipe demonstrates how to use the package to wrap and unwrap errors, as well as basic stack trace functionality. The documentation for the package also provides some other useful examples such as printing partial stacks. Dave Cheney, the author of this library, has also written a number of helpful blogs and given talks on the subject; you can go to `https://dave.cheney.net/2016/04/27/dont-just-check-errors-handle-them-gracefully` to find out more.

Using the log package and understanding when to log errors

Logging should typically occur when an error is the final result. In other words, it's useful to log when something exceptional or unexpected occurs. It might also be appropriate, if you use a log that provides log levels, to sprinkle debug or info statements at key parts of your code to quickly debug issues during development. Too much logging will make it difficult to find anything useful, but not enough logging can result in broken systems with no insight into the root cause. This recipe will demonstrate the use of the default Go `log` package and some useful options, and also showcase when a log should likely occur.

How to do it...

These steps cover the writing and running of your application:

1. From your Terminal/console application, create a new directory called `~/projects/go-programming-cookbook/chapter4/log` and navigate to this directory.

2. Run the following command:

   $ go mod init github.com/PacktPublishing/Go-Programming-Cookbook-Second-Edition/chapter4/log

   You should see a file called `go.mod` that contains the following:

   ```
   module github.com/PacktPublishing/Go-Programming-Cookbook-Second-Edition/chapter4/log
   ```

3. Copy tests from `~/projects/go-programming-cookbook-original/chapter4/log`, or use this as an exercise to write some of your own code!

4. Create a file called `log.go` with the following content:

   ```go
   package log

   import (
       "bytes"
       "fmt"
       "log"
   )

   // Log uses the setup logger
   func Log() {
       // we'll configure the logger to write
       // to a bytes.Buffer
       buf := bytes.Buffer{}

       // second argument is the prefix last argument is about
       // options you combine them with a logical or.
       logger := log.New(&buf, "logger: ",
       log.Lshortfile|log.Ldate)

       logger.Println("test")

       logger.SetPrefix("new logger: ")

       logger.Printf("you can also add args(%v) and use Fatalln to
   ```

```
        log and crash", true)

        fmt.Println(buf.String())
}
```

5. Create a file called `error.go` with the following content:

```
package log

import "github.com/pkg/errors"
import "log"

// OriginalError returns the error original error
func OriginalError() error {
    return errors.New("error occurred")
}

// PassThroughError calls OriginalError and
// forwards the error along after wrapping.
func PassThroughError() error {
    err := OriginalError()
    // no need to check error
    // since this works with nil
    return errors.Wrap(err, "in passthrougherror")
}

// FinalDestination deals with the error
// and doesn't forward it
func FinalDestination() {
    err := PassThroughError()
    if err != nil {
        // we log because an unexpected error occurred!
        log.Printf("an error occurred: %s\n", err.Error())
        return
    }
}
```

6. Create a new directory named `example` and navigate to it.

7. Create a `main.go` file with the following content:

```
package main

import (
    "fmt"

    "github.com/PacktPublishing/
    Go-Programming-Cookbook-Second-Edition/
    chapter4/log"
```

```
    )

    func main() {
        fmt.Println("basic logging and modification of logger:")
        log.Log()
        fmt.Println("logging 'handled' errors:")
        log.FinalDestination()
    }
```

8. Run `go run main.go`.

9. You may also run the following commands:

    $ go build
    $ ./example

    You should see the following output:

    $ go run main.go
    basic logging and modification of logger:
    logger: 2017/02/05 log.go:19: test
    new logger: 2017/02/05 log.go:23: you can also add args(true)
    and use Fataln to log and crash

    logging 'handled' errors:
    2017/02/05 18:36:11 an error occurred: in passthrougherror:
    error occurred

10. The `go.mod` file gets updated and the `go.sum` file should now be present in the top-level recipe directory.

11. If you copied or wrote your own tests, then go up one directory and run `go test`. Ensure that all the tests pass.

How it works...

You can either initialize a logger and pass it around using `log.NewLogger()`, or use the `log` package level logger to log messages. The `log.go` file in this recipe does the former and `error.go` does the latter. It also shows when logging might make sense after an error has reached its final destination; otherwise, it's likely that you'll log multiple times for one event.

There are a few issues with this approach. First, you may have additional context in one of the intermediate functions, such as the variables you'd like to log. Second, logging a bunch of variables can get messy, making it confusing and difficult to read. The next recipe explores structured logging that provides flexibility in logging variables, and, in a later recipe, we will explore implementing a global package-level logger as well.

Structured logging with the apex and logrus packages

The primary reason to log information is to examine the state of the system when events occur or have occurred in the past. Basic log messages are tricky to comb over when you have a large number of microservices that are logging.

There's a variety of third-party packages for combing over logs if you can get the logs into a data format they understand. These packages provide indexing functionality, searchability, and more. The `sirupsen/logrus` and `apex/log` packages provide a way to do structured logging where you can log a number of fields that can be reformatted to fit these third-party log readers. For example, it's simple to emit logs in JSON format to be parsed by a variety of services.

How to do it...

These steps cover the writing and running of your application:

1. From your Terminal/console application, create a new directory called `~/projects/go-programming-cookbook/chapter4/structured` and navigate to this directory.
2. Run the following command:

   ```
   $ go mod init github.com/PacktPublishing/Go-Programming-Cookbook-
   Second-Edition/chapter4/structured
   ```

   You should see a file called `go.mod` that contains the following:

   ```
   module github.com/PacktPublishing/Go-Programming-Cookbook-Second-
   Edition/chapter4/structured
   ```

3. Copy tests from ~/projects/go-programming-cookbook-original/chapter4/structured, or use this as an exercise to write some of your own code!

4. Create a file called logrus.go with the following content:

```go
package structured

import "github.com/sirupsen/logrus"

// Hook will implement the logrus
// hook interface
type Hook struct {
    id string
}

// Fire will trigger whenever you log
func (hook *Hook) Fire(entry *logrus.Entry) error {
    entry.Data["id"] = hook.id
    return nil
}

// Levels is what levels this hook will fire on
func (hook *Hook) Levels() []logrus.Level {
    return logrus.AllLevels
}

// Logrus demonstrates some basic logrus functionality
func Logrus() {
    // we're emitting in json format
    logrus.SetFormatter(&logrus.TextFormatter{})
    logrus.SetLevel(logrus.InfoLevel)
    logrus.AddHook(&Hook{"123"})

    fields := logrus.Fields{}
    fields["success"] = true
    fields["complex_struct"] = struct {
        Event string
        When  string
    }{"Something happened", "Just now"}

    x := logrus.WithFields(fields)
    x.Warn("warning!")
    x.Error("error!")
}
```

5. Create a file called `apex.go` with the following content:

```go
package structured

import (
    "errors"
    "os"

    "github.com/apex/log"
    "github.com/apex/log/handlers/text"
)

// ThrowError throws an error that we'll trace
func ThrowError() error {
    err := errors.New("a crazy failure")
    log.WithField("id", "123").Trace("ThrowError").Stop(&err)
    return err
}

// CustomHandler splits to two streams
type CustomHandler struct {
    id      string
    handler log.Handler
}

// HandleLog adds a hook and does the emitting
func (h *CustomHandler) HandleLog(e *log.Entry) error {
    e.WithField("id", h.id)
    return h.handler.HandleLog(e)
}

// Apex has a number of useful tricks
func Apex() {
    log.SetHandler(&CustomHandler{"123", text.New(os.Stdout)})
    err := ThrowError()

    //With error convenience function
    log.WithError(err).Error("an error occurred")
}
```

6. Create a new directory named `example` and navigate to it.

7. Create a `main.go` file with the following content:

```go
package main

import (
    "fmt"
```

```
            "github.com/PacktPublishing/
            Go-Programming-Cookbook-Second-Edition/
            chapter4/structured"
    )

    func main() {
        fmt.Println("Logrus:")
        structured.Logrus()

        fmt.Println()
        fmt.Println("Apex:")
        structured.Apex()
    }
```

8. Run go run main.go.

9. You may also run the following commands:

    ```
    $ go build
    $ ./example
    ```

    You should now see the following output:

    ```
    $ go run main.go
    Logrus:
    WARN[0000] warning! complex_struct={Something happened Just now}
    id=123 success=true
    ERRO[0000] error! complex_struct={Something happened Just now}
    id=123 success=true

    Apex:
    INFO[0000] ThrowError id=123
    ERROR[0000] ThrowError duration=133ns error=a crazy failure
    id=123
    ERROR[0000] an error occurred error=a crazy failure
    ```

10. The go.mod file should be updated and the go.sum file should now be present in the top-level recipe directory.

11. If you copied or wrote your own tests, then go up one directory and run go test. Ensure that all the tests pass.

How it works...

The `sirupsen/logrus` and `apex/log` packages are both excellent structured loggers. Both provide hooks for either emitting to multiple events or to add extra fields to a log entry. It would be relatively simple, for example, to use the `logrus` hook or the `apex` custom handler to add line numbers to all of your logs, as well as service names. Another use for a hook might include `traceID`, in order to trace a request across different services.

While `logrus` splits the hook and the formatter, `apex` combines them. In addition to this, `apex` adds some convenience functions such as `WithError` to add an `error` field as well as tracing, both of which are demonstrated in this recipe. It's also relatively simple to adapt hooks from `logrus` to the `apex` handlers. For both solutions, it would be a simple change to convert to JSON formatting, instead of ANSI-colored text.

Logging with the context package

This recipe will demonstrate a way to pass log fields between various functions. The Go `pkg/context` package is an excellent way to pass additional variables and cancellations between functions. This recipe will explore using this functionality to distribute variables between functions for logging purposes.

This style can be adapted to `logrus` or `apex` from the previous recipe. We'll use `apex` for this recipe.

How to do it...

These steps cover the writing and running of your application:

1. From your Terminal/console application, create a new directory called `~/projects/go-programming-cookbook/chapter4/context` and navigate to this directory.
2. Run the following command:

   ```
   $ go mod init github.com/PacktPublishing/Go-Programming-Cookbook-
   Second-Edition/chapter4/context
   ```

   You should see a file called `go.mod` that contains the following:

   ```
   module github.com/PacktPublishing/Go-Programming-Cookbook-Second-
   Edition/chapter4/context
   ```

3. Copy tests from `~/projects/go-programming-cookbook-original/chapter4/context`, or use this as an exercise to write some of your own code!

4. Create a file called `log.go` with the following content:

```go
package context

import (
    "context"

    "github.com/apex/log"
)

type key int

// logFields is a key we use
// for our context logging
const logFields key = 0
func getFields(ctx context.Context) *log.Fields {
    fields, ok := ctx.Value(logFields).(*log.Fields)
    if !ok {
        f := make(log.Fields)
        fields = &f
    }
    return fields
}

// FromContext takes an entry and a context
// then returns an entry populated from the context object
func FromContext(ctx context.Context, l log.Interface)
(context.Context, *log.Entry) {
    fields := getFields(ctx)
    e := l.WithFields(fields)
    ctx = context.WithValue(ctx, logFields, fields)
    return ctx, e
}

// WithField adds a log field to the context
func WithField(ctx context.Context, key string, value
    interface{}) context.Context {
        return WithFields(ctx, log.Fields{key: value})
}

// WithFields adds many log fields to the context
func WithFields(ctx context.Context, fields log.Fielder)
context.Context {
    f := getFields(ctx)
```

```
        for key, val := range fields.Fields() {
            (*f)[key] = val
        }
        ctx = context.WithValue(ctx, logFields, f)
        return ctx
    }
```

5. Create a file called `collect.go` with the following content:

```
package context

import (
    "context"
    "os"

    "github.com/apex/log"
    "github.com/apex/log/handlers/text"
)

// Initialize calls 3 functions to set up, then
// logs before terminating
func Initialize() {
    // set basic log up
    log.SetHandler(text.New(os.Stdout))
    // initialize our context
    ctx := context.Background()
    // create a logger and link it to
    // the context
    ctx, e := FromContext(ctx, log.Log)

    // set a field
    ctx = WithField(ctx, "id", "123")
    e.Info("starting")
    gatherName(ctx)
    e.Info("after gatherName")
    gatherLocation(ctx)
    e.Info("after gatherLocation")
    }

    func gatherName(ctx context.Context) {
        ctx = WithField(ctx, "name", "Go Cookbook")
    }

    func gatherLocation(ctx context.Context) {
        ctx = WithFields(ctx, log.Fields{"city": "Seattle",
        "state": "WA"})
    }
```

6. Create a new directory named `example` and navigate to it.

7. Create a `main.go` file with the following content:

```
package main

import "github.com/PacktPublishing/
        Go-Programming-Cookbook-Second-Edition/
        chapter4/context"

func main() {
    context.Initialize()
}
```

8. Run `go run main.go`.

9. You may also run the following commands:

```
$ go build
$ ./example
```

You should see the following output:

```
$ go run main.go
INFO[0000] starting id=123
INFO[0000] after gatherName id=123 name=Go Cookbook
INFO[0000] after gatherLocation city=Seattle id=123 name=Go
Cookbook state=WA
```

10. The `go.mod` file gets updated and the `go.sum` file should now be present in the top-level recipe directory.

11. If you copied or wrote your own tests, then go up one directory and run `go test`. Ensure that all the tests pass.

How it works...

The `context` package now appears in a variety of packages, including the database and HTTP packages. This recipe will allow you to attach log fields to a context and use them for logging purposes. The idea is that separate methods can attach more fields to a context as it is passed around, and then the final call site can perform logging and aggregate variables.

This recipe mimics the `WithField` and `WithFields` methods found in the logging packages in the previous recipe. These modify a single value stored in the context and also provide the other benefits of using a context: cancellation, timeouts, and thread safety.

Using package-level global variables

The `apex` and `logrus` packages in the earlier examples both used a package-level global variable. Sometimes, it's useful to structure your libraries to support both structures with a variety of methods and top-level functions so that you can use them directly without passing them around.

This recipe also demonstrates using `sync.Once` to ensure that the global logger will only be initialized once. It can also be bypassed by the `Set` method. The recipe only exports `WithField` and `Debug`, but you can imagine exporting every method attached to a `log` object.

How to do it...

These steps cover the writing and running of your application:

1. From your Terminal/console application, create a new directory called `~/projects/go-programming-cookbook/chapter4/global` and navigate to this directory.

2. Run the following command:

   ```
   $ go mod init github.com/PacktPublishing/Go-Programming-Cookbook-
   Second-Edition/chapter4/global
   ```

   You should see a file called `go.mod` that contains the following:

   ```
   module github.com/PacktPublishing/Go-Programming-Cookbook-Second-
   Edition/chapter4/global
   ```

3. Copy tests from `~/projects/go-programming-cookbook-original/chapter4/global`, or use this as an exercise to write some of your own code!

4. Create a file called `global.go` with the following content:

   ```
   package global

   import (
       "errors"
       "os"
       "sync"

       "github.com/sirupsen/logrus"
   ```

```
    )

    // we make our global package level
    // variable lower case
    var (
        log *logrus.Logger
        initLog sync.Once
    )

    // Init sets up the logger initially
    // if run multiple times, it returns
    // an error
    func Init() error {
        err := errors.New("already initialized")
        initLog.Do(func() {
            err = nil
            log = logrus.New()
            log.Formatter = &logrus.JSONFormatter{}
            log.Out = os.Stdout
            log.Level = logrus.DebugLevel
        })
        return err
    }

    // SetLog sets the log
    func SetLog(l *logrus.Logger) {
        log = l
    }

    // WithField exports the logs withfield connected
    // to our global log
    func WithField(key string, value interface{}) *logrus.Entry {
        return log.WithField(key, value)
    }

    // Debug exports the logs Debug connected
    // to our global log
    func Debug(args ...interface{}) {
        log.Debug(args...)
    }
```

5. Create a file called `log.go` with the following content:

```
    package global

    // UseLog demonstrates using our global
    // log
    func UseLog() error {
```

```
        if err := Init(); err != nil {
            return err
    }

    // if we were in another package these would be
    // global.WithField and
    // global.Debug
    WithField("key", "value").Debug("hello")
    Debug("test")

    return nil
    }
```

6. Create a new directory named `example` and navigate to it.
7. Create a `main.go` file with the following content:

```
package main

import "github.com/PacktPublishing/
        Go-Programming-Cookbook-Second-Edition/
        chapter4/global"

func main() {
    if err := global.UseLog(); err != nil {
        panic(err)
    }
}
```

8. Run `go run main.go`.
9. You may also run the following commands:

```
$ go build
$ ./example
```

You should see the following output:

```
$ go run main.go
{"key":"value","level":"debug","msg":"hello","time":"2017-02-
12T19:22:50-08:00"}
{"level":"debug","msg":"test","time":"2017-02-12T19:22:50-
08:00"}
```

10. The `go.mod` file gets updated and the `go.sum` file should now be present in the top-level recipe directory.
11. If you copied or wrote your own tests, then go up one directory and run `go test`. Ensure that all the tests pass.

How it works...

A common pattern for these `global` package-level objects is to keep the `global` variable unexported and expose only the desired functionality through methods. Typically, you could also include a method to return a copy of the `global` logger for packages that want a `logger` object.

The `sync.Once` type is a newly introduced structure. This structure, in conjunction with the `Do` method, will only execute in the code once. We use this in our initialization code, and the `Init` function will throw an error if `Init` is called more than once. We use a custom `Init` function instead of the built-in `init()` function, if we want to pass in parameters to our `global` log.

Although this example uses a log, you can also imagine cases where this might be useful with a database connection, data streams, and a number of other use cases.

Catching panics for long-running processes

When implementing long-running processes, it's possible that certain code paths will result in a panic. This is usually common for things such as uninitialized maps and pointers, as well as division by zero problems in the case of poorly validated user input.

Having a program crash completely in these cases is frequently much worse than the panic itself, and so it can be helpful to catch and handle panics.

How to do it...

These steps cover the writing and running of your application:

1. From your Terminal/console application, create a new directory called `~/projects/go-programming-cookbook/chapter4/panic` and navigate to this directory.
2. Run the following command:

```
$ go mod init github.com/PacktPublishing/Go-Programming-Cookbook-
Second-Edition/chapter4/panic
```

You should see a file called `go.mod` that contains the following:

```
module github.com/PacktPublishing/Go-Programming-Cookbook-Second-
Edition/chapter4/panic
```

3. Copy tests from `~/projects/go-programming-cookbook-
original/chapter4/panic`, or use this as an exercise to write some of your
own code!

4. Create a file called `panic.go` with the following content:

```go
package panic

import (
    "fmt"
    "strconv"
)

// Panic panics with a divide by zero
func Panic() {
    zero, err := strconv.ParseInt("0", 10, 64)
    if err != nil {
        panic(err)
    }
    a := 1 / zero
    fmt.Println("we'll never get here", a)
}

// Catcher calls Panic
func Catcher() {
    defer func() {
        if r := recover(); r != nil {
            fmt.Println("panic occurred:", r)
        }
    }()
    Panic()
}
```

5. Create a new directory named `example` and navigate to it.

6. Create a `main.go` file with the following content:

```go
package main

import (
    "fmt"

    "github.com/PacktPublishing/
    Go-Programming-Cookbook-Second-Edition/
```

```
            chapter4/panic"
)

func main() {
    fmt.Println("before panic")
    panic.Catcher()
    fmt.Println("after panic")
}
```

7. Run `go run main.go`.

8. You may also run the following commands:

```
$ go build
$ ./example
```

You should see the following output:

```
$ go run main.go
before panic
panic occurred: runtime error: integer divide by zero
after panic
```

9. If you copied or wrote your own tests, then go up one directory and run `go test`. Ensure that all the tests pass.

How it works...

This recipe is a very basic example of how to catch panics. You can imagine with more complex middleware how you can defer a recover and catch it after running many nested functions. Within the recover, you can, essentially, do anything you want, although emitting a log is common.

In most web applications, it's common to catch panics and emit an `http.InternalServerError` message when a panic occurs.

5
Network Programming

The Go standard library provides a lot of support for network operations. It includes packages that allow you to manage TCP/IP, UDP, DNS, mail, and RPC using HTTP. Third-party packages can also fill in the gaps from what's included in the standard library, including `gorilla/websockets` (`https://github.com/gorilla/websocket/`) for a WebSocket implementation that can be used in a normal HTTP handler. This chapter explores these libraries and demonstrates some simple recipes for how you can make use of each of them. These recipes will assist developers who are unable to use a higher-level abstraction such as REST or GRPC, but need network connectivity. It's also useful for DevOps applications that need to perform DNS lookups or work with raw emails. After reading this chapter, you should've gained some mastery of basic networking programming and be prepared to dive deeper.

In this chapter, the following recipes will be covered:

- Writing a TCP/IP echo server and client
- Writing a UDP server and client
- Working with domain name resolution
- Working with WebSockets
- Working with net/rpc for calling remote methods
- Using net/mail for parsing emails

Technical requirements

In order to proceed with all the recipes in this chapter, configure your environment according to these steps:

1. Download and install Go 1.12.6 or greater on your operating system from `https://golang.org/doc/install`.

2. Open a Terminal or console application, and then create and navigate to a project directory such as `~/projects/go-programming-cookbook`. All code will be run and modified from this directory.

3. Clone the latest code into `~/projects/go-programming-cookbook-original` and you have the option to work from that directory rather than typing the examples manually:

```
$ git clone git@github.com:PacktPublishing/Go-Programming-Cookbook-
Second-Edition.git go-programming-cookbook-original
```

Writing a TCP/IP echo server and client

TCP/IP is a common network protocol and the HTTP protocol was built on top of it. TCP requires a client to connect to a server in order to send and receive data. This recipe will use the `net` package to make a TCP connection between a client and a server. The client will send user input to the server and the server will respond with the same string inputted, but converted to uppercase using the results of `strings.ToUpper()`. The client will print any messages received from the server so it should output the uppercase version of our input.

How to do it...

These steps cover writing and running your application:

1. From your Terminal or console application, create a new directory called `~/projects/go-programming-cookbook/chapter5/tcp` and navigate to this directory.

2. Run the following command:

```
$ go mod init github.com/PacktPublishing/Go-Programming-Cookbook-
Second-Edition/chapter5/tcp
```

You should see a file called `go.mod` that contains the following:

```
module github.com/PacktPublishing/Go-Programming-Cookbook-Second-
Edition/chapter5/tcp
```

3. Copy tests from `~/projects/go-programming-cookbook-original/chapter5/tcp` or use this as an exercise to write some of your own code!

4. Create a new directory named `server` and navigate to it.

5. Create a file called `main.go` with the following content:

```go
package main

import (
  "bufio"
  "fmt"
  "net"
  "strings"
)

const addr = "localhost:8888"

func echoBackCapitalized(conn net.Conn) {
  // set up a reader on conn (an io.Reader)
  reader := bufio.NewReader(conn)

  // grab the first line of data encountered
  data, err := reader.ReadString('\n')
  if err != nil {
    fmt.Printf("error reading data: %s\n", err.Error())
    return
  }
  // print then send back the data
  fmt.Printf("Received: %s", data)
  conn.Write([]byte(strings.ToUpper(data)))
  // close up the finished connection
  conn.Close()
}

func main() {
  ln, err := net.Listen("tcp", addr)
  if err != nil {
    panic(err)
  }
  defer ln.Close()
  fmt.Printf("listening on: %s\n", addr)
  for {
    conn, err := ln.Accept()
    if err != nil {
      fmt.Printf("encountered an error accepting connection: %s\n",
                 err.Error())
      // if there's an error try again
      continue
    }
    // handle this asynchronously
```

```
          // potentially a good use-case
          // for a worker pool
          go echoBackCapitalized(conn)
      }
  }
```

6. Navigate to the previous directory.
7. Create a new directory named `client` and navigate to it.
8. Create a file called `main.go` with the following content:

```go
package main

import (
  "bufio"
  "fmt"
  "net"
  "os"
)

const addr = "localhost:8888"

func main() {
  reader := bufio.NewReader(os.Stdin)
  for {
    // grab a string input from the clie
    fmt.Printf("Enter some text: ")
    data, err := reader.ReadString('\n')
    if err != nil {
      fmt.Printf("encountered an error reading input: %s\n",
            err.Error())
      continue
    }
    // connect to the addr
    conn, err := net.Dial("tcp", addr)
    if err != nil {
      fmt.Printf("encountered an error connecting: %s\n",
            err.Error())
    }

    // write the data to the connection
    fmt.Fprintf(conn, data)

    // read back the response
    status, err := bufio.NewReader(conn).ReadString('\n')
    if err != nil {
      fmt.Printf("encountered an error reading response: %s\n",
            err.Error())
```

```
    }
    fmt.Printf("Received back: %s", status)
    // close up the finished connection
    conn.Close()
  }
}
```

9. Navigate to the previous directory.

10. Run go run ./server and you will see the following output:

    ```
    $ go run ./server
    listening on: localhost:8888
    ```

11. In a separate Terminal, run go run ./client from the tcp directory and you will see the following output:

    ```
    $ go run ./client
    Enter some text:
    ```

12. Type this is a test and hit *Enter*. You will see the following:

    ```
    $ go run ./client
    Enter some text: this is a test
    Received back: THIS IS A TEST
    Enter some text:
    ```

13. Press *Ctrl + C* to exit.

14. If you copied or wrote your own tests, go up one directory and run go test. Ensure that all the tests pass.

How it works...

The server is listening on port 8888. Whenever a request comes in, the server must pick up the request and manage the client connection. In the case of this program, it dispatches a Goroutine that reads the request from the client, capitalizes the data it receives, sends it back to the client, and, lastly, closes the connection. The server immediately loops again, waiting to receive new client connections while the previous connection is handled separately.

The client reads input from STDIN, connects to the address via a TCP connection, writes the message that was read from the input, and then prints back the response from the server. Afterward, it closes the connection and loops the reading once again from STDIN. It's also possible for you to rework this example to have the client stay connected until the program exits rather than on each request.

Writing a UDP server and client

The UDP protocol is often used for games and in places where speed is more important than reliability. UDP servers and clients do not need to connect with one another. This recipe will create a UDP server that will listen for messages from clients, add their IPs to its list, and broadcast messages to each of the previously seen clients.

The server will write a message to STDOUT whenever a client connects and it will broadcast the same message to all of its clients. The text of this message should be Sent <count>, where <count> will increment each time the server broadcasts to all of its clients. As a result, count may have different values depending on how long it takes you to connect to your client as the server will broadcast regardless of the number of clients it sends a message to.

How to do it...

These steps cover the process of writing and running your application:

1. From your Terminal or console application, create a new directory called ~/projects/go-programming-cookbook/chapter5/udp and navigate to this directory.

2. Run the following command:

```
$ go mod init github.com/PacktPublishing/Go-Programming-Cookbook-
Second-Edition/chapter5/udp
```

You should see a file called go.mod that contains the following:

```
module github.com/PacktPublishing/Go-Programming-Cookbook-Second-
Edition/chapter5/udp
```

3. Copy tests from ~/projects/go-programming-cookbook-original/chapter5/udp or use this as an exercise to write some of your own code!

4. Create a new directory named server and navigate to it.

5. Create a file called `broadcast.go` with the following content:

```go
package main

import (
  "fmt"
  "net"
  "sync"
  "time"
)

type connections struct {
  addrs map[string]*net.UDPAddr
  // lock for modifying the map
  mu sync.Mutex
}

func broadcast(conn *net.UDPConn, conns *connections) {
  count := 0
  for {
    count++
    conns.mu.Lock()
    // loop over known addresses
    for _, retAddr := range conns.addrs {

      // send a message to them all
      msg := fmt.Sprintf("Sent %d", count)
      if _, err := conn.WriteToUDP([]byte(msg), retAddr); err !=
nil {
        fmt.Printf("error encountered: %s", err.Error())
        continue
      }

    }
    conns.mu.Unlock()
    time.Sleep(1 * time.Second)
  }
}
```

6. Create a file called `main.go` with the following content:

```go
package main

import (
  "fmt"
  "net"
)
```

```
const addr = "localhost:8888"

func main() {
  conns := &connections{
    addrs: make(map[string]*net.UDPAddr),
  }

  fmt.Printf("serving on %s\n", addr)

  // construct a udp addr
  addr, err := net.ResolveUDPAddr("udp", addr)
  if err != nil {
    panic(err)
  }

  // listen on our specified addr
  conn, err := net.ListenUDP("udp", addr)
  if err != nil {
    panic(err)
  }
  // cleanup
  defer conn.Close()

  // async send messages to all known clients
  go broadcast(conn, conns)

  msg := make([]byte, 1024)
  for {
    // receive a message to gather the ip address
    // and port to send back to
    _, retAddr, err := conn.ReadFromUDP(msg)
    if err != nil {
      continue
    }

    //store it in a map
    conns.mu.Lock()
    conns.addrs[retAddr.String()] = retAddr
    conns.mu.Unlock()
    fmt.Printf("%s connected\n", retAddr)
  }
}
```

7. Navigate to the previous directory.
8. Create a new directory named `client` and navigate to it.

9. Create a file called `main.go` with the following content:

```go
package main

import (
  "fmt"
  "net"
)

const addr = "localhost:8888"

func main() {
  fmt.Printf("client for server url: %s\n", addr)

  addr, err := net.ResolveUDPAddr("udp", addr)
  if err != nil {
    panic(err)
  }

  conn, err := net.DialUDP("udp", nil, addr)
  if err != nil {
    panic(err)
  }
  defer conn.Close()

  msg := make([]byte, 512)
  n, err := conn.Write([]byte("connected"))
  if err != nil {
    panic(err)
  }
  for {
    n, err = conn.Read(msg)
    if err != nil {
      continue
    }
    fmt.Printf("%s\n", string(msg[:n]))
  }
}
```

10. Navigate to the previous directory.

11. Run `go run ./server` and you will see the following output:

```
$ go run ./server
serving on localhost:8888
```

12. In a separate Terminal, run `go run ./client` from the `udp` directory and you will see the following output, although the counts may differ:

```
$ go run ./client
client for server url: localhost:8888
Sent 3
Sent 4
Sent 5
```

13. Navigate to the Terminal that is running the server and you should see something similar to the following:

```
$ go run ./server
serving on localhost:8888
127.0.0.1:64242 connected
```

14. Press *Ctrl* + *C* to exit both the server and client.

15. If you copied or wrote your own tests, go up one directory and run `go test`. Ensure that all the tests pass.

How it works...

The server is listening on port `8888` just like in the previous recipe. If a client starts, it sends a message to the server and the server adds its address to a list of addresses. Because clients can connect asynchronously, the server must use a mutex before modifying or reading from the list.

A separate broadcast Goroutine runs separately and sends the same message to all client addresses that have previously sent it messages. Assuming they're still listening, they'll receive the same message from the server at roughly the same time. You may also connect with more clients to see this in effect.

Working with domain name resolution

The `net` package provides a number of useful functions around DNS lookup. This information is comparable to what you might get from using the Unix `dig` command. This information can be extremely useful for you to implement any kind of network programming that requires dynamically determining IP addresses.

This recipe will explore how you might gather this data. To demonstrate this, we'll implement a simplified dig command. We'll seek to map a URL to all of its IPv4 and IPv6 addresses. By modifying GODEBUG=netdns= to be set to go or cgo, it will either use the pure Go DNS resolver or the cgo resolver. By default, the pure Go DNS resolver is used.

How to do it...

These steps cover writing and running your application:

1. From your Terminal or console application, create a new directory called ~/projects/go-programming-cookbook/chapter5/dns and navigate to this directory.
2. Run the following command:

   ```
   $ go mod init github.com/PacktPublishing/Go-Programming-Cookbook-
   Second-Edition/chapter5/dns
   ```

   You should see a file called go.mod that contains the following:

   ```
   module github.com/PacktPublishing/Go-Programming-Cookbook-Second-
   Edition/chapter5/dns
   ```

3. Copy tests from ~/projects/go-programming-cookbook-original/chapter5/dns or use this as an exercise to write some of your own code!
4. Create a dns.go file with the following content:

   ```go
   package dns

   import (
     "fmt"
     "net"

     "github.com/pkg/errors"
   )

   // Lookup holds the DNS information we care about
   type Lookup struct {
     cname string
     hosts []string
   }

   // We can use this to print the lookup object
   func (d *Lookup) String() string {
   ```

```
        result := ""
        for _, host := range d.hosts {
          result += fmt.Sprintf("%s IN A %s\n", d.cname, host)
        }
        return result
    }

    // LookupAddress returns a DNSLookup consisting of a cname and host
    // for a given address
    func LookupAddress(address string) (*Lookup, error) {
      cname, err := net.LookupCNAME(address)
      if err != nil {
        return nil, errors.Wrap(err, "error looking up CNAME")
      }
      hosts, err := net.LookupHost(address)
      if err != nil {
        return nil, errors.Wrap(err, "error looking up HOST")
      }

      return &Lookup{cname: cname, hosts: hosts}, nil
    }
```

5. Create a new directory named `example` and navigate to it.

6. Create a `main.go` file with the following content:

```
    package main

    import (
      "fmt"
      "log"
      "os"

      "github.com/PacktPublishing/Go-Programming-Cookbook-Second-
    Edition/chapter5/dns"
    )

    func main() {
      if len(os.Args) < 2 {
        fmt.Printf("Usage: %s <address>\n", os.Args[0])
        os.Exit(1)
      }
      address := os.Args[1]
      lookup, err := dns.LookupAddress(address)
      if err != nil {
        log.Panicf("failed to lookup: %s", err.Error())
      }
      fmt.Println(lookup)
    }
```

7. Run the `go run main.go golang.org` command.

8. You may also run the following:

```
$ go build
$ ./example golang.org
```

You should see the following output:

```
$ go run main.go golang.org
golang.org.  IN A 172.217.5.17
golang.org.  IN A 2607:f8b0:4009:809::2011
```

9. The `go.mod` file may be updated and the `go.sum` file should now be present in the top-level recipe directory.

10. If you copied or wrote your own tests, go up one directory and run `go test`. Ensure that all the tests pass.

How it works...

This recipe performed a `CNAME` and host lookup of the address provided. In our case, we used `golang.org`. We store the result in a lookup structure that prints the output results using the `String()` method. This method will be called automatically when we print our object as a string, or we can call the method directly. We implement some basic argument checking in `main.go` to ensure that an address is provided when the program is run.

Working with WebSockets

WebSockets allow a server application to connect to a web-based client written in JavaScript. This allows you to create web applications with two-way communication and to create updates such as chat rooms and more.

This recipe will explore writing a WebSocket server in Go and also demonstrate the process of a client consuming and communicating with a WebSocket server. It uses `github.com/gorilla/websocket` to upgrade a standard handler into a WebSocket handler and also to create the client application.

How to do it...

These steps cover writing and running your application:

1. From your Terminal or console application, create a new directory called `~/projects/go-programming-cookbook/chapter5/websocket` and navigate to this directory.

2. Run the following command:

   $ go mod init github.com/PacktPublishing/Go-Programming-Cookbook-Second-Edition/chapter5/websocket

   You should see a file called `go.mod` that contains the following:

   ```
   module github.com/PacktPublishing/Go-Programming-Cookbook-Second-Edition/chapter5/websocket
   ```

3. Copy tests from `~/projects/go-programming-cookbook-original/chapter5/websocket` or use this as an exercise to write some of your own code!

4. Create a new directory named `server` and navigate to it.

5. Create a file called `handler.go` with the following content:

   ```go
   package main

   import (
     "log"
     "net/http"

     "github.com/gorilla/websocket"
   )

   // upgrader takes an http connection and converts it
   // to a websocket one, we're using some recommended
   // basic buffer sizes
   var upgrader = websocket.Upgrader{
     ReadBufferSize: 1024,
     WriteBufferSize: 1024,
   }

   func wsHandler(w http.ResponseWriter, r *http.Request) {
     // upgrade the connection
     conn, err := upgrader.Upgrade(w, r, nil)
     if err != nil {
       log.Println("failed to upgrade connection: ", err)
       return
   ```

```
    }
    for {
      // read and echo back messages in a loop
      messageType, p, err := conn.ReadMessage()
      if err != nil {
        log.Println("failed to read message: ", err)
        return
      }
      log.Printf("received from client: %#v", string(p))
      if err := conn.WriteMessage(messageType, p); err != nil {
        log.Println("failed to write message: ", err)
        return
      }
    }
  }
}
```

6. Create a file called `main.go` with the following content:

```
package main

import (
  "fmt"
  "log"
  "net/http"
)

func main() {
  fmt.Println("Listening on port :8000")
 // we mount our single handler on port localhost:8000 to handle all
  // requests
  log.Panic(http.ListenAndServe("localhost:8000",
http.HandlerFunc(wsHandler)))
}
```

7. Navigate to the previous directory.
8. Create a new directory named `client` and navigate to it.
9. Create a file called `process.go` with the following content:

```
package main

import (
  "bufio"
  "fmt"
  "log"
  "os"
  "strings"
```

```
      "github.com/gorilla/websocket"
)

func process(c *websocket.Conn) {
  reader := bufio.NewReader(os.Stdin)
  for {
    fmt.Printf("Enter some text: ")
    // this will block ctrl-c, to exit press it then hit enter
    // or kill from another location
    data, err := reader.ReadString('\n')
    if err != nil {
      log.Println("failed to read stdin", err)
    }

    // trim off the space from reading the string
    data = strings.TrimSpace(data)

    // write the message as a byte across the websocket
    err = c.WriteMessage(websocket.TextMessage, []byte(data))
    if err != nil {
      log.Println("failed to write message:", err)
      return
    }

    // this is an echo server, so we can always read after the
write
    _, message, err := c.ReadMessage()
    if err != nil {
      log.Println("failed to read:", err)
      return
    }
    log.Printf("received back from server: %#v\n", string(message))
  }
}
```

10. Create a file called main.go with the following content:

```
package main

import (
  "log"
  "os"
  "os/signal"

  "github.com/gorilla/websocket"
)

// catchSig cleans up our websocket conenction if we kill the
```

```
program
// with a ctrl-c
func catchSig(ch chan os.Signal, c *websocket.Conn) {
  // block on waiting for a signal
  <-ch
  err := c.WriteMessage(websocket.CloseMessage,
websocket.FormatCloseMessage(websocket.CloseNormalClosure, ""))
  if err != nil {
    log.Println("write close:", err)
  }
  return
}

func main() {
  // connect the os signal to our channel
  interrupt := make(chan os.Signal, 1)
  signal.Notify(interrupt, os.Interrupt)

  // use the ws:// Scheme to connect to the websocket
  u := "ws://localhost:8000/"
  log.Printf("connecting to %s", u)

  c, _, err := websocket.DefaultDialer.Dial(u, nil)
  if err != nil {
    log.Fatal("dial:", err)
  }
  defer c.Close()

  // dispatch our signal catcher
  go catchSig(interrupt, c)

  process(c)
}
```

11. Navigate to the previous directory.

12. Run `go run ./server` and you will see the following output:

    ```
    $ go run ./server
    Listening on port :8000
    ```

13. In a separate Terminal, run `go run ./client` from the `websocket` directory and you will see the following output:

    ```
    $ go run ./client
    2019/05/26 11:53:20 connecting to ws://localhost:8000/
    Enter some text:
    ```

14. Enter the `test` string and you should see the following:

```
$ go run ./client
2019/05/26 11:53:20 connecting to ws://localhost:8000/
Enter some text: test
2019/05/26 11:53:22 received back from server: "test"
Enter some text:
```

15. Navigate to the Terminal running the server and you should see something similar to the following:

```
$ go run ./server
Listening on port :8000
2019/05/26 11:53:22 received from client: "test"
```

16. Press *Ctrl + C* to exit both the server and client. You may also have to hit *Enter* after pressing *Ctrl + C* on the client.

17. The `go.mod` file may be updated and the `go.sum` file should now be present in the top-level recipe directory.

18. If you copied or wrote your own tests, go up one directory and run `go test`. Ensure that all the tests pass.

How it works...

The server is listening on port `8000` for WebSocket connections. When a request comes in, the `github.com/gorilla/websocket` package is used to upgrade the request to a WebSocket connection. Similar to earlier echo server examples, the server waits for a message on the WebSocket connection and responds with the same message back to the client. Because it's a handler, it can handle many WebSocket connections asynchronously and they will remain connected until the client terminates.

In the client, we added a `catchsig` function to handle the *Ctrl + C* event. This allows us to cleanly terminate the connection with the server when the client exits. Otherwise, the client just takes user input on `STDIN` and sends it to the server, logs the response, and then repeats.

Working with net/rpc for calling remote methods

Go provides your system with basic RPC functionality with the net/rpc package. This is a potential alternative to making RPC calls without relying on GRPC or other more complex RPC packages. However, its functionality is rather limited and any function you may wish to export must conform to a very specific function signature.

The comments in the code note some of these restrictions for a method that can be called remotely. This recipe demonstrates how to create a shared function that has a number of parameters passed in via a structure and can be called remotely.

How to do it...

These steps cover writing and running your application:

1. From your Terminal or console application, create a new directory called ~/projects/go-programming-cookbook/chapter5/rpc and navigate to this directory.

2. Run the following command:

   ```
   $ go mod init github.com/PacktPublishing/Go-Programming-Cookbook-
   Second-Edition/chapter5/rpc
   ```

   You should see a file called go.mod that contains the following:

   ```
   module github.com/PacktPublishing/Go-Programming-Cookbook-Second-
   Edition/chapter5/rpc
   ```

3. Copy tests from ~/projects/go-programming-cookbook-original/chapter5/rpc or use this as an exercise to write some of your own code!

4. Create a new directory named tweak and navigate to it.

5. Create a file called tweak.go with the following content:

   ```go
   package tweak

   import (
     "strings"
   )

   // StringTweaker is a type of string
   ```

```
// that can reverse itself
type StringTweaker struct{}

// Args are a list of options for how to tweak
// the string
type Args struct {
  String string
  ToUpper bool
  Reverse bool
}

// Tweak conforms to the RPC library which require:
// - the method's type is exported.
// - the method is exported.
// - the method has two arguments, both exported (or builtin)
types.
// - the method's second argument is a pointer.
// - the method has return type error.
func (s StringTweaker) Tweak(args *Args, resp *string) error {

  result := string(args.String)
  if args.ToUpper {
    result = strings.ToUpper(result)
  }
  if args.Reverse {
    runes := []rune(result)
    for i, j := 0, len(runes)-1; i < j; i, j = i+1, j-1 {
      runes[i], runes[j] = runes[j], runes[i]
    }
    result = string(runes)

  }
  *resp = result
  return nil
}
```

6. Navigate to the previous directory.
7. Create a new directory named `server` and navigate to it.
8. Create a file called `main.go` with the following content:

```
package main

import (
  "fmt"
  "log"
  "net"
  "net/http"
```

```
  "net/rpc"

  "github.com/PacktPublishing/Go-Programming-Cookbook-Second-
  Edition/chapter5/rpc/tweak"
)

func main() {
  s := new(tweak.StringTweaker)
  if err := rpc.Register(s); err != nil {
    log.Fatal("failed to register:", err)
  }

  rpc.HandleHTTP()

  l, err := net.Listen("tcp", ":1234")
  if err != nil {
    log.Fatal("listen error:", err)
  }

  fmt.Println("listening on :1234")
  log.Panic(http.Serve(l, nil))
}
```

9. Navigate to the previous directory.

10. Create a new directory named `client` and navigate to it.

11. Create a file called `main.go` with the following content:

```
package main

import (
  "fmt"
  "log"
  "net/rpc"

  "github.com/PacktPublishing/Go-Programming-Cookbook-Second-
  Edition/chapter5/rpc/tweak"
)

func main() {
  client, err := rpc.DialHTTP("tcp", "localhost:1234")
  if err != nil {
    log.Fatal("error dialing:", err)
  }

  args := tweak.Args{
    String: "this string should be uppercase and reversed",
    ToUpper: true,
```

```
        Reverse: true,
    }
    var result string
    err = client.Call("StringTweaker.Tweak", args, &result)
    if err != nil {
      log.Fatal("client call with error:", err)
    }
    fmt.Printf("the result is: %s", result)
}
```

12. Navigate to the previous directory.

13. Run `go run ./server` and you will see the following output:

    ```
    $ go run ./server
    Listening on :1234
    ```

14. In a separate Terminal, run `go run ./client` from the `rpc` directory and you will see the following output:

    ```
    $ go run ./client
    the result is: DESREVER DNA ESACREPPU EB DLUOHS GNIRTS SIHT
    ```

15. Press *Ctrl + C* to exit the server.

16. If you copied or wrote your own tests, go up one directory and run `go test`. Ensure that all the tests pass.

How it works...

The `StringTweaker` structure is put into a separate library so that its exported types can be accessed by the client (to set arguments) and the server (to register the RPC and start the server). It also conforms to the rules mentioned at the start of this recipe in order to work with `net/rpc`.

`StringTweaker` can be used to take an input string and, optionally, reverse and uppercase all the characters contained within it, depending on the options passed. This pattern can be extended to create far more complex functions and you can also use extra functions to make the code more readable as it grows.

Using net/mail for parsing emails

The net/mail package provides a number of useful functions that assist you when working with email. If you have the raw text of the email, it can be parsed into extract headers, information about the send date, and much more. This recipe will demonstrate a number of these functions by parsing a raw email hardcoded as a string.

How to do it...

These steps cover writing and running your application:

1. From your Terminal or console application, create a new directory called ~/projects/go-programming-cookbook/chapter5/mail and navigate to this directory.

2. Run the following command:

```
$ go mod init github.com/PacktPublishing/Go-Programming-Cookbook-
Second-Edition/chapter5/mail
```

You should see a file called go.mod that contains the following:

```
module github.com/PacktPublishing/Go-Programming-Cookbook-Second-
Edition/chapter5/mail
```

3. Copy tests from ~/projects/go-programming-cookbook-original/chapter5/mail or use this as an exercise to write some of your own code!

4. Create a header.go file with the following content:

```go
package main

import (
  "fmt"
  "net/mail"
  "strings"
)

// extract header info and print it nicely
func printHeaderInfo(header mail.Header) {

  // this works because we know it's a single address
  // otherwise use ParseAddressList
  toAddress, err := mail.ParseAddress(header.Get("To"))
  if err == nil {
```

```
      fmt.Printf("To: %s <%s>\n", toAddress.Name, toAddress.Address)
   }
   fromAddress, err := mail.ParseAddress(header.Get("From"))
   if err == nil {
      fmt.Printf("From: %s <%s>\n", fromAddress.Name,
            fromAddress.Address)
   }

   fmt.Println("Subject:", header.Get("Subject"))

   // this works for a valid RFC5322 date
   // it does a header.Get("Date"), then a
   // mail.ParseDate(that_result)
   if date, err := header.Date(); err == nil {
      fmt.Println("Date:", date)
   }

   fmt.Println(strings.Repeat("=", 40))
   fmt.Println()
}
```

5. Create a `main.go` file with the following content:

```
package main

import (
  "io"
  "log"
  "net/mail"
  "os"
  "strings"
)

// an example email message
const msg string = `Date: Thu, 24 Jul 2019 08:00:00 -0700
From: Aaron <fake_sender@example.com>
To: Reader <fake_receiver@example.com>
Subject: Gophercon 2019 is going to be awesome!

Feel free to share my book with others if you're attending.
This recipe can be used to process and parse email information.
`

func main() {
  r := strings.NewReader(msg)
  m, err := mail.ReadMessage(r)
  if err != nil {
    log.Fatal(err)
```

```
    }

    printHeaderInfo(m.Header)

    // after printing the header, dump the body to stdout
    if _, err := io.Copy(os.Stdout, m.Body); err != nil {
      log.Fatal(err)
    }
  }
```

6. Run the `go run .` command.

7. You may also run the following:

```
$ go build
$ ./mail
```

You should see the following output:

```
$ go run .
To: Reader <fake_receiver@example.com>
From: Aaron <fake_sender@example.com>
Subject: Gophercon 2019 is going to be awesome!
Date: 2019-07-24 08:00:00 -0700 -0700
==========================================

Feel free to share my book with others if you're attending.
This recipe can be used to process and parse email information.
```

8. If you copied or wrote your own tests, go up one directory and run `go test`. Ensure that all the tests pass.

How it works...

The `printHeaderInfo` function does the majority of the work for this recipe. It parses the addresses from the header into a `*mail.Address` structure and parses the date header into a date object. Then, it takes all of the information in the message and formats it into a readable format. The main function parses the initial email and passes this header along.

6
All about Databases and Storage

Go applications frequently need to make use of long-term storage. This is usually in the form of relational and non-relational databases, as well as key-value stores and more. When working with these storage applications, it helps to wrap your operations in an interface. The recipes in this chapter will examine various storage interfaces, consider parallel access with things such as connection pools, and look at general tips for integrating a new library, which is often the case when using a new storage technology.

In this chapter, the following recipes will be covered:

- Using the database/sql package with MySQL
- Executing a database transaction interface
- Connection pooling, rate limiting, and timeouts for SQL
- Working with Redis
- Using NoSQL with MongoDB
- Creating storage interfaces for data portability

Using the database/sql package with MySQL

Relational databases are some of the most well understood and common database options. MySQL and PostgreSQL are two of the most popular open-source relational databases. This recipe will demonstrate the `database/sql` package, which provides hooks for a number of relational databases and automatically handles connection pooling and connection duration, and gives access to a number of basic database operations.

This recipe will make use of a MySQL database to establish a connection, insert some simple data, and query it. It will clean up the database after use by dropping the table.

Getting ready

Configure your environment according to these steps:

1. Download and install Go 1.12.6 or greater on your operating system at `https://golang.org/doc/install`.

2. Open a Terminal or console application, create a project directory such as `~/projects/go-programming-cookbook` and navigate to this directory. All code will be run and modified from this directory.

3. Clone the latest code into `~/projects/go-programming-cookbook-original` and optionally work from that directory rather than typing the examples manually, as follows:

   ```
   $ git clone git@github.com:PacktPublishing/Go-Programming-Cookbook-
   Second-Edition.git go-programming-cookbook-original
   ```

4. Install and configure MySQL using `https://dev.mysql.com/doc/mysql-getting-started/en/`.

5. Run the `export MYSQLUSERNAME=<your mysql username>` command.

6. Run the `export MYSQLPASSWORD=<your mysql password>` command.

How to do it...

These steps cover writing and running your application:

1. From your Terminal or console application, create a new directory called `~/projects/go-programming-cookbook/chapter6/database` and navigate to this directory.

2. Run the following command:

   ```
   $ go mod init github.com/PacktPublishing/Go-Programming-Cookbook-
   Second-Edition/chapter6/database
   ```

   You should see a file called `go.mod` that containing the following:

   ```
   module github.com/PacktPublishing/Go-Programming-Cookbook-Second-
   Edition/chapter6/database
   ```

3. Copy tests from `~/projects/go-programming-cookbook-original/chapter6/database`, or use this as an exercise to write some code of your own!

4. Create a file called `config.go` with the following content:

```go
package database

import (
    "database/sql"
    "fmt"
    "os"
    "time"

    _ "github.com/go-sql-driver/mysql" //we import supported
    libraries for database/sql
)

// Example hold the results of our queries
type Example struct {
    Name string
    Created *time.Time
}

// Setup configures and returns our database
// connection poold
func Setup() (*sql.DB, error) {
    db, err := sql.Open("mysql",
    fmt.Sprintf("%s:%s@/gocookbook?
    parseTime=true", os.Getenv("MYSQLUSERNAME"),
    os.Getenv("MYSQLPASSWORD")))
    if err != nil {
        return nil, err
    }
    return db, nil
}
```

5. Create a file called `create.go` with the following content:

```go
package database

import (
    "database/sql"

    _ "github.com/go-sql-driver/mysql" //we import supported
    libraries for database/sql
)
```

```go
// Create makes a table called example
// and populates it
func Create(db *sql.DB) error {
    // create the database
    if _, err := db.Exec("CREATE TABLE example (name
    VARCHAR(20), created DATETIME)"); err != nil {
        return err
    }

    if _, err := db.Exec(`INSERT INTO example (name, created)
    values ("Aaron", NOW())`); err != nil {
        return err
    }

    return nil
}
```

6. Create a file called `query.go` with the following content:

```go
package database

import (
    "database/sql"
    "fmt"

    _ "github.com/go-sql-driver/mysql" //we import supported
    libraries for database/sql
)

// Query grabs a new connection
// creates tables, and later drops them
// and issues some queries
func Query(db *sql.DB, name string) error {
    name := "Aaron"
    rows, err := db.Query("SELECT name, created FROM example
    where name=?", name)
    if err != nil {
        return err
    }
    defer rows.Close()
    for rows.Next() {
        var e Example
        if err := rows.Scan(&e.Name, &e.Created); err != nil {
            return err
        }
        fmt.Printf("Results:\n\tName: %s\n\tCreated: %v\n",
        e.Name, e.Created)
    }
```

```
        return rows.Err()
    }
```

7. Create a file called `exec.go` with the following content:

```go
package database

// Exec replaces the Exec from the previous
// recipe
func Exec(db DB) error {

    // uncaught error on cleanup, but we always
    // want to cleanup
    defer db.Exec("DROP TABLE example")

    if err := Create(db); err != nil {
        return err
    }

    if err := Query(db, "Aaron"); err != nil {
        return err
    }
    return nil
}
```

8. Create and navigate to the `example` directory.

9. Create a file called `main.go` with the following content:

```go
package main

import (
    "PacktPublishing/Go-Programming-Cookbook-Second-Edition/
    go-cookbook/chapter6/database"
    _ "github.com/go-sql-driver/mysql" //we import supported
    libraries for database/sql
)

func main() {
    db, err := database.Setup()
    if err != nil {
        panic(err)
    }

    if err := database.Exec(db); err != nil {
        panic(err)
    }
}
```

10. Run `go run main.go`.

11. You could also run the following command:

```
$ go build
$ ./example
```

You should see the following output:

```
$ go run main.go
Results:
 Name: Aaron
 Created: 2017-02-16 19:02:36 +0000 UTC
```

13. The `go.mod` file may be updated and `go.sum` file should now be present in the top-level recipe directory.

14. If you copied or wrote your own tests, go up one directory and run `go test`. Ensure that all the tests pass.

How it works...

The _ `"github.com/go-sql-driver/mysql"` line of code is how you connect various database connectors to the `database/sql` package. There are also alternative MySQL packages that can be imported in the same way for similar results. The commands would be similar if you were to connect to PostgreSQL, SQLite, or any others that implement the `database/sql` interfaces.

Once connected, the package sets up a connection pool that is covered in the *Connection pooling, rate limiting, and timeouts for SQL* recipe, and you can either execute SQL on the connection directly, or create transaction objects that can do everything a connection can do with the `commit` and `rollback` commands.

The `mysql` package provides some convenience support for Go time objects when talking to the database. This recipe also retrieves the username and password from the `MYSQLUSERNAME` and `MYSQLPASSWORD` environment variables.

Executing a database transaction interface

When working with connections to services such as database, it can be difficult to write tests. This is because it's difficult in Go to mock or duck-type things at runtime. Although I recommend using a storage interface when working with databases, it's still useful to mock a database transaction interface inside this interface. The *Creating storage interfaces for data portability* recipe will cover storage interfaces; this recipe will focus on an interface to wrap database connections and transaction objects.

To show the use of such an interface, we'll rewrite the create and query files from the previous recipe to use our interface. The final output will be the same, but the create and query operations will all be performed in a transaction.

Getting ready

Refer to the *Getting ready* section in the *Using the database/sql package with MySQL* recipe.

How to do it...

These steps cover writing and running your application:

1. From your Terminal or console application, create a new directory called `~/projects/go-programming-cookbook/chapter6/dbinterface` and navigate to this directory.
2. Run the following command:

   ```
   $ go mod init github.com/PacktPublishing/Go-Programming-Cookbook-
   Second-Edition/chapter6/dbinterface
   ```

   You should see a file called `go.mod` that containing the following:

   ```
   module github.com/PacktPublishing/Go-Programming-Cookbook-Second-
   Edition/chapter6/dbinterface
   ```

3. Copy tests from `~/projects/go-programming-cookbook-original/chapter6/dbinterface`, or use this as an exercise to write some code of your own!

4. Create a file called `transaction.go` with the following content:

```go
package dbinterface

import "database/sql"

// DB is an interface that is satisfied
// by an sql.DB or an sql.Transaction
type DB interface {
  Exec(query string, args ...interface{}) (sql.Result, error)
  Prepare(query string) (*sql.Stmt, error)
  Query(query string, args ...interface{}) (*sql.Rows, error)
  QueryRow(query string, args ...interface{}) *sql.Row
}

// Transaction can do anything a Query can do
// plus Commit, Rollback, or Stmt
type Transaction interface {
  DB
  Commit() error
  Rollback() error
}
```

5. Create a file called `create.go` with the following content:

```go
package dbinterface

import _ "github.com/go-sql-driver/mysql" //we import supported
libraries for database/sql

// Create makes a table called example
// and populates it
func Create(db DB) error {
  // create the database
  if _, err := db.Exec("CREATE TABLE example (name VARCHAR(20),
created DATETIME)"); err != nil {
    return err
  }

  if _, err := db.Exec(`INSERT INTO example (name, created) values
("Aaron", NOW())`); err != nil {
    return err
  }

  return nil
}
```

6. Create a file called `query.go` with the following content:

```go
package dbinterface

import (
  "fmt"

  "github.com/PacktPublishing/Go-Programming-Cookbook-Second-Edition/chapter6/database"
)

// Query grabs a new connection
// creates tables, and later drops them
// and issues some queries
func Query(db DB) error {
  name := "Aaron"
  rows, err := db.Query("SELECT name, created FROM example where name=?", name)
  if err != nil {
    return err
  }
  defer rows.Close()
  for rows.Next() {
    var e database.Example
    if err := rows.Scan(&e.Name, &e.Created); err != nil {
      return err
    }
    fmt.Printf("Results:\n\tName: %s\n\tCreated: %v\n", e.Name,
               e.Created)
  }
  return rows.Err()
}
```

7. Create a file called `exec.go` with the following content:

```go
package dbinterface

// Exec replaces the Exec from the previous
// recipe
func Exec(db DB) error {

  // uncaught error on cleanup, but we always
  // want to cleanup
  defer db.Exec("DROP TABLE example")

  if err := Create(db); err != nil {
    return err
  }
```

```
      if err := Query(db); err != nil {
        return err
      }
      return nil
    }
```

8. Navigate to `example`.

9. Create a file called `main.go` with the following content:

```
package main

import (
  "github.com/PacktPublishing/Go-Programming-Cookbook-Second-
Edition/chapter6/database"
  "github.com/PacktPublishing/Go-Programming-Cookbook-Second-
Edition/chapter6/dbinterface"
  _ "github.com/go-sql-driver/mysql" //we import supported
libraries for database/sql
)

func main() {
  db, err := database.Setup()
  if err != nil {
    panic(err)
  }

  tx, err := db.Begin()
  if err != nil {
    panic(err)
  }
  // this wont do anything if commit is successful
  defer tx.Rollback()

  if err := dbinterface.Exec(tx); err != nil {
    panic(err)
  }
  if err := tx.Commit(); err != nil {
    panic(err)
```

10. Run `go run main.go`.

11. You could also run the following command:

```
$ go build
$ ./example
```

You should see the following output:

```
$ go run main.go
Results:
 Name: Aaron
 Created: 2017-02-16 20:00:00 +0000 UTC
```

12. The go.mod file may be updated and go.sum file should now be present in the top-level recipe directory.
13. If you copied or wrote your own tests, go up one directory and run go test. Ensure that all the tests pass.

How it works...

This recipe works in a very similar way to the previous database recipe *Using the database/sql package with MySQL*. This recipe performs the same operation of creating data and querying it, but also demonstrates using transactions and making generic database functions that work with both sql.DB connections and sql.Transaction objects.

Code written in this way allows us to reuse function that perform database operations that can be run individually or in groups using a transaction. This allows for more code reuse while still isolating functionality to functions or methods operating on a database. For example you can have Update(db DB) functions for multiple tables and pass them all a shared transaction to perform multiple updates atomically. It's also simpler to mock these interfaces, as you'll see in Chapter 9, *Testing Go Code*.

Connection pooling, rate limiting, and timeouts for SQL

Although the database/sql package provides support for connection pooling, rate limiting, and timeouts, it's often important to tweak the defaults to better accommodate your database configuration. This can become important when you have horizontal scaling on microservices and don't want to hold too many active connections to the database.

Getting ready

Refer to the *Getting ready* section in the *Using the database/sql package with MySQL* recipe.

How to do it...

These steps cover writing and running your application:

1. From your Terminal or console application, create a new directory called `~/projects/go-programming-cookbook/chapter6/pools` and navigate to this directory.

2. Run the following command:

   $ go mod init github.com/PacktPublishing/Go-Programming-Cookbook-Second-Edition/chapter6/pools

   You should see a file called `go.mod` that containing the following:

   ```
   module github.com/PacktPublishing/Go-Programming-Cookbook-Second-Edition/chapter6/pools
   ```

3. Copy tests from `~/projects/go-programming-cookbook-original/chapter6/pools`, or use this as an exercise to write some code of your own!

4. Create a file called `pools.go` with the following content:

   ```go
   package pools

   import (
       "database/sql"
       "fmt"
       "os"

       _ "github.com/go-sql-driver/mysql" //we import supported
       libraries for database/sql
   )

   // Setup configures the db along with pools
   // number of connections and more
   func Setup() (*sql.DB, error) {
       db, err := sql.Open("mysql",
       fmt.Sprintf("%s:%s@/gocookbook?
       parseTime=true", os.Getenv("MYSQLUSERNAME"),
       os.Getenv("MYSQLPASSWORD")))
       if err != nil {
           return nil, err
       }

       // there will only ever be 24 open connections
       db.SetMaxOpenConns(24)
   ```

```
    // MaxIdleConns can never be less than max open
    // SetMaxOpenConns otherwise it'll default to that value
    db.SetMaxIdleConns(24)

    return db, nil
}
```

5. Create a file called `timeout.go` with the following content:

```
package pools

import (
  "context"
  "time"
)

// ExecWithTimeout will timeout trying
// to get the current time
func ExecWithTimeout() error {
  db, err := Setup()
  if err != nil {
    return err
  }

  ctx := context.Background()

  // we want to timeout immediately
  ctx, cancel := context.WithDeadline(ctx, time.Now())

  // call cancel after we complete
  defer cancel()

  // our transaction is context aware
  _, err = db.BeginTx(ctx, nil)
  return err
}
```

6. Navigate to `example`.

7. Create a file called `main.go` with the following content:

```
package main

import "PacktPublishing/
        Go-Programming-Cookbook-Second-Edition/
        go-cookbook/chapter6/pools"

func main() {
    if err := pools.ExecWithTimeout(); err != nil {
```

```
        panic(err)
      }
   }
```

8. Run `go run main.go`.

9. You could also run the following:

   ```
   $ go build
   $ ./example
   ```

   You should see the following output:

   ```
   $ go run main.go
   panic: context deadline exceeded

   goroutine 1 [running]:
   main.main()
   /go/src/PacktPublishing/Go-Programming-Cookbook-Second-
   Edition/go-cookbook/chapter6/pools/example/main.go:7 +0x4e
   exit status 2
   ```

10. The `go.mod` file may be updated and `go.sum` file should now be present in the top-level recipe directory.

11. If you copied or wrote your own tests, go up one directory and run `go test`. Ensure that all tests pass.

How it works...

Being able to control the depth of our connection pool is very useful. This will prevent us from overloading a database, but it's important to consider what it will mean in the context of timeouts. If you enforce both a set number of connections and strict context-based timeouts, as we did in this recipe, there will be cases where you'll have requests frequently timing out on an overloaded application trying to establish too many connections.

This is because connections will time-out waiting for a connection to become available. The newly added context functionality for `database/sql` makes it much simpler to have a shared timeout for the entire request, including the steps involved in performing the query.

With this and the other recipes, it makes sense to use a global `config` object to be passed into the `Setup()` function, although this recipe just uses environment variables.

Working with Redis

Sometimes you need persistent storage or additional functionality provided by third-party libraries and services. This recipe will explore Redis as a form of non-relational data storage and showcase how a language such as Go can interact with these third-party services.

Since Redis supports key-value storage with a simple interface, it's an excellent candidate for session storage or temporary data that has a duration. The ability to specify a timeout on data stored in Redis is extremely valuable. This recipe will explore basic Redis usage from configuration, to querying, to using custom sorting.

Getting ready

Configure your environment according to these steps:

1. Download and install Go 1.11.1 or above on your operating system from `https://golang.org/doc/install`.

2. Install Consul from `https://www.consul.io/intro/getting-started/install.html`.

3. Open a Terminal or console application and create and navigate to a project directory such as `~/projects/go-programming-cookbook`. All the code will be run and modified from this directory.

4. Clone the latest code into `~/projects/go-programming-cookbook-original` and (optionally) work from that directory rather than typing in the examples manually:

   ```
   $ git clone git@github.com:PacktPublishing/Go-Programming-Cookbook-
   Second-Edition.git go-programming-cookbook-original
   ```

5. Install and configure Redis using `https://redis.io/topics/quickstart`.

How to do it...

These steps cover writing and running your application:

1. From your Terminal or console application, create a new directory called `~/projects/go-programming-cookbook/chapter6/redis` and navigate to this directory.

2. Run the following command:

```
$ go mod init github.com/PacktPublishing/Go-Programming-Cookbook-
Second-Edition/chapter6/redis
```

You should see a file called `go.mod` that containing the following:

```
module github.com/PacktPublishing/Go-Programming-Cookbook-Second-
Edition/chapter6/redis
```

3. Copy tests from `~/projects/go-programming-cookbook-
original/chapter6/redis`, or use this as an exercise to write some code of
your own!

4. Create a file called `config.go` with the following content:

```go
package redis

import (
    "os"

    redis "gopkg.in/redis.v5"
)

// Setup initializes a redis client
func Setup() (*redis.Client, error) {
    client := redis.NewClient(&redis.Options{
        Addr: "localhost:6379",
        Password: os.Getenv("REDISPASSWORD"),
        DB: 0, // use default DB
   })

  _, err := client.Ping().Result()
  return client, err
 }
```

5. Create a file called `exec.go` with the following content:

```go
package redis

import (
    "fmt"
    "time"

    redis "gopkg.in/redis.v5"
)

// Exec performs some redis operations
```

```go
func Exec() error {
    conn, err := Setup()
    if err != nil {
        return err
    }

    c1 := "value"
    // value is an interface, we can store whatever
    // the last argument is the redis expiration
    conn.Set("key", c1, 5*time.Second)

    var result string
    if err := conn.Get("key").Scan(&result); err != nil {
        switch err {
        // this means the key
        // was not found
        case redis.Nil:
            return nil
        default:
            return err
        }
    }

    fmt.Println("result =", result)

    return nil
}
```

6. Create a file called `sort.go` with the following content:

```go
package redis

import (
    "fmt"

    redis "gopkg.in/redis.v5"
)

// Sort performs a sort redis operations
func Sort() error {
    conn, err := Setup()
    if err != nil {
        return err
    }

    listkey := "list"
    if err := conn.LPush(listkey, 1).Err(); err != nil {
        return err
```

```
    }
    // this will clean up the list key if any of the subsequent
commands error
    defer conn.Del(listkey)

    if err := conn.LPush(listkey, 3).Err(); err != nil {
        return err
    }
    if err := conn.LPush(listkey, 2).Err(); err != nil {
        return err
    }

    res, err := conn.Sort(listkey, redis.Sort{Order: "ASC"}).Result()
    if err != nil {
        return err
    }
    fmt.Println(res)

    return nil
}
```

7. Navigate to `example`.
8. Create a file called `main.go` with the following content:

```
package main

import "PacktPublishing/
        Go-Programming-Cookbook-Second-Edition/
        go-cookbook/chapter6/redis"

func main() {
    if err := redis.Exec(); err != nil {
        panic(err)
    }

    if err := redis.Sort(); err != nil {
        panic(err)
    }
}
```

9. Run `go run main.go`.
10. You could also run the following command:

```
$ go build
$ ./example
```

You should see the following output:

```
$ go run main.go
result = value
[1 2 3]
```

11. The `go.mod` file may be updated and `go.sum` file should now be present in the top-level recipe directory.
12. If you copied or wrote your own tests, go up one directory and run `go test`. Ensure that all tests pass.

How it works...

Working with Redis in Go is very similar to working with MySQL. Although there's no standard library, a lot of the same conventions are followed with functions such as `Scan()` to read data from Redis into Go types. It can be challenging to pick the best library to use in cases like this and I suggest surveying what's available periodically, as things can rapidly change.

This recipe uses a `redis` package to do basic setting and getting, a more complex sort function, and basic configuration. Like `database/sql`, you can set additional configuration in the form of write timeouts, poolsize, and more. Redis itself also provides a lot of additional functionality, including Redis cluster support, Zscore and counter objects, and distributed locks.

As in the preceding recipe, I recommend using a `config` object, which stores your Redis settings and configuration details for ease of setup and security.

Using NoSQL with MongoDB

You may initially think that Go is better suited to relational databases due to Go structures and because Go is a typed language. When working with something like the `github.com/mongodb/mongo-go-driver` package, Go can nearly arbitrarily store and retrieve structure objects. If you version your objects, your schema can adapt and it can provide a very flexible development environment.

Some libraries do a better job of hiding or elevating these abstractions. The `mongo-go-driver` package is an example of a library that does an excellent job of the former. The following recipe will create a connection in a similar way to Redis and MySQL, but will store and retrieve an object without even defining a concrete schema.

Getting ready

Configure your environment according to these steps:

1. Download and install Go 1.11.1 or above on your operating system from `https://golang.org/doc/install`.
2. Install Consul from `https://www.consul.io/intro/getting-started/install.html`.
3. Open a Terminal or console application and create and navigate to a project directory such as `~/projects/go-programming-cookbook`. All the code will be run and modified from this directory.
4. Clone the latest code into `~/projects/go-programming-cookbook-original` and (optionally) work from that directory rather than typing in the examples manually:

   ```
   $ git clone git@github.com:PacktPublishing/Go-Programming-Cookbook-Second-Edition.git go-programming-cookbook-original
   ```

5. Install and configure MongoDB (`https://docs.mongodb.com/getting-started/shell/`.)

How to do it...

These steps cover writing and running your application:

1. From your Terminal or console application, create a new directory called `~/projects/go-programming-cookbook/chapter6/mongodb` and navigate to this directory.
2. Run the following command:

   ```
   $ go mod init github.com/PacktPublishing/Go-Programming-Cookbook-Second-Edition/chapter6/mongodb
   ```

   You should see a file called `go.mod` that containing the following:

   ```
   module github.com/PacktPublishing/Go-Programming-Cookbook-Second-Edition/chapter6/mongodb
   ```

3. Copy tests from `~/projects/go-programming-cookbook-original/chapter6/mongodb`, or use this as an exercise to write some code of your own!

4. Create a file called `config.go` with the following content:

```
package mongodb

import (
  "context"
  "time"

  "github.com/mongodb/mongo-go-driver/mongo"
  "go.mongodb.org/mongo-driver/mongo/options"
)

// Setup initializes a mongo client
func Setup(ctx context.Context, address string) (*mongo.Client,
error) {
  ctx, cancel := context.WithTimeout(ctx, 10*time.Second)
  // cancel will be called when setup exits
  defer cancel()

  client, err :=
mongo.NewClient(options.Client().ApplyURI(address))
  if err != nil {
    return nil, err
  }

  if err := client.Connect(ctx); err != nil {
    return nil, err
  }
  return client, nil
}
```

5. Create a file called `exec.go` with the following content:

```
package mongodb

import (
  "context"
  "fmt"

  "github.com/mongodb/mongo-go-driver/bson"
)

// State is our data model
type State struct {
  Name string `bson:"name"`
  Population int `bson:"pop"`
}
```

```
// Exec creates then queries an Example
func Exec(address string) error {
  ctx := context.Background()
  db, err := Setup(ctx, address)
  if err != nil {
    return err
  }

  coll := db.Database("gocookbook").Collection("example")

  vals := []interface{}{&State{"Washington", 7062000},
&State{"Oregon", 3970000}}

  // we can inserts many rows at once
  if _, err := coll.InsertMany(ctx, vals); err != nil {
    return err
  }

  var s State
  if err := coll.FindOne(ctx, bson.M{"name":
"Washington"}).Decode(&s); err != nil {
    return err
  }

  if err := coll.Drop(ctx); err != nil {
    return err
  }

  fmt.Printf("State: %#v\n", s)
  return nil
}
```

6. Navigate to `example`.

7. Create a file called `main.go` with the following content:

```
package main

import "github.com/PacktPublishing/Go-Programming-Cookbook-Second-
Edition/chapter6/mongodb"

func main() {
  if err := mongodb.Exec("mongodb://localhost"); err != nil {
    panic(err)
  }
}
```

8. Run `go run main.go`.

9. You could also run the following command:

```
$ go build
$ ./example
```

You should see the following output:

```
$ go run main.go
State: mongodb.State{Name:"Washington", Population:7062000}
```

10. The `go.mod` file may be updated and `go.sum` file should now be present in the top-level recipe directory.

11. If you copied or wrote your own tests, go up one directory and run `go test`. Ensure that all tests pass.

How it works...

The `mongo-go-driver` package also provides connection pooling, and many ways to tweak and configure your connections to the `mongodb` database. This recipe's examples are fairly basic, but they illustrate how easy it is to reason about and query a document-based database. The package implements a BSON data type, and marshaling to and from it is very similar to working with JSON.

Consistency guarantees and best practices for `mongodb` are outside the scope of this book. However, it's a pleasure to work with these in the Go language.

Creating storage interfaces for data portability

When working with external storage interfaces, it can be helpful to abstract your operations behind an interface. This is for ease of mocking, portability in the event you change storage backends, and isolation of concerns. The downside to this approach may come if you need to perform multiple operations inside a transaction. In that case, it makes sense to make composite operations, or to allow them to be passed in via a context object or additional function arguments.

This recipe will implement a very simple interface for working with items in MongoDB. These items will have a name and price and we'll use an interface to persist and retrieve these objects.

Getting ready

Refer to the steps given in the *Getting ready* section in the *Using NoSQL with MongoDB* recipe.

How to do it...

These steps cover writing and running your application:

1. From your Terminal or console application, create a new directory called `~/projects/go-programming-cookbook/chapter6/storage` and navigate to this directory.

2. Run the following command:

```
$ go mod init github.com/PacktPublishing/Go-Programming-Cookbook-Second-Edition/chapter6/storage
```

You should see a file called `go.mod` that containing the following:

```
module github.com/PacktPublishing/Go-Programming-Cookbook-Second-Edition/chapter6/storage
```

3. Copy tests from `~/projects/go-programming-cookbook-original/chapter6/storage`, or use this as an exercise to write some code of your own!

4. Create a file called `storage.go` with the following content:

```go
package storage

import "context"

// Item represents an item at
// a shop
type Item struct {
    Name  string
    Price int64
}

// Storage is our storage interface
```

```
    // We'll implement it with Mongo
    // storage
    type Storage interface {
        GetByName(context.Context, string) (*Item, error)
        Put(context.Context, *Item) error
    }
```

5. Create a file called `mongoconfig.go` with the following content:

```go
package storage

import (
  "context"
  "time"

  "github.com/mongodb/mongo-go-driver/mongo"
)

// MongoStorage implements our storage interface
type MongoStorage struct {
  *mongo.Client
  DB string
  Collection string
}

// NewMongoStorage initializes a MongoStorage
func NewMongoStorage(ctx context.Context, connection, db,
collection string) (*MongoStorage, error) {
  ctx, cancel := context.WithTimeout(ctx, 10*time.Second)
  defer cancel()

  client, err := mongo.Connect(ctx, "mongodb://localhost")
  if err != nil {
    return nil, err
  }

  ms := MongoStorage{
    Client: client,
    DB: db,
    Collection: collection,
  }
  return &ms, nil
}
```

6. Create a file called `mongointerface.go` with the following content:

```go
package storage

import (
  "context"

  "github.com/mongodb/mongo-go-driver/bson"
)

// GetByName queries mongodb for an item with
// the correct name
func (m *MongoStorage) GetByName(ctx context.Context, name string)
(*Item, error) {
  c := m.Client.Database(m.DB).Collection(m.Collection)
  var i Item
  if err := c.FindOne(ctx, bson.M{"name": name}).Decode(&i); err !=
nil {
    return nil, err
  }

  return &i, nil
}

// Put adds an item to our mongo instance
func (m *MongoStorage) Put(ctx context.Context, i *Item) error {
  c := m.Client.Database(m.DB).Collection(m.Collection)
  _, err := c.InsertOne(ctx, i)
  return err
}
```

7. Create a file called `exec.go` with the following content:

```go
package storage

import (
  "context"
  "fmt"
)

// Exec initializes storage, then performs operations
// using the storage interface
func Exec() error {
  ctx := context.Background()
  m, err := NewMongoStorage(ctx, "localhost", "gocookbook",
"items")
  if err != nil {
    return err
```

```
    }
    if err := PerformOperations(m); err != nil {
      return err
    }

    if err :=
m.Client.Database(m.DB).Collection(m.Collection).Drop(ctx); err !=
nil {
      return err
    }

    return nil
  }

  // PerformOperations creates a candle item
  // then gets it
  func PerformOperations(s Storage) error {
    ctx := context.Background()
    i := Item{Name: "candles", Price: 100}
    if err := s.Put(ctx, &i); err != nil {
      return err
    }

    candles, err := s.GetByName(ctx, "candles")
    if err != nil {
      return err
    }
    fmt.Printf("Result: %#v\n", candles)
    return nil
  }
```

8. Navigate to `example`.

9. Create a file called `main.go` with the following content:

```
package main

import "PacktPublishing/Go-Programming-Cookbook-Second-Edition/
    go-cookbook/chapter6/storage"

func main() {
    if err := storage.Exec(); err != nil {
        panic(err)
    }
}
```

10. Run `go run main.go`.

11. You could also run the following command:

```
$ go build
$ ./example
```

You should see the following output:

```
$ go run main.go
Result: &storage.Item{Name:"candles", Price:100}
```

12. The `go.mod` file may be updated and `go.sum` file should now be present in the top-level recipe directory.

13. If you copied or wrote your own tests, go up one directory and run `go test`. Ensure that all tests pass.

How it works...

The most important function for demonstrating this recipe is `PerformOperations`. This function takes an interface to `Storage` as a parameter. This means we can dynamically replace the underlying storage without even modifying this function. It would be simple, for example, to connect storage to a separate API in order to consume and modify it.

We use the context for these interfaces to add additional flexibility and allow the interface to handle timeouts as well. Separating your application logic from the underlying storage provides a variety of benefits, but it can be difficult to pick the right places to draw boundaries, and this will vary widely by application.

Web Clients and APIs

7

Working with APIs and writing web clients can be a tricky business. Different APIs have different types of authorization, authentication, and protocol. We'll explore the `http.Client` structure object, work with OAuth2 clients and long-term token storage, and finish off with GRPC and an additional REST interface.

By the end of this chapter, you should have an idea of how to interface with third-party or in-house APIs and have some patterns for common operations, such as async requests to APIs.

In this chapter, we will cover the following recipes:

- Initializing, storing, and passing http.Client structures
- Writing a client for a REST API
- Executing parallel and async client requests
- Making use of OAuth2 clients
- Implementing an OAuth2 token storage interface
- Wrapping a client in added functionality and function composition
- Understanding GRPC clients
- Using twitchtv/twirp for RPC

Technical requirements

In order to proceed with all the recipes in this chapter, configure your environment according to these steps:

1. Download and install Go 1.12.6 or higher on your operating system at `https://golang.org/doc/install`.

2. Open a Terminal or console application, create a project directory such as `~/projects/go-programming-cookbook`, and navigate to this directory. All code will be run and modified from this directory.

3. Clone the latest code into `~/projects/go-programming-cookbook-original` and optionally work from that directory rather than typing the examples manually, as follows:

```
$ git clone git@github.com:PacktPublishing/Go-Programming-Cookbook-
Second-Edition.git go-programming-cookbook-original
```

Initializing, storing, and passing http.Client structures

The Go `net/http` package exposes a flexible `http.Client` structure for working with HTTP APIs. This structure has separate transport functionality and makes it relatively simple to short-circuit requests, modify headers for each client operation, and handle any REST operations. Creating clients is a very common operation, and this recipe will start with the basics of working and creating an `http.Client` object.

How to do it...

These steps cover writing and running of your application:

1. From your Terminal or console application, create a new directory called `~/projects/go-programming-cookbook/chapter7/client`, and navigate to this directory.

2. Run the following command:

```
$ go mod init github.com/PacktPublishing/Go-Programming-Cookbook-
Second-Edition/chapter7/client
```

You should see a file called `go.mod` containing the following:

```
module github.com/PacktPublishing/Go-Programming-Cookbook-Second-
Edition/chapter7/client
```

3. Copy tests from `~/projects/go-programming-cookbook-original/chapter7/client`, or use this as an exercise to write some code of your own!

4. Create a file called `client.go` with the following content:

```go
package client

import (
    "crypto/tls"
    "net/http"
)

// Setup configures our client and redefines
// the global DefaultClient
func Setup(isSecure, nop bool) *http.Client {
    c := http.DefaultClient

    // Sometimes for testing, we want to
    // turn off SSL verification
    if !isSecure {
        c.Transport = &http.Transport{
        TLSClientConfig: &tls.Config{
            InsecureSkipVerify: false,
        },
    }
}
if nop {
    c.Transport = &NopTransport{}
}
http.DefaultClient = c
return c
}

// NopTransport is a No-Op Transport
type NopTransport struct {
}

// RoundTrip Implements RoundTripper interface
func (n *NopTransport) RoundTrip(*http.Request)
(*http.Response, error) {
    // note this is an unitialized Response
    // if you're looking at headers etc
    return &http.Response{StatusCode: http.StatusTeapot}, nil
}
```

5. Create a file called `exec.go` with the following content:

```go
package client

import (
    "fmt"
    "net/http"
)

// DoOps takes a client, then fetches
// google.com
func DoOps(c *http.Client) error {
    resp, err := c.Get("http://www.google.com")
    if err != nil {
        return err
    }
    fmt.Println("results of DoOps:", resp.StatusCode)

    return nil
}

// DefaultGetGolang uses the default client
// to get golang.org
func DefaultGetGolang() error {
    resp, err := http.Get("https://www.golang.org")
    if err != nil {
        return err
    }
    fmt.Println("results of DefaultGetGolang:",
    resp.StatusCode)
    return nil
}
```

6. Create a file called `store.go` with the following content:

```go
package client

import (
    "fmt"
    "net/http"
)

// Controller embeds an http.Client
// and uses it internally
type Controller struct {
    *http.Client
}
```

```
    // DoOps with a controller object
    func (c *Controller) DoOps() error {
        resp, err := c.Client.Get("http://www.google.com")
        if err != nil {
            return err
        }
        fmt.Println("results of client.DoOps", resp.StatusCode)
        return nil
    }
```

7. Create a new directory called `example` and navigate to it.

8. Create a file named `main.go` with the following content:

```
package main

import "github.com/PacktPublishing/
        Go-Programming-Cookbook-Second-Edition/
        chapter7/client"

func main() {
    // secure and op!
    cli := client.Setup(true, false)

    if err := client.DefaultGetGolang(); err != nil {
        panic(err)
    }

    if err := client.DoOps(cli); err != nil {
        panic(err)
    }

    c := client.Controller{Client: cli}
    if err := c.DoOps(); err != nil {
        panic(err)
    }

    // secure and noop
    // also modifies default
    client.Setup(true, true)

    if err := client.DefaultGetGolang(); err != nil {
        panic(err)
    }
}
```

9. Run `go run main.go`.

10. You may also run the following command:

```
$ go build
$ ./example
```

You should now see the following output:

```
$ go run main.go
results of DefaultGetGolang: 200
results of DoOps: 200
results of client.DoOps 200
results of DefaultGetGolang: 418
```

11. If you copied or wrote your own tests, go up one directory and run `go test`. Ensure that all the tests pass.

How it works...

The `net/http` package exposes a `DefaultClient` package variable, which is used by the following internal operations: `Do`, `GET`, `POST`, and so on. Our `Setup()` function returns a client and sets the default client to be the same client. When setting up a client, most of your modifications will take place in the transport, which only needs to implement the `RoundTripper` interface.

This recipe gives an example of a no-op round tripper that always returns a 418 status code. You can imagine how this might be useful for testing. It also demonstrates passing in clients as function arguments, using them as structure parameters, and using the default client to process requests.

Writing a client for a REST API

Writing a client for a REST API will not only help you better understand the API in question, it will also give you a useful tool for all future applications using that API. This recipe will explore structuring a client and show some strategies that you can immediately take advantage of.

For this client, we'll assume that the authentication is handled by the basic auth, but it should also be possible to hit an endpoint to retrieve a token, and so on. For the sake of simplicity, we'll assume that our API exposes one endpoint, GetGoogle(), which returns that status code returned from doing a GET request to https://www.google.com.

How to do it...

These steps cover writing and running of your application:

1. From your Terminal or console application, create a new directory called ~/projects/go-programming-cookbook/chapter7/rest, and navigate to this directory.

2. Run the following command:

   $ go mod init github.com/PacktPublishing/Go-Programming-Cookbook-Second-Edition/chapter7/rest

   You should see a file called go.mod containing the following:

   ```
   module github.com/PacktPublishing/Go-Programming-Cookbook-Second-
   Edition/chapter7/rest
   ```

3. Copy tests from ~/projects/go-programming-cookbook-original/chapter7/rest, or use this as an exercise to write some code of your own!

4. Create a file called client.go with the following content:

   ```go
   package rest

   import "net/http"

   // APIClient is our custom client
   type APIClient struct {
       *http.Client
   }

   // NewAPIClient constructor initializes the client with our
   // custom Transport
   func NewAPIClient(username, password string) *APIClient {
       t := http.Transport{}
       return &APIClient{
           Client: &http.Client{
               Transport: &APITransport{
                   Transport: &t,
   ```

```
                    username: username,
                    password: password,
            },
        },
    }
}

// GetGoogle is an API Call - we abstract away
// the REST aspects
func (c *APIClient) GetGoogle() (int, error) {
    resp, err := c.Get("http://www.google.com")
    if err != nil {
        return 0, err
    }
    return resp.StatusCode, nil
}
```

5. Create a file called `transport.go` with the following content:

```
package rest

import "net/http"

// APITransport does a SetBasicAuth
// for every request
type APITransport struct {
    *http.Transport
    username, password string
}

// RoundTrip does the basic auth before deferring to the
// default transport
func (t *APITransport) RoundTrip(req *http.Request)
(*http.Response, error) {
    req.SetBasicAuth(t.username, t.password)
    return t.Transport.RoundTrip(req)
}
```

6. Create a file called `exec.go` with the following content:

```
package rest

import "fmt"

// Exec creates an API Client and uses its
// GetGoogle method, then prints the result
func Exec() error {
    c := NewAPIClient("username", "password")
```

```
StatusCode, err := c.GetGoogle()
if err != nil {
    return err
}
fmt.Println("Result of GetGoogle:", StatusCode)
return nil
}
```

7. Create a new directory called `example` and navigate to it.
8. Create a file named `main.go` with the following content:

```
package main

import "github.com/PacktPublishing/
        Go-Programming-Cookbook-Second-Edition/
        chapter7/rest"

func main() {
    if err := rest.Exec(); err != nil {
        panic(err)
    }
}
```

9. Run `go run main.go`.
10. You may also run the following command:

```
$ go build
$ ./example
```

You should now see the following output:

```
$ go run main.go
Result of GetGoogle: 200
```

11. If you copied or wrote your own tests, go up one directory and run `go test`. Ensure that all the tests pass.

How it works...

This code demonstrates how to hide logic such as authentication, and performing a token refresh using the `Transport` interface. It also demonstrates how to expose an API call via a method. Had we been implementing against something such as a user API, we would expect methods such as the following:

```
type API interface{
  GetUsers() (Users, error)
  CreateUser(User) error
  UpdateUser(User) error
  DeleteUser(User)
}
```

If you've read `Chapter 5`, *All about Databases and Storage*, this may look similar to the recipe entitled *Executing a database transaction interface*. This composition through interfaces, especially common interfaces such as the `RoundTripper` interface, provides a lot of flexibility for writing APIs. In addition, it may be useful to write a top-level interface as we did earlier and pass the interface around instead of to the client directly. We'll explore this in more detail in the next recipe as we explore writing an OAuth2 client.

Executing parallel and async client requests

Performing client requests in parallel is relatively simple in Go. In the following recipe, we'll use a client to retrieve multiple URLs using Go buffered channels. Responses and errors will both go to a separate channel that is readily accessible by anyone with access to the client.

In the case of this recipe, creating the client, reading the channels, and handling responses and errors will all be done in the `main.go` file.

How to do it...

These steps cover writing and running of your application:

1. From your Terminal or console application, create a new directory called `~/projects/go-programming-cookbook/chapter7/async`, and navigate to this directory.

2. Run the following command:

```
$ go mod init github.com/PacktPublishing/Go-Programming-Cookbook-
Second-Edition/chapter7/async
```

You should see a file called `go.mod` containing the following:

```
module github.com/PacktPublishing/Go-Programming-Cookbook-Second-
Edition/chapter7/async
```

3. Copy tests from `~/projects/go-programming-cookbook-original/chapter7/async`, or use this as an exercise to write some code of your own!

4. Create a file called `config.go` with the following content:

```go
package async

import "net/http"

// NewClient creates a new client and
// sets its appropriate channels
func NewClient(client *http.Client, bufferSize int) *Client {
    respch := make(chan *http.Response, bufferSize)
    errch := make(chan error, bufferSize)
    return &Client{
        Client: client,
        Resp: respch,
        Err: errch,
    }
}

// Client stores a client and has two channels to aggregate
// responses and errors
type Client struct {
    *http.Client
    Resp chan *http.Response
    Err chan error
}

// AsyncGet performs a Get then returns
// the resp/error to the appropriate channel
func (c *Client) AsyncGet(url string) {
    resp, err := c.Get(url)
    if err != nil {
        c.Err <- err
        return
    }
```

```
            c.Resp <- resp
    }
```

5. Create a file called `exec.go` with the following content:

```
package async

// FetchAll grabs a list of urls
func FetchAll(urls []string, c *Client) {
    for _, url := range urls {
        go c.AsyncGet(url)
    }
}
```

6. Create a new directory called `example` and navigate to it.
7. Create a file named `main.go` with the following content:

```
package main

import (
    "fmt"
    "net/http"

    "github.com/PacktPublishing/
     Go-Programming-Cookbook-Second-Edition/chapter7/async"
)

func main() {
    urls := []string{
        "https://www.google.com",
        "https://golang.org",
        "https://www.github.com",
    }
    c := async.NewClient(http.DefaultClient, len(urls))
    async.FetchAll(urls, c)

    for i := 0; i < len(urls); i++ {
        select {
            case resp := <-c.Resp:
            fmt.Printf("Status received for %s: %d\n",
            resp.Request.URL, resp.StatusCode)
            case err := <-c.Err:
            fmt.Printf("Error received: %s\n", err)
        }
    }
}
```

8. Run `go run main.go`.

9. You may also run the following command:

```
$ go build
$ ./example
```

You should now see the following output:

```
$ go run main.go
Status received for https://www.google.com: 200
Status received for https://golang.org: 200
Status received for https://github.com/: 200
```

10. If you copied or wrote your own tests, go up one directory and run `go test`. Ensure that all the tests pass.

How it works...

This recipe creates a framework for processing requests in a fan-out `async` way using a single client. It will attempt to retrieve as many URLs as you specify as quickly as it can. In many cases, you'll want to restrict this further with something such as a worker pool. It may also make sense to handle these `async` Go routines outside the client and for specific storage or retrieval interfaces.

This recipe also explores using a case statement to switch on multiple channels. Because the fetches are being executed asynchronously, there must be some mechanism to wait for them to complete. In this case, the program will only terminate when the main function has read the same number of responses and errors as there were URLs in the original list. In cases such as this, it's also important to consider whether your application should time-out or whether there is some other way to cancel its operation early.

Making use of OAuth2 clients

OAuth2 is a relatively common protocol for speaking with APIs. The `golang.org/x/oauth2` package provides a pretty flexible client for working with OAuth2. It has subpackages that specify endpoints for various providers such as Facebook, Google, and GitHub.

This recipe will demonstrate how to create a new GitHub OAuth2 client and some of its basic usages.

Getting ready

After completing the initial setup steps mentioned in the *Technical requirements* section at the beginning of this chapter, proceed with the following steps:

1. Configure an OAuth Client at `https://github.com/settings/applications/new`.
2. Set the environment variables with your client ID and secret:
   - `export GITHUB_CLIENT="your_client"`
   - `export GITHUB_SECRET="your_secret"`
3. Brush up on the GitHub API documentation at `https://developer.github.com/v3/`.

How to do it...

These steps cover writing and running of your application:

1. From your Terminal or console application, create a new directory called `~/projects/go-programming-cookbook/chapter7/oauthcli`, and navigate to this directory.
2. Run the following command:

   ```
   $ go mod init github.com/PacktPublishing/Go-Programming-Cookbook-
   Second-Edition/chapter7/oauthcli
   ```

   You should see a file called `go.mod` containing the following:

   ```
   module github.com/PacktPublishing/Go-Programming-Cookbook-Second-
   Edition/chapter7/oauthcli
   ```

3. Copy tests from `~/projects/go-programming-cookbook-original/chapter7/oauthcli`, or use this as an exercise to write some code of your own!
4. Create a file called `config.go` with the following content:

   ```go
   package oauthcli

   import (
       "context"
       "fmt"
       "os"
   ```

```
    "golang.org/x/oauth2"
    "golang.org/x/oauth2/github"
)

// Setup return an oauth2Config configured to talk
// to github, you need environment variables set
// for your id and secret
func Setup() *oauth2.Config {
    return &oauth2.Config{
        ClientID: os.Getenv("GITHUB_CLIENT"),
        ClientSecret: os.Getenv("GITHUB_SECRET"),
        Scopes: []string{"repo", "user"},
        Endpoint: github.Endpoint,
    }
}

// GetToken retrieves a github oauth2 token
func GetToken(ctx context.Context, conf *oauth2.Config)
(*oauth2.Token, error) {
    url := conf.AuthCodeURL("state")
    fmt.Printf("Type the following url into your browser and
    follow the directions on screen: %v\n", url)
    fmt.Println("Paste the code returned in the redirect URL
    and hit Enter:")

    var code string
    if _, err := fmt.Scan(&code); err != nil {
        return nil, err
    }
    return conf.Exchange(ctx, code)
}
```

5. Create a file called `exec.go` with the following content:

```
package oauthcli

import (
    "fmt"
    "net/http"
)

// GetUsers uses an initialized oauth2 client to get
// information about a user
func GetUser(client *http.Client) error {
    url := fmt.Sprintf("https://api.github.com/user")

    resp, err := client.Get(url)
    if err != nil {
```

```
                return err
        }
        defer resp.Body.Close()
        fmt.Println("Status Code from", url, ":", resp.StatusCode)
        io.Copy(os.Stdout, resp.Body)
        return nil
}
```

6. Create a new directory called `example` and navigate to it.

7. Create a `main.go` file with the following content:

```
package main

import (
    "context"

    "github.com/PacktPublishing/
    Go-Programming-Cookbook-Second-Edition/
    chapter7/oauthcli"
)

func main() {
    ctx := context.Background()
    conf := oauthcli.Setup()

    tok, err := oauthcli.GetToken(ctx, conf)
    if err != nil {
        panic(err)
    }
    client := conf.Client(ctx, tok)

    if err := oauthcli.GetUser(client); err != nil {
        panic(err)
    }

}
```

8. Run `go run main.go`.

9. You may also run the following command:

```
$ go build
$ ./example
```

You should now see the following output:

```
$ go run main.go
Visit the URL for the auth dialog:
https://github.com/login/oauth/authorize?
```

```
access_type=offline&client_id=
<your_id>&response_type=code&scope=repo+user&state=state
Paste the code returned in the redirect URL and hit Enter:
<your_code>
Status Code from https://api.github.com/user: 200
{<json_payload>}
```

10. The `go.mod` file may be updated and `go.sum` file should now be present in the top-level recipe directory.

11. If you copied or wrote your own tests, go up one directory and run `go test`. Ensure that all the tests pass.

How it works...

The standard OAuth2 flow is redirect-based and ends with the server redirecting to an endpoint you specify. Your server is then responsible for grabbing the code and exchanging it for a token. This recipe bypasses that requirement by allowing us to use a URL such as `https://localhost` or `https://a-domain-you-own`, manually copying/pasting the code, and then hitting *Enter*. Once the token has been exchanged, the client will intelligently refresh the token as required.

It's important to note that we're not storing the token in any way. If the program crashes, it must re-exchange for the token. It's also important to note that we need to retrieve the token explicitly only once unless the refresh token expires, is lost, or is corrupted. Once the client is configured, it should be able to perform all typical HTTP operations for the API as long as the appropriate scopes were requested during the OAuth2 flow. This recipe requests the `"repo"` and `"user"` scopes, but more or less can be added as needed.

Implementing an OAuth2 token storage interface

In the previous recipe, we retrieved a token for our client and performed API requests. The downside of this approach is that we have no long-term storage for our token. In an HTTP server, for example, we'd like to have consistent storage of the token between requests.

This recipe will explore modifying the OAuth2 client to store a token between requests and retrieve it as required using a key. For the sake of simplicity, this key will be a file, but it could also be a database, Redis, and so on.

Getting ready

Refer to the *Getting ready* section in the *Making use of OAuth2 clients* recipe.

How to do it...

These steps cover writing and running of your application:

1. From your Terminal or console application, create a new directory called `~/projects/go-programming-cookbook/chapter7/oauthstore`, and navigate to this directory.

2. Run the following command:

   ```
   $ go mod init github.com/PacktPublishing/Go-Programming-Cookbook-
   Second-Edition/chapter7/oauthstore
   ```

   You should see a file called `go.mod` containing the following:

   ```
   module github.com/PacktPublishing/Go-Programming-Cookbook-Second-
   Edition/chapter7/oauthstore
   ```

3. Copy tests from `~/projects/go-programming-cookbook-original/chapter7/oauthstore`, or use this as an exercise to write some code of your own!

4. Create a file called `config.go` with the following content:

   ```go
   package oauthstore

   import (
       "context"
       "net/http"

       "golang.org/x/oauth2"
   )

   // Config wraps the default oauth2.Config
   // and adds our storage
   type Config struct {
       *oauth2.Config
       Storage
   }

   // Exchange stores a token after retrieval
   func (c *Config) Exchange(ctx context.Context, code string)
   ```

```
(*oauth2.Token, error) {
    token, err := c.Config.Exchange(ctx, code)
    if err != nil {
        return nil, err
    }
    if err := c.Storage.SetToken(token); err != nil {
        return nil, err
    }
    return token, nil
}
// TokenSource can be passed a token which
// is stored, or when a new one is retrieved,
// that's stored
func (c *Config) TokenSource(ctx context.Context, t
*oauth2.Token) oauth2.TokenSource {
    return StorageTokenSource(ctx, c, t)
}


// Client is attached to our TokenSource
func (c *Config) Client(ctx context.Context, t *oauth2.Token)
*http.Client {
    return oauth2.NewClient(ctx, c.TokenSource(ctx, t))
}
```

5. Create a file called `tokensource.go` with the following content:

```
package oauthstore

import (
    "context"

    "golang.org/x/oauth2"
)

type storageTokenSource struct {
    *Config
    oauth2.TokenSource
}

// Token satisfies the TokenSource interface
func (s *storageTokenSource) Token() (*oauth2.Token, error) {
    if token, err := s.Config.Storage.GetToken(); err == nil &&
    token.Valid() {
        return token, err
    }
    token, err := s.TokenSource.Token()
    if err != nil {
        return token, err
```

```
    }
    if err := s.Config.Storage.SetToken(token); err != nil {
        return nil, err
    }
    return token, nil
}

// StorageTokenSource will be used by out configs TokenSource
// function
func StorageTokenSource(ctx context.Context, c *Config, t
*oauth2.Token) oauth2.TokenSource {
    if t == nil || !t.Valid() {
        if tok, err := c.Storage.GetToken(); err == nil {
            t = tok
        }
    }
    ts := c.Config.TokenSource(ctx, t)
    return &storageTokenSource{c, ts}
}
```

6. Create a file called `storage.go` with the following content:

```
package oauthstore

import (
    "context"
    "fmt"

    "golang.org/x/oauth2"
)

// Storage is our generic storage interface
type Storage interface {
    GetToken() (*oauth2.Token, error)
    SetToken(*oauth2.Token) error
}

// GetToken retrieves a github oauth2 token
func GetToken(ctx context.Context, conf Config) (*oauth2.Token,
error) {
    token, err := conf.Storage.GetToken()
    if err == nil && token.Valid() {
        return token, err
    }
    url := conf.AuthCodeURL("state")
    fmt.Printf("Type the following url into your browser and
    follow the directions on screen: %v\n", url)
    fmt.Println("Paste the code returned in the redirect URL
```

```
    and hit Enter:")

    var code string
    if _, err := fmt.Scan(&code); err != nil {
        return nil, err
    }
    return conf.Exchange(ctx, code)
}
```

7. Create a file called `filestorage.go` with the following content:

```go
package oauthstore

import (
    "encoding/json"
    "errors"
    "os"
    "sync"

    "golang.org/x/oauth2"
)

// FileStorage satisfies our storage interface
type FileStorage struct {
    Path string
    mu sync.RWMutex
}

// GetToken retrieves a token from a file
func (f *FileStorage) GetToken() (*oauth2.Token, error) {
    f.mu.RLock()
    defer f.mu.RUnlock()
    in, err := os.Open(f.Path)
    if err != nil {
        return nil, err
    }
    defer in.Close()
    var t *oauth2.Token
    data := json.NewDecoder(in)
    return t, data.Decode(&t)
}

// SetToken creates, truncates, then stores a token
// in a file
func (f *FileStorage) SetToken(t *oauth2.Token) error {
    if t == nil || !t.Valid() {
        return errors.New("bad token")
    }
```

```
        f.mu.Lock()
        defer f.mu.Unlock()
        out, err := os.OpenFile(f.Path,
        os.O_RDWR|os.O_CREATE|os.O_TRUNC, 0755)
        if err != nil {
            return err
        }
        defer out.Close()
        data, err := json.Marshal(&t)
        if err != nil {
            return err
        }

        _, err = out.Write(data)
        return err
    }
```

8. Create a new directory called example and navigate to it.

9. Create a file named main.go with the following content:

```
package main

import (
    "context"
    "io"
    "os"
    "github.com/PacktPublishing/
    Go-Programming-Cookbook-Second-Edition/
    chapter7/oauthstore"

    "golang.org/x/oauth2"
    "golang.org/x/oauth2/github"
)

func main() {
    conf := oauthstore.Config{
        Config: &oauth2.Config{
            ClientID: os.Getenv("GITHUB_CLIENT"),
            ClientSecret: os.Getenv("GITHUB_SECRET"),
            Scopes: []string{"repo", "user"},
            Endpoint: github.Endpoint,
        },
        Storage: &oauthstore.FileStorage{Path: "token.txt"},
    }
    ctx := context.Background()
    token, err := oauthstore.GetToken(ctx, conf)
    if err != nil {
        panic(err)
```

```
    }

    cli := conf.Client(ctx, token)
    resp, err := cli.Get("https://api.github.com/user")
    if err != nil {
        panic(err)
    }
    defer resp.Body.Close()
    io.Copy(os.Stdout, resp.Body)
}
```

10. Run `go run main.go`.

11. You may also run the following command:

    ```
    $ go build
    $ ./example
    ```

    You should now see the following output:

    ```
    $ go run main.go
    Visit the URL for the auth dialog:
    https://github.com/login/oauth/authorize?
    access_type=offline&client_id=
    <your_id>&response_type=code&scope=repo+user&state=state
    Paste the code returned in the redirect URL and hit Enter:
    <your_code>
    {<json_payload>}

    $ go run main.go
    {<json_payload>}
    ```

12. The `go.mod` file may be updated and `go.sum` file should now be present in the top-level recipe directory.

13. If you copied or wrote your own tests, go up one directory and run `go test`. Ensure that all the tests pass.

How it works...

This recipe takes care of storing and retrieving the contents of a token to/from a file. If it's a first run, it must execute the entire code exchange, but subsequent runs will reuse the access token, and, if one is available, it will refresh using the refresh token.

There is currently no way in this code to differentiate between users/tokens, but that could be accomplished with cookies as a key for a filename or a row in the database as well. Let's walk through what this code does:

- The `config.go` file wraps the standard OAuth2 config. For every method that involves retrieving a token, we first check whether we have a valid token in local storage. If not, we retrieve one using the standard config and then store it.
- The `tokensource.go` file implements our custom `TokenSource` interface, which pairs with `Config`. Similar to `Config`, we always first try to retrieve our token from a file; failing this, we set it with the new token.

- The `storage.go` file is the `storage` interface used by `Config` and `TokenSource`. It only defines two methods and we also include a helper function to bootstrap the OAuth2 code-based flow similar to what we did in the previous recipe, but if a file with a valid token already exists, it will be used instead.
- The `filestorage.go` file implements the `storage` interface. When we store a new token, we first truncate the file and write a JSON representation of the `token` struct. Otherwise, we decode the file and return `token`.

Wrapping a client in added functionality and function composition

In 2015, Tomás Senart gave an excellent talk on wrapping an `http.Client` structure with an interface, allowing you to take advantage of middleware and function composition. You can find out more on this at `https://github.com/gophercon/2015-talks`. This recipe borrows from his ideas and demonstrates an example of performing the same action on the `Transport` interface of the `http.Client` structure, in a similar way to our earlier recipe, *Writing a client for a REST API*.

The following recipe will implement logging and basic auth middleware for a standard `http.Client` structure. It also includes a `decorate` function that can be used when required with a large variety of middleware.

How to do it...

These steps cover writing and running of your application:

1. From your Terminal or console application, create a new directory called
   `~/projects/go-programming-cookbook/chapter7/decorator`, and
   navigate to this directory.
2. Run the following command:

   ```
   $ go mod init github.com/PacktPublishing/Go-Programming-Cookbook-
   Second-Edition/chapter7/decorator
   ```

   You should see a file called `go.mod` containing the following:

   ```
   module github.com/PacktPublishing/Go-Programming-Cookbook-Second-
   Edition/chapter7/decorator
   ```

3. Copy tests from `~/projects/go-programming-cookbook-
   original/chapter7/decorator`, or use this as an exercise to write some code
   of your own!
4. Create a file called `config.go` with the following content:

   ```go
   package decorator

   import (
       "log"
       "net/http"
       "os"
   )

   // Setup initializes our ClientInterface
   func Setup() *http.Client {
       c := http.Client{}

       t := Decorate(&http.Transport{},
           Logger(log.New(os.Stdout, "", 0)),
           BasicAuth("username", "password"),
       )
       c.Transport = t
       return &c
   }
   ```

5. Create a file called `decorator.go` with the following content:

```go
package decorator

import "net/http"

// TransportFunc implements the RountTripper interface
type TransportFunc func(*http.Request) (*http.Response, error)

// RoundTrip just calls the original function
func (tf TransportFunc) RoundTrip(r *http.Request)
(*http.Response, error) {
    return tf(r)
}

// Decorator is a convenience function to represent our
// middleware inner function
type Decorator func(http.RoundTripper) http.RoundTripper

// Decorate is a helper to wrap all the middleware
func Decorate(t http.RoundTripper, rts ...Decorator)
http.RoundTripper {
    decorated := t
    for _, rt := range rts {
        decorated = rt(decorated)
    }
    return decorated
}
```

6. Create a file called `middleware.go` with the following content:

```go
package decorator

import (
    "log"
    "net/http"
    "time"
)

// Logger is one of our 'middleware' decorators
func Logger(l *log.Logger) Decorator {
    return func(c http.RoundTripper) http.RoundTripper {
        return TransportFunc(func(r *http.Request)
        (*http.Response, error) {
            start := time.Now()
            l.Printf("started request to %s at %s", r.URL,
            start.Format("2006-01-02 15:04:05"))
            resp, err := c.RoundTrip(r)
```

```
            l.Printf("completed request to %s in %s", r.URL,
            time.Since(start))
            return resp, err
        })
    }
}

// BasicAuth is another of our 'middleware' decorators
func BasicAuth(username, password string) Decorator {
    return func(c http.RoundTripper) http.RoundTripper {
        return TransportFunc(func(r *http.Request)
        (*http.Response, error) {
            r.SetBasicAuth(username, password)
            resp, err := c.RoundTrip(r)
            return resp, err
        })
    }
}
```

7. Create a file called `exec.go` with the following content:

```
package decorator

import "fmt"

// Exec creates a client, calls google.com
// then prints the response
func Exec() error {
    c := Setup()

    resp, err := c.Get("https://www.google.com")
    if err != nil {
        return err
    }
    fmt.Println("Response code:", resp.StatusCode)
    return nil
}
```

8. Create a new directory called `example` and navigate to it.

9. Create a `main.go` file with the following content:

```
package main

import "github.com/PacktPublishing/
        Go-Programming-Cookbook-Second-Edition/
        chapter7/decorator"

func main() {
```

```
            if err := decorator.Exec(); err != nil {
                panic(err)
            }
        }
```

10. Run `go run main.go`.

11. You may also run the following command:

    ```
    $ go build
    $ ./example
    ```

    You should now see the following output:

    ```
    $ go run main.go
    started request to https://www.google.com at 2017-01-01 13:38:42
    completed request to https://www.google.com in 194.013054ms
    Response code: 200
    ```

12. If you copied or wrote your own tests, go up one directory and run `go test`. Ensure that all the tests pass.

How it works...

This recipe takes advantage of closures as first-class citizens and interfaces. The main trick in achieving this is having a function implement an interface. This allows us to wrap an interface implemented by a structure with an interface implemented by a function.

The `middleware.go` file contains two example client middleware functions. These could be extended to contain additional middleware, such as a more sophisticated auth, and metrics. This recipe can also be combined with the previous recipe to produce an OAuth2 client that can be extended by additional middleware.

The `Decorator` function is a convenience function that allows the following:

```
Decorate(RoundTripper, Middleware1, Middleware2, etc)

vs

var t RoundTripper
t = Middleware1(t)
t = Middleware2(t)
etc
```

The advantage of this approach compared to wrapping the client is that we can keep the interface sparse. If you want a fully featured client, you'll also need to implement methods such as GET, POST, and PostForm.

Understanding GRPC clients

GRPC is a high-performance RPC framework that is built using protocol buffers (https://developers.google.com/protocol-buffers) and HTTP/2 (https://http2.github.io). Creating a GRPC client in Go involves many of the same intricacies as working with Go HTTP clients. In order to demonstrate basic client usage, it's easiest to also implement a server. This recipe will create a greeter service, which takes a greeting and a name and returns the sentence <greeting> <name>!. In addition, the server can specify whether to exclaim ! or not . (full stop).

There are some details about GRPC, such as streaming, that this recipe won't explore; however, it will hopefully serve as an introduction to creating a very basic server and client.

Getting ready

After completing the initial setup steps mentioned in the *Technical requirements* section at the beginning of this chapter, install GRPC (https://grpc.io/docs/quickstart/go/) and run the following commands:

- go get -u github.com/golang/protobuf/{proto,protoc-gen-go}
- go get -u google.golang.org/grpc

How to do it...

These steps cover writing and running of your application:

1. From your Terminal or console application, create a new directory called `~/projects/go-programming-cookbook/chapter7/grpc`, and navigate to this directory.
2. Run the following command:

```
$ go mod init github.com/PacktPublishing/Go-Programming-Cookbook-
Second-Edition/chapter7/grpc
```

You should see a file called go.mod containing the following:

```
module github.com/PacktPublishing/Go-Programming-Cookbook-Second-
Edition/chapter7/grpc
```

3. Copy tests from ~/projects/go-programming-cookbook-original/chapter7/grpc, or use this as an exercise to write some code of your own!
4. Create a directory called greeter and navigate to it.
5. Create a file called greeter.proto with the following content:

```
syntax = "proto3";

package greeter;

service GreeterService{
    rpc Greet(GreetRequest) returns (GreetResponse) {}
}

message GreetRequest {
    string greeting = 1;
    string name = 2;
}

message GreetResponse{
    string response = 1;
}
```

6. Navigate back up a directory to grpc.
7. Run the following command:

```
$ protoc --go_out=plugins=grpc:. greeter/greeter.proto
```

8. Create a new directory called server and navigate to it.
9. Create a file called greeter.go with the following content. Ensure that you modify the greeter import to use the path you set up in step 3:

```
package main

import (
    "fmt"

    "github.com/PacktPublishing/
    Go-Programming-Cookbook-Second-Edition/
    chapter7/grpc/greeter"
    "golang.org/x/net/context"
```

```
)

// Greeter implements the interface
// generated by protoc
type Greeter struct {
    Exclaim bool
}

// Greet implements grpc Greet
func (g *Greeter) Greet(ctx context.Context, r
*greeter.GreetRequest) (*greeter.GreetResponse, error) {
    msg := fmt.Sprintf("%s %s", r.GetGreeting(), r.GetName())
    if g.Exclaim {
        msg += "!"
    } else {
        msg += "."
    }
    return &greeter.GreetResponse{Response: msg}, nil
}
```

10. Create a file called `server.go` with the following content. Ensure that you modify the `greeter` import to use the path you set up in step 3:

```
package main

import (
    "fmt"
    "net"

    "github.com/PacktPublishing/
    Go-Programming-Cookbook-Second-Edition/
    chapter7/grpc/greeter"
    "google.golang.org/grpc"
)

func main() {
    grpcServer := grpc.NewServer()
    greeter.RegisterGreeterServiceServer(grpcServer,
    &Greeter{Exclaim: true})
    lis, err := net.Listen("tcp", ":4444")
    if err != nil {
        panic(err)
    }
    fmt.Println("Listening on port :4444")
    grpcServer.Serve(lis)
}
```

11. Navigate back up a directory to `grpc`.

12. Create a new directory called `client` and navigate to it.

13. Create a file called `client.go` with the following content. Ensure that you modify the `greeter` import to use the path you set up in step 3:

```
package main

import (
    "context"
    "fmt"

    "github.com/PacktPublishing/
     Go-Programming-Cookbook-Second-Edition/
     chapter7/grpc/greeter"
    "google.golang.org/grpc"
)

func main() {
    conn, err := grpc.Dial(":4444", grpc.WithInsecure())
    if err != nil {
        panic(err)
    }
    defer conn.Close()

    client := greeter.NewGreeterServiceClient(conn)

    ctx := context.Background()
    req := greeter.GreetRequest{Greeting: "Hello", Name:
    "Reader"}
    resp, err := client.Greet(ctx, &req)
    if err != nil {
        panic(err)
    }
    fmt.Println(resp)

    req.Greeting = "Goodbye"
    resp, err = client.Greet(ctx, &req)
    if err != nil {
        panic(err)
    }
    fmt.Println(resp)
}
```

14. Navigate back up a directory to `grpc`.

15. Run `go run ./server`, and you will see the following output:

```
$ go run ./server
Listening on port :4444
```

16. In a separate Terminal, run `go run ./client` from the `grpc` directory, and you will see the following output:

```
$ go run ./client
response:"Hello Reader!"
response:"Goodbye Reader!"
```

17. The `go.mod` file may be updated and `go.sum` file should now be present in the top-level recipe directory.

18. If you copied or wrote your own tests, go up one directory and run `go test`. Ensure that all the tests pass.

How it works...

The GRPC server is set up to listen on port `4444`. Once the client connects, it can send requests and receive responses from the server. The structure of the requests, responses, and supported methods is dictated by the `.proto` file we created in step 4. In practice, when integrating against GRPC servers, they should provide the `.proto` file, which can be used to automatically generate a client.

In addition to the client, the `protoc` command generates the stubs for the server, and all that's required is to fill in the implementation details. The generated Go code also has JSON tags and the same structures could be reused for JSON REST services. Our code sets up an insecure client. To handle GRPC securely, you need to use an SSL certificate.

Using twitchtv/twirp for RPC

The `twitchtv/twirp` RPC framework affords many of the benefits of GRPC, including building models with protocol buffers (`https://developers.google.com/protocol-buffers`), and allows for communication over HTTP 1.1. It can also communicate using JSON, so it's possible to use the `curl` command to communicate with a `twirp` RPC service. This recipe will implement the same `greeter` as the GRPC section before it. This service takes a greeting and a name and returns the sentence `<greeting> <name>!`. In addition, the server can specify whether to exclaim `!` or not `.`.

This recipe won't explore the other features of `twitchtv/twirp`, and will focus primarily on basic client-server communication. For more information on what is supported, visit their GitHub page (`https://github.com/twitchtv/twirp`).

Getting ready

After completing the initial setup steps mentioned in the *Technical requirements* section at the beginning of this chapter, install twirp `https://twitchtv.github.io/twirp/docs/install.html` and run the following commands:

- `go get -u github.com/golang/protobuf/{proto,protoc-gen-go}`
- `go get github.com/twitchtv/twirp/protoc-gen-twirp`

How to do it...

These steps cover writing and running of your application:

1. From your Terminal or console application, create a new directory called `~/projects/go-programming-cookbook/chapter7/twirp`, and navigate to this directory.
2. Run the following command:

   ```
   $ go mod init github.com/PacktPublishing/Go-Programming-Cookbook-Second-Edition/chapter7/twirp
   ```

   You should see a file called `go.mod` containing the following:

   ```
   module github.com/PacktPublishing/Go-Programming-Cookbook-Second-Edition/chapter7/twirp
   ```

3. Copy tests from `~/projects/go-programming-cookbook-original/chapter7/twirp`, or use this as an exercise to write some code of your own!
4. Create a directory called `rpc/greeter` and navigate to it.

5. Create a file called `greeter.proto` with the following content:

```
syntax = "proto3";

package greeter;

service GreeterService{
    rpc Greet(GreetRequest) returns (GreetResponse) {}
}

message GreetRequest {
    string greeting = 1;
    string name = 2;
}

message GreetResponse{
    string response = 1;
}
```

6. Navigate back up a directory to `twirp`.
7. Run the following command:

```
$ protoc --proto_path=$GOPATH/src:. --twirp_out=. --go_out=.
./rpc/greeter/greeter.proto
```

8. Create a new directory called `server` and navigate to it.
9. Create a file called `greeter.go` with the following content. Ensure that you modify the `greeter` import to use the path you set up in step 3:

```go
package main

import (
  "context"
  "fmt"

  "github.com/PacktPublishing/
  Go-Programming-Cookbook-Second-Edition/
  chapter7/twirp/rpc/greeter"
)

// Greeter implements the interface
// generated by protoc
type Greeter struct {
  Exclaim bool
}

// Greet implements twirp Greet
```

```
func (g *Greeter) Greet(ctx context.Context, r
*greeter.GreetRequest) (*greeter.GreetResponse, error) {
  msg := fmt.Sprintf("%s %s", r.GetGreeting(), r.GetName())
  if g.Exclaim {
    msg += "!"
  } else {
    msg += "."
  }
  return &greeter.GreetResponse{Response: msg}, nil
}
```

10. Create a file called `server.go` with the following content. Ensure that you modify the `greeter` import to use the path you set up in step 3:

```
package main

import (
  "fmt"
  "net/http"

  "github.com/PacktPublishing/Go-Programming-Cookbook-Second-
Edition/chapter7/twirp/rpc/greeter"
)

func main() {
  server := &Greeter{}
  twirpHandler := greeter.NewGreeterServiceServer(server, nil)

  fmt.Println("Listening on port :4444")
  http.ListenAndServe(":4444", twirpHandler)
}
```

11. Navigate back up a directory to `twirp`.
12. Create a new directory called `client` and navigate to it.
13. Create a file called `client.go` with the following content. Ensure that you modify the `greeter` import to use the path you set up in step 3:

```
package main

import (
  "context"
  "fmt"
  "net/http"

  "github.com/PacktPublishing/Go-Programming-Cookbook-Second-
Edition/chapter7/twirp/rpc/greeter"
)
```

```
func main() {
  // you can put in a custom client for tighter controls on
  timeouts etc.
    client :=
  greeter.NewGreeterServiceProtobufClient("http://localhost:4444",
  &http.Client{})

    ctx := context.Background()
    req := greeter.GreetRequest{Greeting: "Hello", Name: "Reader"}
    resp, err := client.Greet(ctx, &req)
    if err != nil {
      panic(err)
    }
    fmt.Println(resp)

    req.Greeting = "Goodbye"
    resp, err = client.Greet(ctx, &req)
    if err != nil {
      panic(err)
    }
    fmt.Println(resp)
}
```

14. Navigate back up a directory to `twirp`.

15. Run `go run ./server`, and you will see the following output:

    ```
    $ go run ./server
    Listening on port :4444
    ```

16. In a separate Terminal, run `go run ./client` from the `twirp` directory. You should see the following output:

    ```
    $ go run ./client
    response:"Hello Reader."
    response:"Goodbye Reader."
    ```

17. The `go.mod` file may be updated and `go.sum` file should now be present in the top-level recipe directory.

18. If you copied or wrote your own tests, go up one directory and run `go test`. Ensure that all the tests pass.

How it works...

We set up the `twitchtv/twirp` RPC server to listen on port `4444`. Like GRPC, `protoc` can be used to generate clients for a number of languages and, for example, generate Swagger (`https://swagger.io/`) documentation.

Like GRPC, we define our models first as `.proto` files, generate Go bindings, and finally implement the interface generated. Thanks to the use of `.proto` files, the code is relatively portable between GRPC and `twitchtv/twirp` as long as you're not relying on more advanced features of either framework.

In addition, because the `twitchtv/twirp` server supports HTTP 1.1, we can `curl` it as follows:

```
$ curl --request "POST" \
    --location "http://localhost:4444/twirp/greeter.GreeterService/Greet" \
    --header "Content-Type:application/json" \
    --data '{"greeting": "Greetings to", "name":"you"}'

{"response":"Greetings to you."}
```

8
Microservices for Applications in Go

Out of the box, Go is an excellent choice for writing web applications. The built-in `net/http` packages combined with packages such as `html/template` allow for fully featured modern web applications out of the box. It's so easy that it encourages spinning up web interfaces for the management of even basic long-running applications. Although the standard library is fully featured, there is still a large variety of third-party web packages for everything from routes to full-stack frameworks, including the following:

- https://github.com/urfave/negroni
- https://github.com/gin-gonic/gin
- https://github.com/labstack/echo
- http://www.gorillatoolkit.org/
- https://github.com/julienschmidt/httprouter

The recipes in this chapter will focus on basic tasks you might run into when working with handlers, when navigating response and request objects, and in dealing with concepts such as middleware.

In this chapter, the following recipes will be covered:

- Working with web handlers, requests, and ResponseWriter instances
- Using structures and closures for stateful handlers
- Validating input for Go structures and user inputs
- Rendering and content negotiation
- Implementing and using middleware
- Building a reverse proxy application
- Exporting GRPC as a JSON API

Technical requirements

In order to proceed with all the recipes in this chapter, configure your environment according to these steps:

1. Download and install Go 1.12.6 or greater on your operating system from `https://golang.org/doc/install`.

2. Open a Terminal or console application; create a project directory such as `~/projects/go-programming-cookbook` and navigate to this directory. All code will be run and modified from this directory.

3. Clone the latest code into `~/projects/go-programming-cookbook-original` and optionally work from that directory rather than typing the examples manually, as follows:

   ```
   $ git clone git@github.com:PacktPublishing/Go-Programming-Cookbook-
   Second-Edition.git go-programming-cookbook-original
   ```

4. Install the `curl` command from `https://curl.haxx.se/download.html`.

Working with web handlers, requests, and ResponseWriter instances

Go defines `HandlerFunc` and a `Handler` interface with the following signatures:

```
// HandlerFunc implements the Handler interface
type HandlerFunc func(http.ResponseWriter, *http.Request)

type Handler interface {
    ServeHTTP(http.ResponseWriter, *http.Request)
}
```

By default, the `net/http` package makes extensive use of these types. For example, a route can be attached to a `Handler` or `HandlerFunc` interface. This recipe will explore creating a `Handler` interface, listening on a local port, and performing some operations on an `http.ResponseWriter` interface after processing `http.Request`. This should be considered the basis for Go web applications and RESTful APIs.

How to do it...

The following steps cover the writing and running of your application:

1. From your Terminal or console application, create a new directory called `~/projects/go-programming-cookbook/chapter8/handlers`, and navigate to this directory.

2. Run the following command:

   $ go mod init github.com/PacktPublishing/Go-Programming-Cookbook-Second-Edition/chapter8/handlers

   You should see a file called `go.mod` that contains the following:

   ```
   module github.com/PacktPublishing/Go-Programming-Cookbook-Second-Edition/chapter8/handlers
   ```

3. Copy tests from `~/projects/go-programming-cookbook-original/chapter8/handlers`, or use this as an exercise to write some of your own code!

4. Create a file called `get.go` with the following contents:

   ```go
   package handlers

   import (
       "fmt"
       "net/http"
   )

   // HelloHandler takes a GET parameter "name" and responds
   // with Hello <name>! in plaintext
   func HelloHandler(w http.ResponseWriter, r *http.Request) {
       w.Header().Set("Content-Type", "text/plain")
       if r.Method != http.MethodGet {
           w.WriteHeader(http.StatusMethodNotAllowed)
           return
       }
       name := r.URL.Query().Get("name")

       w.WriteHeader(http.StatusOK)
       w.Write([]byte(fmt.Sprintf("Hello %s!", name)))
   }
   ```

5. Create a file called `post.go` with the following contents:

```
package handlers

import (
    "encoding/json"
    "net/http"
)

// GreetingResponse is the JSON Response that
// GreetingHandler returns
type GreetingResponse struct {
    Payload struct {
        Greeting string `json:"greeting,omitempty"`
        Name string `json:"name,omitempty"`
        Error string `json:"error,omitempty"`
    } `json:"payload"`
    Successful bool `json:"successful"`
}

// GreetingHandler returns a GreetingResponse which either has
// errors or a useful payload
func GreetingHandler(w http.ResponseWriter, r *http.Request) {
    w.Header().Set("Content-Type", "application/json")
    if r.Method != http.MethodPost {
        w.WriteHeader(http.StatusMethodNotAllowed)
        return
    }
    var gr GreetingResponse
    if err := r.ParseForm(); err != nil {
        gr.Payload.Error = "bad request"
        if payload, err := json.Marshal(gr); err == nil {
            w.Write(payload)
        } else if err != nil {
            w.WriteHeader(http.StatusInternalServerError)
        }
    }
    name := r.FormValue("name")
    greeting := r.FormValue("greeting")

    w.WriteHeader(http.StatusOK)
    gr.Successful = true
    gr.Payload.Name = name
    gr.Payload.Greeting = greeting
    if payload, err := json.Marshal(gr); err == nil {
        w.Write(payload)
    }
}
```

6. Create a new directory named `example` and navigate to it.

7. Create a file called `main.go` with the following contents:

```
package main

import (
    "fmt"
    "net/http"

    "github.com/PacktPublishing/
    Go-Programming-Cookbook-Second-Edition/
    $ chapter8/handlers"
)

func main() {
    http.HandleFunc("/name", handlers.HelloHandler)
    http.HandleFunc("/greeting", handlers.GreetingHandler)
    fmt.Println("Listening on port :3333")
    err := http.ListenAndServe(":3333", nil)
    panic(err)
}
```

8. Run `go run main.go`.

9. You could also run the following command:

```
$ go build
$ ./example
```

You should see the following output:

```
$ go run main.go
Listening on port :3333
```

10. In a separate Terminal, run the following commands:

```
$ curl "http://localhost:3333/name?name=Reader" -X GET
$ curl "http://localhost:3333/greeting" -X POST -d
  'name=Reader;greeting=Goodbye'
```

You should see the following output:

```
$ curl "http://localhost:3333/name?name=Reader" -X GET
Hello Reader!

$ curl "http://localhost:3333/greeting" -X POST -d
'name=Reader;greeting=Goodbye'
{"payload":{"greeting":"Goodbye","name":"Reader"},"successful":true
}
```

11. The `go.mod` file may be updated and the `go.sum` file should now be present in the top-level recipe directory.
12. If you copied or wrote your own tests, go up one directory and run `go test`. Ensure that all tests pass.

How it works...

For this recipe, we set up two handlers. The first handler expects a GET request with a GET parameter called `name`. When we `curl` it, it returns the plain text string `Hello <name>!`.

The second handler expects a POST method with `PostForm` requests. This is what you'd get if you used a standard HTML form without any AJAX calls. Alternatively, we could parse JSON out of the request body instead. This is commonly done with `json.Decoder`. I recommend trying this as an exercise as well. Lastly, the handler sends a JSON-formatted response and sets all the appropriate headers.

Although all of this was written explicitly, there are a number of methods for making the code less verbose, including the following:

- Using `https://github.com/unrolled/render` to handle responses
- Using various web frameworks mentioned in the *Working with web handlers, requests, and ResponseWriters* recipe of this chapter to parse route arguments, restrict routes to specific HTTP verbs, handle graceful shutdown, and more

Using structures and closures for stateful handlers

Due to the sparse signatures of HTTP handler functions, it may seem tricky to add state to a handler. For example, there are a variety of ways to include a database connection. Two approaches to doing this are to pass in the state via closures, which is useful for achieving flexibility on a single handler, or by using a structure.

This recipe will demonstrate both. We'll use a `struct` controller to store a storage interface and create two routes with a single handler that are modified by an outer function.

How to do it...

The following steps cover the writing and running of your application:

1. From your Terminal or console application, create a new directory called `~/projects/go-programming-cookbook/chapter8/controllers`, and navigate to this directory.

2. Run the following command:

   ```
   $ go mod init github.com/PacktPublishing/Go-Programming-Cookbook-
   Second-Edition/chapter8/controllers
   ```

   You should see a file called `go.mod` that contains the following:

   ```
   module github.com/PacktPublishing/Go-Programming-Cookbook-Second-
   Edition/chapter8/controllers
   ```

3. Copy the tests from `~/projects/go-programming-cookbook-original/chapter8/controllers`, or use this as an exercise to write some of your own code!

4. Create a file called `controller.go` with the following contents:

   ```go
   package controllers

   // Controller passes state to our handlers
   type Controller struct {
       storage Storage
   }

   // New is a Controller 'constructor'
   func New(storage Storage) *Controller {
       return &Controller{
           storage: storage,
       }
   }

   // Payload is our common response
   type Payload struct {
       Value string `json:"value"`
   }
   ```

5. Create a file called `storage.go` with the following contents:

   ```go
   package controllers

   // Storage Interface Supports Get and Put
   ```

```
// of a single value
type Storage interface {
    Get() string
    Put(string)
}

// MemStorage implements Storage
type MemStorage struct {
    value string
}

// Get our in-memory value
func (m *MemStorage) Get() string {
    return m.value
}

// Put our in-memory value
func (m *MemStorage) Put(s string) {
    m.value = s
}
```

6. Create a file called `post.go` with the following contents:

```
package controllers

import (
    "encoding/json"
    "net/http"
)

// SetValue modifies the underlying storage of the controller
// object
func (c *Controller) SetValue(w http.ResponseWriter, r
*http.Request) {
    if r.Method != http.MethodPost {
        w.WriteHeader(http.StatusMethodNotAllowed)
        return
    }
    if err := r.ParseForm(); err != nil {
        w.WriteHeader(http.StatusInternalServerError)
        return
    }
    value := r.FormValue("value")
    c.storage.Put(value)
    w.WriteHeader(http.StatusOK)
    p := Payload{Value: value}
    if payload, err := json.Marshal(p); err == nil {
        w.Write(payload)
```

```
    } else if err != nil {
        w.WriteHeader(http.StatusInternalServerError)
    }


}
```

7. Create a file called `get.go` with the following contents:

```go
package controllers

import (
    "encoding/json"
    "net/http"
)

// GetValue is a closure that wraps a HandlerFunc, if
// UseDefault is true value will always be "default" else it'll
// be whatever is stored in storage
func (c *Controller) GetValue(UseDefault bool) http.HandlerFunc
{
    return func(w http.ResponseWriter, r *http.Request) {
        w.Header().Set("Content-Type", "application/json")
        if r.Method != http.MethodGet {
            w.WriteHeader(http.StatusMethodNotAllowed)
            return
        }
        value := "default"
        if !UseDefault {
            value = c.storage.Get()
        }
        w.WriteHeader(http.StatusOK)
        p := Payload{Value: value}
        if payload, err := json.Marshal(p); err == nil {
            w.Write(payload)
        }
    }
}
```

8. Create a new directory named `example` and navigate to it.
9. Create a file called `main.go` with the following contents:

```go
package main

import (
    "fmt"
    "net/http"

    "github.com/PacktPublishing/
```

```
            Go-Programming-Cookbook-Second-Edition/
            chapter8/controllers"
    )

    func main() {
        storage := controllers.MemStorage{}
        c := controllers.New(&storage)
        http.HandleFunc("/get", c.GetValue(false))
        http.HandleFunc("/get/default", c.GetValue(true))
        http.HandleFunc("/set", c.SetValue)

        fmt.Println("Listening on port :3333")
        err := http.ListenAndServe(":3333", nil)
        panic(err)
    }
```

10. Run `go run main.go`.

11. You could also run the following:

    ```
    $ go build
    $ ./example
    ```

    You should see the following output:

    ```
    $ go run main.go
    Listening on port :3333
    ```

12. In a separate Terminal, run the following commands:

    ```
    $ curl "http://localhost:3333/set" -X POST -d "value=value"
    $ curl "http://localhost:3333/get" -X GET
    $ curl "http://localhost:3333/get/default" -X GET
    ```

    You should see the following output:

    ```
    $ curl "http://localhost:3333/set" -X POST -d "value=value"
    {"value":"value"}

    $ curl "http://localhost:3333/get" -X GET
    {"value":"value"}

    $ curl "http://localhost:3333/get/default" -X GET
    {"value":"default"}
    ```

13. The `go.mod` file may be updated and the `go.sum` file should now be present in the top-level recipe directory.

14. If you copied or wrote your own tests, go up one directory and run `go test`. Ensure that all tests pass.

How it works...

These strategies work because Go allows methods to satisfy typed functions such as `http.HandlerFunc`. By using a structure, we can inject various pieces in `main.go`, which could include database connections, logging, and more. In this recipe, we inserted a `Storage` interface. All handlers connected to the controller can make use of its methods and attributes.

The `GetValue` method doesn't have an `http.HandlerFunc` signature, and instead, returns one. This is how we can use a closure to inject state. In `main.go`, we define two routes—one with `UseDefault` set to `false`, and the other with it set to `true`. This could be used when defining a function that spans multiple routes, or when using a structure where your handlers feel too cumbersome.

Validating input for Go structures and user inputs

Validation for web can be a problem. This recipe will explore using closures to support the easy mocking of validation functions and to allow flexibility in the type of validation performed when initializing a controller structure as described by the previous recipe.

We'll perform this validation on a structure, but not explore how to populate the structure. We can assume that the data will be populated by parsing a JSON payload, populating explicitly from the form input, or other methods.

How to do it...

The following steps cover the writing and running of your application:

1. From your Terminal or console application, create a new directory called `~/projects/go-programming-cookbook/chapter8/validation`, and navigate to this directory.

2. Run the following command:

```
$ go mod init github.com/PacktPublishing/Go-Programming-Cookbook-
Second-Edition/chapter8/validation
```

You should see a file called `go.mod` that contains the following:

```
module github.com/PacktPublishing/Go-Programming-Cookbook-Second-
Edition/chapter8/validation
```

3. Copy the tests from `~/projects/go-programming-cookbook-
original/chapter8/validation`, or use this as an exercise to write some of
your own code!

4. Create a file called `controller.go` with the following contents:

```go
package validation

// Controller holds our validation functions
type Controller struct {
    ValidatePayload func(p *Payload) error
}

// New initializes a controller with our
// local validation, it can be overwritten
func New() *Controller {
    return &Controller{
        ValidatePayload: ValidatePayload,
    }
}
```

5. Create a file called `validate.go` with the following contents:

```go
package validation

import "errors"

// Verror is an error that occurs
// during validation, we can
// return this to a user
type Verror struct {
    error
}

// Payload is the value we
// process
type Payload struct {
    Name string `json:"name"`
```

```
        Age int `json:"age"`
}

// ValidatePayload is 1 implementation of
// the closure in our controller
func ValidatePayload(p *Payload) error {
    if p.Name == "" {
        return Verror{errors.New("name is required")}
    }

    if p.Age <= 0 || p.Age >= 120 {
        return Verror{errors.New("age is required and must be a
        value greater than 0 and less than 120")}
    }
    return nil
}
```

6. Create a file called `process.go` with the following contents:

```
package validation

import (
    "encoding/json"
    "fmt"
    "net/http"
)

// Process is a handler that validates a post payload
func (c *Controller) Process(w http.ResponseWriter, r
*http.Request) {
    if r.Method != http.MethodPost {
        w.WriteHeader(http.StatusMethodNotAllowed)
        return
    }

    decoder := json.NewDecoder(r.Body)
    defer r.Body.Close()
    var p Payload

    if err := decoder.Decode(&p); err != nil {
        fmt.Println(err)
        w.WriteHeader(http.StatusBadRequest)
        return
    }

    if err := c.ValidatePayload(&p); err != nil {
        switch err.(type) {
        case Verror:
```

```
                    w.WriteHeader(http.StatusBadRequest)
                    // pass the Verror along
                    w.Write([]byte(err.Error()))
                    return
               default:
                    w.WriteHeader(http.StatusInternalServerError)
                    return
               }
          }
     }
```

7. Create a new directory named `example` and navigate to it.

8. Create a file called `main.go` with the following contents:

```
package main

import (
     "fmt"
     "net/http"

     "github.com/PacktPublishing/
     Go-Programming-Cookbook-Second-Edition/
     chapter8/validation"
)

func main() {
     c := validation.New()
     http.HandleFunc("/", c.Process)
     fmt.Println("Listening on port :3333")
     err := http.ListenAndServe(":3333", nil)
     panic(err)
}
```

9. Run `go run main.go`.

10. You could also run the following:

```
$ go build
$ ./example
```

You should see the following output:

```
$ go run main.go
Listening on port :3333
```

11. In a separate Terminal, run the following commands:

```
$ curl "http://localhost:3333/" -X POST -d '{}'
$ curl "http://localhost:3333/" -X POST -d '{"name":"test"}'
$ curl "http://localhost:3333/" -X POST -d '{"name":"test",
  "age": 5}' -v
```

You should see the following output:

```
$ curl "http://localhost:3333/" -X POST -d '{}'
name is required

$ curl "http://localhost:3333/" -X POST -d '{"name":"test"}'
age is required and must be a value greater than 0 and
less than 120

$ curl "http://localhost:3333/" -X POST -d '{"name":"test",
"age": 5}' -v

<lots of output, should contain a 200 OK status code>
```

12. The `go.mod` file may be updated and the `go.sum` file should now be present in the top-level recipe directory.
13. If you copied or wrote your own tests, go up one directory and run `go test`. Ensure that all tests pass.

How it works...

We handle validation by passing in a closure to our controller structure. For any input that the controller might need to validate, we'd need one of these closures. The advantage to this approach is that we can mock and replace the validation functions at runtime, so testing becomes far simpler. In addition, we're not bound to a single function signature and we can pass in things such as a database connection to our validation functions.

The other thing this recipe demonstrates is returning a typed error called `Verror`. This type holds validation error messages that can be displayed to users. One shortcoming of this approach is that it doesn't handle multiple validation messages at once. This would be possible by modifying the `Verror` type to allow for more state, for example, by including a map, in order to house a number of validation errors before it returns from our `ValidatePayload` function.

Rendering and content negotiation

Web handlers can return a variety of content types; for example, they can return JSON, plain text, images, and more. Frequently, when communicating with APIs, it's possible to specify and accept a content type to clarify what format you'll pass data in as and what data you want to receive back out.

This recipe will explore using `unrolled/render` and a custom function to negotiate the content type and respond accordingly.

How to do it...

The following steps cover the writing and running of your application:

1. From your Terminal or console application, create a new directory called `~/projects/go-programming-cookbook/chapter8/negotiate`, and navigate to this directory.

2. Run the following command:

```
$ go mod init github.com/PacktPublishing/Go-Programming-Cookbook-
Second-Edition/chapter8/negotiate
```

You should see a file called `go.mod` that contains the following:

```
module github.com/PacktPublishing/Go-Programming-Cookbook-Second-
Edition/chapter8/negotiate
```

3. Copy the tests from `~/projects/go-programming-cookbook-
original/chapter8/negotiate`, or use this as an exercise to write some of your own code!

4. Create a file called `negotiate.go` with the following contents:

```go
package negotiate

import (
    "net/http"

    "github.com/unrolled/render"
)

// Negotiator wraps render and does
// some switching on ContentType
type Negotiator struct {
```

```
        ContentType string
        *render.Render
}

// GetNegotiator takes a request, and figures
// out the ContentType from the Content-Type header
func GetNegotiator(r *http.Request) *Negotiator {
    contentType := r.Header.Get("Content-Type")

    return &Negotiator{
        ContentType: contentType,
        Render: render.New(),
    }
}
```

5. Create a file called `respond.go` with the following contents:

```
package negotiate

import "io"
import "github.com/unrolled/render"

// Respond switches on Content Type to determine
// the response
func (n *Negotiator) Respond(w io.Writer, status int, v
interface{}) {
    switch n.ContentType {
        case render.ContentJSON:
            n.Render.JSON(w, status, v)
        case render.ContentXML:
            n.Render.XML(w, status, v)
        default:
            n.Render.JSON(w, status, v)
    }
}
```

6. Create a file called `handler.go` with the following contents:

```
package negotiate

import (
    "encoding/xml"
    "net/http"
)

// Payload defines it's layout in xml and json
type Payload struct {
    XMLName xml.Name `xml:"payload" json:"-"`
```

```
        Status string `xml:"status" json:"status"`
    }

    // Handler gets a negotiator using the request,
    // then renders a Payload
    func Handler(w http.ResponseWriter, r *http.Request) {
        n := GetNegotiator(r)

        n.Respond(w, http.StatusOK, &Payload{Status:
        "Successful!"})
    }
```

7. Create a new directory named `example` and navigate to it.

8. Create a file called `main.go` with the following contents:

```
    package main

    import (
        "fmt"
        "net/http"

        "github.com/PacktPublishing/
        Go-Programming-Cookbook-Second-Edition/
        chapter8/negotiate"
    )

    func main() {
        http.HandleFunc("/", negotiate.Handler)
        fmt.Println("Listening on port :3333")
        err := http.ListenAndServe(":3333", nil)
        panic(err)
    }
```

9. Run `go run main.go`.

10. You could also run the following:

```
    $ go build
    $ ./example
```

You should see the following output:

```
    $ go run main.go
    Listening on port :3333
```

11. In a separate Terminal, run the following commands:

```
$ curl "http://localhost:3333" -H "Content-Type: text/xml"
$ curl "http://localhost:3333" -H "Content-Type: application/json"
```

You should see the following output:

```
$ curl "http://localhost:3333" -H "Content-Type: text/xml"
<payload><status>Successful!</status></payload>

$ curl "http://localhost:3333" -H "Content-Type: application/json"
{"status":"Successful!"}
```

12. The `go.mod` file may be updated and the `go.sum` file should now be present in the top-level recipe directory.

13. If you copied or wrote your own tests, go up one directory and run `go test`. Ensure that all tests pass.

How it works...

The `github.com/unrolled/render` package does the heavy lifting for this recipe. There are a huge number of other options you can input if you need to work with HTML templates and more. This recipe can be used to auto negotiate when working through web handlers as demonstrated here by passing in various content type headers, or by directly manipulating the structure.

A similar pattern can be applied to accept headers, but beware that these headers often include multiple values and your code will have to take that into account.

Implementing and using middleware

Middleware for handlers in Go is an area that has been widely explored. There are a variety of packages for handling middleware. This recipe will create middleware from scratch and implement an `ApplyMiddleware` function to chain together a bunch of middlewares.

It will also explore setting values in the request context object and retrieving them later using middleware. This will all be done with a very basic handler to help demonstrate how to decouple middleware logic from your handlers.

How to do it...

The following steps cover the writing and running of your application:

1. From your Terminal or console application, create a new directory called `~/projects/go-programming-cookbook/chapter8/middleware`, and navigate to this directory.

2. Run the following command:

   ```
   $ go mod init github.com/PacktPublishing/Go-Programming-Cookbook-
   Second-Edition/chapter8/middleware
   ```

   You should see a file called `go.mod` that contains the following:

   ```
   module github.com/PacktPublishing/Go-Programming-Cookbook-Second-
   Edition/chapter8/middleware
   ```

3. Copy the tests from `~/projects/go-programming-cookbook-original/chapter8/middleware`, or use this as an exercise to write some of your own code!

4. Create a file called `middleware.go` with the following contents:

   ```go
   package middleware

   import (
       "log"
       "net/http"
       "time"
   )

   // Middleware is what all middleware functions will return
   type Middleware func(http.HandlerFunc) http.HandlerFunc

   // ApplyMiddleware will apply all middleware, the last
   // arguments will be the
   // outer wrap for context passing purposes
   func ApplyMiddleware(h http.HandlerFunc, middleware
   ...Middleware) http.HandlerFunc {
       applied := h
       for _, m := range middleware {
           applied = m(applied)
       }
       return applied
   }

   // Logger logs requests, this will use an id passed in via
   ```

```
// SetID()
func Logger(l *log.Logger) Middleware {
    return func(next http.HandlerFunc) http.HandlerFunc {
        return func(w http.ResponseWriter, r *http.Request) {
            start := time.Now()
            l.Printf("started request to %s with id %s", r.URL,
            GetID(r.Context()))
            next(w, r)
            l.Printf("completed request to %s with id %s in
            %s", r.URL, GetID(r.Context()), time.Since(start))
        }
    }
}
```

5. Create a file called `context.go` with the following contents:

```
package middleware

import (
    "context"
    "net/http"
    "strconv"
)

// ContextID is our type to retrieve our context
// objects
type ContextID int

// ID is the only ID we've defined
const ID ContextID = 0

// SetID updates context with the id then
// increments it
func SetID(start int64) Middleware {
    return func(next http.HandlerFunc) http.HandlerFunc {
        return func(w http.ResponseWriter, r *http.Request) {
            ctx := context.WithValue(r.Context(), ID,
            strconv.FormatInt(start, 10))
            start++
            r = r.WithContext(ctx)
            next(w, r)
        }
    }
}

// GetID grabs an ID from a context if set
// otherwise it returns an empty string
func GetID(ctx context.Context) string {
```

```
    if val, ok := ctx.Value(ID).(string); ok {
        return val
    }
    return ""
}
```

6. Create a file called `handler.go` with the following contents:

```
package middleware

import (
    "net/http"
)

// Handler is very basic
func Handler(w http.ResponseWriter, r *http.Request) {
    w.WriteHeader(http.StatusOK)
    w.Write([]byte("success"))
}
```

7. Create a new directory named `example` and navigate to it.

8. Create a file called `main.go` with the following contents:

```
package main

import (
    "fmt"
    "log"
    "net/http"
    "os"

    "github.com/PacktPublishing/
     Go-Programming-Cookbook-Second-Edition/
     chapter8/middleware"
)

func main() {
    // We apply from bottom up
    h := middleware.ApplyMiddleware(
    middleware.Handler,
    middleware.Logger(log.New(os.Stdout, "", 0)),
    middleware.SetID(100),
    )
    http.HandleFunc("/", h)
    fmt.Println("Listening on port :3333")
    err := http.ListenAndServe(":3333", nil)
    panic(err)
}
```

9. Run `go run main.go`.

10. You could also run the following commands:

```
$ go build
$ ./example
```

You should see the following output:

```
$ go run main.go
Listening on port :3333
```

11. In a separate Terminal, run the following `curl` command several times:

```
$ curl http://localhost:3333
```

You should see the following output:

```
$ curl http://localhost:3333
success

$ curl http://localhost:3333
success

$ curl http://localhost:3333
success
```

12. In the original `main.go`, you should see the following:

```
Listening on port :3333
started request to / with id 100
completed request to / with id 100 in 52.284µs
started request to / with id 101
completed request to / with id 101 in 40.273µs
started request to / with id 102
```

13. The `go.mod` file may be updated and the `go.sum` file should now be present in the top-level recipe directory.

14. If you copied or wrote your own tests, go up one directory and run `go test`. Ensure that all tests pass.

How it works...

Middlewares can be used to perform simple operations such as logging, metric collection, and analytics. Middlewares can also be used to dynamically populate variables on each request. This can be done, for example, to collect an X-header from the request to set an ID or generate an ID, like we did in this recipe. Another ID strategy might be to generate a **Universal Unique Identifier** (**UUID**) for every request—this allows us to easily correlate log messages together and trace your request across different applications if multiple microservices are involved in building the response.

When working with context values, it's important to consider the order of your middlewares. Typically, it's better to not make middlewares reliant on one another. For example, in this recipe, it would probably be better to generate the UUID in the logging middleware itself. However, this recipe should serve as a guide for layering middlewares and initializing them in `main.go`.

Building a reverse proxy application

In this recipe, we will develop a reverse proxy application. The idea is, by hitting `http://localhost:3333` in a browser, all traffic will be forwarded to a configurable host and the responses will be forwarded to your browser. The end result should be `https://www.golang.org` rendered in a browser through our proxy application.

This can be combined with port forwarding and SSH tunnels in order to securely hit websites through an intermediate server. This recipe will build a reverse proxy from the ground up, but this functionality is also provided by the `net/http/httputil` package. Using this package, the incoming request can be modified by `Director func(*http.Request)` and the outgoing response can be modified by `ModifyResponse func(*http.Response) error`. In addition, there's support for buffering the response.

How to do it...

The following steps cover the writing and running of your application:

1. From your Terminal or console application, create a new directory called `~/projects/go-programming-cookbook/chapter8/proxy`, and navigate to this directory.

2. Run the following command:

   ```
   $ go mod init github.com/PacktPublishing/Go-Programming-Cookbook-
   Second-Edition/chapter8/proxy
   ```

   You should see a file called `go.mod` that contains the following:

   ```
   module github.com/PacktPublishing/Go-Programming-Cookbook-Second-
   Edition/chapter8/proxy
   ```

3. Copy the tests from `~/projects/go-programming-cookbook-original/chapter8/proxy`, or use this as an exercise to write some of your own code!

4. Create a file called `proxy.go` with the following contents:

   ```go
   package proxy

   import (
       "log"
       "net/http"
   )

   // Proxy holds our configured client
   // and BaseURL to proxy to
   type Proxy struct {
       Client *http.Client
       BaseURL string
   }

   // ServeHTTP means that proxy implements the Handler interface
   // It manipulates the request, forwards it to BaseURL, then
   // returns the response
   func (p *Proxy) ServeHTTP(w http.ResponseWriter, r
   *http.Request) {
       if err := p.ProcessRequest(r); err != nil {
           log.Printf("error occurred during process request: %s",
           err.Error())
           w.WriteHeader(http.StatusBadRequest)
           return
       }

       resp, err := p.Client.Do(r)
       if err != nil {
           log.Printf("error occurred during client operation:
           %s", err.Error())
           w.WriteHeader(http.StatusInternalServerError)
           return
   ```

```
    }
    defer resp.Body.Close()
    CopyResponse(w, resp)
}
```

5. Create a file called `process.go` with the following contents:

```go
package proxy

import (
    "bytes"
    "net/http"
    "net/url"
)

// ProcessRequest modifies the request in accordnance
// with Proxy settings
func (p *Proxy) ProcessRequest(r *http.Request) error {
    proxyURLRaw := p.BaseURL + r.URL.String()

    proxyURL, err := url.Parse(proxyURLRaw)
    if err != nil {
        return err
    }
    r.URL = proxyURL
    r.Host = proxyURL.Host
    r.RequestURI = ""
    return nil
}

// CopyResponse takes the client response and writes everything
// to the ResponseWriter in the original handler
func CopyResponse(w http.ResponseWriter, resp *http.Response) {
    var out bytes.Buffer
    out.ReadFrom(resp.Body)

    for key, values := range resp.Header {
        for _, value := range values {
        w.Header().Add(key, value)
        }
    }

    w.WriteHeader(resp.StatusCode)
    w.Write(out.Bytes())
}
```

6. Create a new directory named `example` and navigate to it.

7. Create a file called `main.go` with the following contents:

```go
package main

import (
    "fmt"
    "net/http"

    "github.com/PacktPublishing/
    Go-Programming-Cookbook-Second-Edition/
    chapter8/proxy"
)

func main() {
    p := &proxy.Proxy{
        Client: http.DefaultClient,
        BaseURL: "https://www.golang.org",
    }
    http.Handle("/", p)
    fmt.Println("Listening on port :3333")
    err := http.ListenAndServe(":3333", nil)
    panic(err)
}
```

8. Run `go run main.go`.

9. You could also run the following:

```
$ go build
$ ./example
```

You should see the following output:

```
$ go run main.go
Listening on port :3333
```

10. Navigate a browser to `localhost:3333/`. You should see the `https://golang.org/` website rendered!

11. The `go.mod` file may be updated and the `go.sum` file should now be present in the top-level recipe directory.

12. If you copied or wrote your own tests, go up one directory and run `go test`. Ensure that all tests pass.

How it works...

Go request and response objects are largely shareable between clients and handlers. This code takes a request obtained by a `Proxy` structure that satisfies a `Handler` interface. The `main.go` file is using `Handle` instead of `HandleFunc` used elsewhere. Once the request is available, it's modified to prepend `Proxy.BaseURL` for the request, which the client then dispatches. Lastly, the response is copied back to the `ResponseWriter` interface. This includes all headers, the body, and the status.

We can also add some additional features such as basic `auth` for requests, token management, and more if needed. This can be useful for token management where the proxy manages sessions for a JavaScript or other client application.

Exporting GRPC as a JSON API

In the *Understanding GRPC clients* recipe from Chapter 7, *Web Clients and APIs*, we wrote a basic GRPC server and client. This recipe will expand on that idea by putting common RPC functions in a package and wrapping them in both a GRPC server and a standard web handler. This can be useful when your API wants to support both types of client, but you don't want to replicate code for common functionality.

Getting ready

Configure your environment according to the following steps:

1. Refer to the steps given in the *Technical requirements* section at the beginning of this chapter.
2. Install GRPC (`https://grpc.io/docs/quickstart/go/`) and run the following commands:
   - `go get -u github.com/golang/protobuf/{proto,protoc-gen-go}`
   - `go get -u google.golang.org/grpc`

How to do it...

The following steps cover the writing and running of your application:

1. From your Terminal or console application, create a new directory called `~/projects/go-programming-cookbook/chapter8/grpcjson`, and navigate to this directory.

2. Run the following command:

   ```
   $ go mod init github.com/PacktPublishing/Go-Programming-Cookbook-
   Second-Edition/chapter8/grpcjson
   ```

   You should see a file called `go.mod` that contains the following:

   ```
   module github.com/PacktPublishing/Go-Programming-Cookbook-Second-
   Edition/chapter8/grpcjson
   ```

3. Copy the tests from `~/projects/go-programming-cookbook-original/chapter8/grpcjson`, or use this as an exercise to write some of your own code!

4. Create a new directory named `keyvalue` and navigate to it.

5. Create a file called `keyvalue.proto` with the following contents:

   ```
   syntax = "proto3";

   package keyvalue;

   service KeyValue{
       rpc Set(SetKeyValueRequest) returns (KeyValueResponse){}
       rpc Get(GetKeyValueRequest) returns (KeyValueResponse){}
   }

   message SetKeyValueRequest {
       string key = 1;
       string value = 2;
   }

   message GetKeyValueRequest{
       string key = 1;
   }

   message KeyValueResponse{
       string success = 1;
       string value = 2;
   }
   ```

6. Run the following command:

```
$ protoc --go_out=plugins=grpc:. keyvalue.proto
```

7. Navigate back up a directory.
8. Create a new directory named `internal`.
9. Create a file called `internal/keyvalue.go` with the following contents:

```go
package internal

import (
    "golang.org/x/net/context"
    "sync"

    "github.com/PacktPublishing/
     Go-Programming-Cookbook-Second-Edition/
     chapter8/grpcjson/keyvalue"
    "google.golang.org/grpc"
    "google.golang.org/grpc/codes"
)

// KeyValue is a struct that holds a map
type KeyValue struct {
    mutex sync.RWMutex
    m map[string]string
}

// NewKeyValue initializes the KeyValue struct and its map
func NewKeyValue() *KeyValue {
    return &KeyValue{
        m: make(map[string]string),
    }
}

// Set sets a value to a key, then returns the value
func (k *KeyValue) Set(ctx context.Context, r
*keyvalue.SetKeyValueRequest) (*keyvalue.KeyValueResponse,
error) {
    k.mutex.Lock()
    k.m[r.GetKey()] = r.GetValue()
    k.mutex.Unlock()
    return &keyvalue.KeyValueResponse{Value: r.GetValue()}, nil
}

// Get gets a value given a key, or say not found if
// it doesn't exist
func (k *KeyValue) Get(ctx context.Context, r
```

```
*keyvalue.GetKeyValueRequest) (*keyvalue.KeyValueResponse,
error) {
    k.mutex.RLock()
    defer k.mutex.RUnlock()
    val, ok := k.m[r.GetKey()]
    if !ok {
        return nil, grpc.Errorf(codes.NotFound, "key not set")
    }
    return &keyvalue.KeyValueResponse{Value: val}, nil
}
```

10. Create a new directory named `grpc`.

11. Create a file called `grpc/main.go` with the following contents:

```
package main

import (
    "fmt"
    "net"

    "github.com/PacktPublishing/
     Go-Programming-Cookbook-Second-Edition/
     chapter8/grpcjson/internal"
    "github.com/PacktPublishing/
     Go-Programming-Cookbook-Second-Edition/
     chapter8/grpcjson/keyvalue"
    "google.golang.org/grpc"
)

func main() {
    grpcServer := grpc.NewServer()
    keyvalue.RegisterKeyValueServer(grpcServer,
    internal.NewKeyValue())
    lis, err := net.Listen("tcp", ":4444")
    if err != nil {
        panic(err)
    }
    fmt.Println("Listening on port :4444")
    grpcServer.Serve(lis)
}
```

12. Create a new directory named `http`.

13. Create a file called `http/set.go` with the following contents:

```go
package main

import (
    "encoding/json"
    "net/http"

    "github.com/PacktPublishing/
     Go-Programming-Cookbook-Second-Edition/
     chapter8/grpcjson/internal"
    "github.com/PacktPublishing/
     Go-Programming-Cookbook-Second-Edition/
     chapter8/grpcjson/keyvalue"
    "github.com/apex/log"
)

// Controller holds an internal KeyValueObject
type Controller struct {
    *internal.KeyValue
}

// SetHandler wraps our GRPC Set
func (c *Controller) SetHandler(w http.ResponseWriter, r
*http.Request) {
    var kv keyvalue.SetKeyValueRequest

    decoder := json.NewDecoder(r.Body)
    if err := decoder.Decode(&kv); err != nil {
        log.Errorf("failed to decode: %s", err.Error())
        w.WriteHeader(http.StatusBadRequest)
        return
    }

    gresp, err := c.Set(r.Context(), &kv)
    if err != nil {
        log.Errorf("failed to set: %s", err.Error())
        w.WriteHeader(http.StatusInternalServerError)
        return
    }

    resp, err := json.Marshal(gresp)
    if err != nil {
        log.Errorf("failed to marshal: %s", err.Error())
        w.WriteHeader(http.StatusInternalServerError)
        return
    }
    w.WriteHeader(http.StatusOK)
```

```
        w.Write(resp)
    }
```

14. Create a file called `http/get.go` with the following contents:

```go
package main

import (
    "encoding/json"
    "net/http"

    "google.golang.org/grpc"
    "google.golang.org/grpc/codes"

    "github.com/PacktPublishing/
     Go-Programming-Cookbook-Second-Edition/
     chapter8/grpcjson/keyvalue"
    "github.com/apex/log"
)

// GetHandler wraps our RPC Get call
func (c *Controller) GetHandler(w http.ResponseWriter, r
*http.Request) {
    key := r.URL.Query().Get("key")
    kv := keyvalue.GetKeyValueRequest{Key: key}

    gresp, err := c.Get(r.Context(), &kv)
    if err != nil {
        if grpc.Code(err) == codes.NotFound {
            w.WriteHeader(http.StatusNotFound)
            return
        }
        log.Errorf("failed to get: %s", err.Error())
        w.WriteHeader(http.StatusInternalServerError)
        return
    }

    w.WriteHeader(http.StatusOK)
    resp, err := json.Marshal(gresp)
    if err != nil {
        log.Errorf("failed to marshal: %s", err.Error())
        w.WriteHeader(http.StatusInternalServerError)
        return
    }
    w.Write(resp)
}
```

15. Create a file called `http/main.go` with the following contents:

```go
package main

import (
    "fmt"
    "net/http"

    "github.com/PacktPublishing/
     Go-Programming-Cookbook-Second-Edition/
     chapter8/grpcjson/internal"
)

func main() {
    c := Controller{KeyValue: internal.NewKeyValue()}
    http.HandleFunc("/set", c.SetHandler)
    http.HandleFunc("/get", c.GetHandler)

    fmt.Println("Listening on port :3333")
    err := http.ListenAndServe(":3333", nil)
    panic(err)
}
```

16. Run the `go run ./http` command. You should see the following output:

```
$ go run ./http
Listening on port :3333
```

17. In a separate Terminal, run the following commands:

```
$ curl "http://localhost:3333/set" -d '{"key":"test",
  "value":"123"}' -v
$ curl "http://localhost:3333/get?key=badtest" -v
$ curl "http://localhost:3333/get?key=test" -v
```

You should see the following output:

```
$ curl "http://localhost:3333/set" -d '{"key":"test",
"value":"123"}' -v
{"value":"123"}

$ curl "http://localhost:3333/get?key=badtest" -v
<should return a 404>

$ curl "http://localhost:3333/get?key=test" -v
{"value":"123"}
```

18. The `go.mod` file may be updated and the `go.sum` file should now be present in the top-level recipe directory.

19. If you copied or wrote your own tests, go up one directory and run `go test`. Ensure that all tests pass.

How it works...

Although this recipe omits the client, you could replicate the steps in the *Understanding GRPC clients* recipe from `Chapter 7`, *Web Clients and APIs*, and you should see identical results to what we see with our curls. Both the `http` and `grpc` directories make use of the same internal package. We have to be careful in this package to return appropriate GRPC error codes and to correctly map those error codes to our HTTP response. In this case, we use `codes.NotFound`, which we map to `http.StatusNotFound`. If you have to handle more than a few errors, a `switch` statement may make more sense than an `if...else` statement.

The other thing you may notice is that GRPC signatures are usually very consistent. They take a request and return an optional response and an error. It's possible to create a generic handler, `shim`, if your GRPC calls are repetitive enough and it also seems like it lends itself well to code generation; you may eventually see something like that with a package such as `goadesign/goa`.

9
Testing Go Code

This chapter will be different from the previous chapters; this chapter will focus on testing and testing methodologies. Go provides excellent testing support out of the box. However, it can be difficult to understand for developers coming from more dynamic languages where monkey patching and mocking are relatively straightforward.

Go testing encourages a specific structure for your code. In particular, testing and mocking interfaces is very straightforward and well supported. Some types of code can be more difficult to test. For example, it can be difficult to test code that makes use of package-level global variables, places that have not been abstracted into interfaces, and structures that have non-exported variables or methods. This chapter will share some recipes for testing Go code.

In this chapter, we will cover the following recipes:

- Mocking using the standard library
- Using the Mockgen package to mock interfaces
- Using table-driven tests to improve coverage
- Using third-party testing tools
- Behavior testing using Go

Technical requirements

In order to proceed with all the recipes in this chapter, configure your environment according to these steps:

1. Download and install Go 1.12.6 or greater on your operating system from `https://golang.org/doc/install`.
2. Open a Terminal or console application, then create and navigate to a project directory such as `~/projects/go-programming-cookbook`. All code will be run and modified from this directory.

3. Clone the latest code into `~/projects/go-programming-cookbook-original`, and you have the option to work from that directory rather than typing the examples manually:

```
$ git clone git@github.com:PacktPublishing/Go-Programming-Cookbook-
Second-Edition.git go-programming-cookbook-original
```

Mocking using the standard library

In Go, mocking typically means implementing an interface with a test version that allows you to control runtime behavior from tests. It may also refer to mocking functions and methods, for which we'll explore another trick in this recipe. This trick uses the `Patch` and `Restore` functions defined at `https://play.golang.org/p/oLF1XnRX3C`.

In general, it's better to compose code so that you can use interfaces frequently and so that the code is in small, testable chunks. Code that contains lots of branching conditions or deeply nested logic can be tricky to test and tests tend to be more brittle at the end. This is because a developer will need to keep track of more mock objects, patches, return values, and states within their tests.

How to do it...

These steps cover writing and running your application:

1. From your Terminal or console application, create a new directory called `~/projects/go-programming-cookbook/chapter9/mocking`, and navigate to this directory.
2. Run the following command:

```
$ go mod init github.com/PacktPublishing/Go-Programming-Cookbook-
Second-Edition/chapter9/mocking
```

You should see a file called `go.mod` that contains the following:

```
module github.com/PacktPublishing/Go-Programming-Cookbook-Second-
Edition/chapter9/mocking
```

3. Create a file called `mock.go` with the following content:

```
package mocking

// DoStuffer is a simple interface
type DoStuffer interface {
    DoStuff(input string) error
}
```

4. Create a file called `patch.go` with the following content:

```
package mocking

import "reflect"

// Restorer holds a function that can be used
// to restore some previous state.
type Restorer func()

// Restore restores some previous state.
func (r Restorer) Restore() {
    r()
}

// Patch sets the value pointed to by the given destination to
// the given value, and returns a function to restore it to its
// original value. The value must be assignable to the element
//type of the destination.
func Patch(dest, value interface{}) Restorer {
    destv := reflect.ValueOf(dest).Elem()
    oldv := reflect.New(destv.Type()).Elem()
    oldv.Set(destv)
    valuev := reflect.ValueOf(value)
    if !valuev.IsValid() {
        // This isn't quite right when the destination type is
        // not nilable, but it's better than the complex
        // alternative.
        valuev = reflect.Zero(destv.Type())
    }
    destv.Set(valuev)
    return func() {
        destv.Set(oldv)
    }
}
```

5. Create a file called `exec.go` with the following content:

```go
package mocking
import "errors"
var ThrowError = func() error {
    return errors.New("always fails")
}

func DoSomeStuff(d DoStuffer) error {

    if err := d.DoStuff("test"); err != nil {
        return err
    }

    if err := ThrowError(); err != nil {
        return err
    }

    return nil
}
```

6. Create a file called `mock_test.go` with the following content:

```go
package mocking
type MockDoStuffer struct {
    // closure to assist with mocking
    MockDoStuff func(input string) error
}
func (m *MockDoStuffer) DoStuff(input string) error {
    if m.MockDoStuff != nil {
        return m.MockDoStuff(input)
    }
    // if we don't mock, return a common case
    return nil
}
```

7. Create a file called `exec_test.go` with the following content:

```go
package mocking
import (
    "errors"
    "testing"
)

func TestDoSomeStuff(t *testing.T) {
    tests := []struct {
        name        string
        DoStuff     error
```

```
            ThrowError error
            wantErr    bool
    }{
        {"base-case", nil, nil, false},
        {"DoStuff error", errors.New("failed"), nil, true},
        {"ThrowError error", nil, errors.New("failed"), true},
    }
    for _, tt := range tests {
        t.Run(tt.name, func(t *testing.T) {
            // An example of mocking an interface
            // with our mock struct
            d := MockDoStuffer{}
            d.MockDoStuff = func(string) error {
            return tt.DoStuff }

            // mocking a function that is declared as a variable
            // will not work for func A(),
            // must be var A = func()
            defer Patch(&ThrowError, func() error { return
            tt.ThrowError }).Restore()

            if err := DoSomeStuff(&d); (err != nil) != tt.wantErr
            {
                t.Errorf("DoSomeStuff() error = %v,
                wantErr %v", err, tt.wantErr)
            }
        })
    }
}
```

8. Fill in tests for the remaining functions and go up one directory and run `go test`. Ensure that all the tests pass:

```
$go test
PASS
ok github.com/PacktPublishing/Go-Programming-Cookbook-Second-
Edition/chapter9/mocking 0.006s
```

9. The `go.mod` file may be updated and the `go.sum` file should now be present in the top-level recipe directory.

How it works...

This recipe demonstrates how to mock interfaces as well as functions that have been declared as variables. There are also certain libraries that can mimic this patch/restore directly on declared functions, but they bypass a lot of Go's type safety to accomplish that feat. If you need to patch functions from an external package, you may use the following trick:

```
// Whatever package you wanna patch
import "github.com/package"

// This is patchable using the method described in this recipe
var packageDoSomething = package.DoSomething
```

For this recipe, we start by setting up our test and using table-driven tests. There's a lot of literature about this technique, such as `https://github.com/golang/go/wiki/TableDrivenTests`, and I recommend exploring it further. Once our tests are set up, we choose outputs for our mocked functions. In order to mock our interface, our mocked objects define closures that can be rewritten at runtime. The patch/restore technique is applied to change our global function and restore it after each loop. This is thanks to `t.Run`, which sets up a new function for each loop of the test.

Using the Mockgen package to mock interfaces

The previous example used our custom mock objects. When you're working with a lot of interfaces, writing these can become cumbersome and error-prone. This is a place where generating code makes a lot of sense. Fortunately, there's a package called `github.com/golang/mock/gomock` that provides a generation of mock objects and gives us a very useful library to use in conjunction with interface testing.

This recipe will explore some of the functionality of `gomock` and will cover trade-offs on where, when, and how to work with and generate mock objects.

Getting ready

Configure your environment according to these steps:

1. Refer to the *Technical requirements* section at the beginning of this chapter.
2. Run the `go get github.com/golang/mock/mockgen` command.

How to do it...

These steps cover writing and running your application:

1. From your Terminal or console application, create a new directory called `~/projects/go-programming-cookbook/chapter9/mockgen` and navigate to this directory.
2. Run the following command:

   $ go mod init github.com/PacktPublishing/Go-Programming-Cookbook-Second-Edition/chapter9/mockgen

   You should see a file called `go.mod` that contains the following:

   ```
   module github.com/PacktPublishing/Go-Programming-Cookbook-Second-
   Edition/chapter9/mockgen
   ```

3. Create a file called `interface.go` with the following content:

   ```
   package mockgen

   // GetSetter implements get a set of a
   // key value pair
   type GetSetter interface {
       Set(key, val string) error
       Get(key string) (string, error)
   }
   ```

4. Create a directory named `internal`.
5. Run the `mockgen -destination internal/mocks.go -package internal github.com/PacktPublishing/Go-Programming-Cookbook-Second-Edition/chapter9/mockgen GetSetter` command. This will create a file named `internal/mocks.go`.

6. Create a file called `exec.go` with the following content:

```go
package mockgen

// Controller is a struct demonstrating
// one way to initialize interfaces
type Controller struct {
    GetSetter
}

// GetThenSet checks if a value is set. If not
// it sets it.
func (c *Controller) GetThenSet(key, value string) error {
    val, err := c.Get(key)
    if err != nil {
        return err
    }

    if val != value {
        return c.Set(key, value)
    }
    return nil
}
```

7. Create a file called `interface_test.go` with the following content:

```go
package mockgen

import (
    "errors"
    "testing"

    "github.com/PacktPublishing/
    Go-Programming-Cookbook-Second-Edition/
    chapter9/mockgen/internal"
    "github.com/golang/mock/gomock"
)

func TestExample(t *testing.T) {
    ctrl := gomock.NewController(t)
    defer ctrl.Finish()

    mockGetSetter := internal.NewMockGetSetter(ctrl)

    var k string
    mockGetSetter.EXPECT().Get("we can put anything
    here!").Do(func(key string) {
        k = key
```

```
    }).Return("", nil)

    customError := errors.New("failed this time")

    mockGetSetter.EXPECT().Get(gomock.Any()).Return("",
    customError)

    if _, err := mockGetSetter.Get("we can put anything
    here!"); err != nil {
        t.Errorf("got %#v; want %#v", err, nil)
    }
    if k != "we can put anything here!" {
        t.Errorf("bad key")
    }

    if _, err := mockGetSetter.Get("key"); err == nil {
        t.Errorf("got %#v; want %#v", err, customError)
    }
}
```

8. Create a file called `exec_test.go` with the following content:

```
package mockgen

import (
    "errors"
    "testing"

    "github.com/PacktPublishing/
     Go-Programming-Cookbook-Second-Edition/
     chapter9/mockgen/internal"
    "github.com/golang/mock/gomock"
)

func TestController_Set(t *testing.T) {
    tests := []struct {
        name string
        getReturnVal string
        getReturnErr error
        setReturnErr error
        wantErr bool
    }{
        {"get error", "value", errors.New("failed"), nil,
        true},
        {"value match", "value", nil, nil, false},
        {"no errors", "not set", nil, nil, false},
        {"set error", "not set", nil, errors.New("failed"),
        true},
```

```
        }
        for _, tt := range tests {
            t.Run(tt.name, func(t *testing.T) {
                ctrl := gomock.NewController(t)
                defer ctrl.Finish()

                mockGetSetter := internal.NewMockGetSetter(ctrl)
                mockGetSetter.EXPECT().Get("key").AnyTimes()
                .Return(tt.getReturnVal, tt.getReturnErr)
                mockGetSetter.EXPECT().Set("key",
                gomock.Any()).AnyTimes().Return(tt.setReturnErr)

                c := &Controller{
                    GetSetter: mockGetSetter,
                }
                if err := c.GetThenSet("key", "value"); (err !=
                nil) != tt.wantErr {
                    t.Errorf("Controller.Set() error = %v, wantErr
                    %v", err, tt.wantErr)
                }
            })
        }
    }
```

9. Fill in tests for the remaining functions, go up one directory, and run `go test`. Ensure that all the tests pass.

10. The `go.mod` file may be updated and the `go.sum` file should now be present in the top-level recipe directory.

How it works...

The mock objects that have been generated allow tests to specify what arguments are expected, the number of times a function will be called, and what to return. They also allow us to set additional artifacts. For example, we could write to a channel directly if the original function had a similar workflow. The `interface_test.go` file showcases some examples of using mock objects while calling them in line. Generally, tests will look more like `exec_test.go`, where we'll want intercept interface function calls performed by our actual code and change their behavior at test time.

The `exec_test.go` file also showcases how you might use mocked objects in a table-driven test environment. The `Any()` function means that the mocked function can be called zero or more times, which is great for cases where the code terminates early.

One last trick demonstrated in this recipe is sticking mocked objects into the `internal` package. This is useful when you need to mock functions declared in packages outside of your own. This allows those methods to be defined in a `non _test.go` file, but they won't be visible to users of your libraries as they cannot import from the internal package. Generally, it's easier to just stick mocked objects into `_test.go` files, using the same package name as the tests you're currently writing.

Using table-driven tests to improve coverage

This recipe will demonstrate the process of how to write a table-driven test, collect test coverage, and improve it. It will also make use of the `github.com/cweill/gotests` package to generate tests. If you've been downloading the test code for other chapters, these should look very familiar. Using a combination of this recipe and the previous two, you should be able to achieve 100% test coverage in all cases with some work.

How to do it...

These steps cover writing and running your application:

1. From your Terminal or console application, create a new directory called `~/projects/go-programming-cookbook/chapter9/coverage`, and navigate to this directory.

2. Run the following command:

   ```
   $ go mod init github.com/PacktPublishing/Go-Programming-Cookbook-
   Second-Edition/chapter9/coverage
   ```

   You should see a file called `go.mod` that contains the following:

   ```
   module github.com/PacktPublishing/Go-Programming-Cookbook-Second-
   Edition/chapter9/coverage
   ```

3. Create a file called `coverage.go` with the following content:

```
package main

import "errors"

// Coverage is a simple function with some branching conditions
func Coverage(condition bool) error {
    if condition {
        return errors.New("condition was set")
    }
    return nil
}
```

4. Run the `gotests -all -w` command.

5. This will generate a file named `coverage_test.go` with the following content:

```
package main

import "testing"

func TestCoverage(t *testing.T) {
    type args struct {
        condition bool
    }
    tests := []struct {
        name string
        args args
        wantErr bool
    }{
        // TODO: Add test cases.
    }
    for _, tt := range tests {
        t.Run(tt.name, func(t *testing.T) {
            if err := Coverage(tt.args.condition); (err != nil)
            != tt.wantErr {
                t.Errorf("Coverage() error = %v, wantErr %v",
                err, tt.wantErr)
            }
        })
    }
}
```

6. Fill in the TODO section with the following:

```
{"no condition", args{true}, true},
```

7. Run the go test -cover command, and you will see the following output:

```
$ go test -cover
PASS
coverage: 66.7% of statements
ok github.com/PacktPublishing/Go-Programming-Cookbook-Second-
Edition/chapter9/coverage 0.007s
```

8. Add the following item to the TODO section:

```
{"condition", args{false}, false},
```

9. Run the go test -cover command, and you will see the following output:

```
$ go test -cover
PASS
coverage: 100.0% of statements
ok github.com/PacktPublishing/Go-Programming-Cookbook-Second-
Edition/chapter9/coverage 0.007s
```

10. Run the following commands:

```
$ go test -coverprofile=cover.out
$ go tool cover -html=cover.out -o coverage.html
```

11. Open the coverage.html file in a browser to see a graphical coverage report.
12. The go.mod file may be updated and the go.sum file should now be present in the top-level recipe directory.

How it works...

The go test -cover command comes with a basic Go installation. It can be used to collect a coverage report of your Go application. In addition, it has the ability to output coverage metrics and an HTML coverage report. This tool is often wrapped by other tools, which will be covered in the next recipe. These table-driven test styles are covered at https://github.com/golang/go/wiki/TableDrivenTests and are an excellent way to make clean tests that can handle many cases without writing a bunch of extra code.

This recipe starts by automatically generating test code, then filling in test cases as needed to help create more coverage. The only time this is especially tricky is when you have non-variable functions or methods being invoked. For example, it can be tricky to make `gob.Encode()` return an error to increase test coverage. It can also seem quirky to use the method described in the *Mocking using the standard library* recipe of this chapter and use `var gobEncode = gob.Encode` to allow patching. For this reason, it can be difficult to advocate for 100% test coverage and instead argue for focusing on testing the external interface extensively—that is, testing many variations of input and output—and in some cases, as we'll see in the *Behavior testing using Go* recipe of this chapter, fuzzing can become useful.

Using third-party testing tools

There are a number of helpful tools for Go testing: tools that make it easier to get an idea of code coverage at a per-function level, tools to implement assertions to reduce testing lines of code, and test runners. This recipe will cover the `github.com/axw/gocov` and `github.com/smartystreets/goconvey` packages in order to demonstrate some of this functionality. There are a number of other notable test frameworks depending on your needs. The `github.com/smartystreets/goconvey` package supports both assertions and is a test runner. It used to be the cleanest way to have labeled subtests prior to Go 1.7.

Getting ready

Configure your environment according to these steps:

1. Refer to the *Technical requirements* section at the beginning of this chapter.
2. Run the `go get github.com/axw/gocov/gocov` command.
3. Run the `go get github.com/smartystreets/goconvey` command.

How to do it...

These steps cover writing and running your application:

1. From your Terminal or console application, create a new directory called `~/projects/go-programming-cookbook/chapter9/tools`, and navigate to this directory.

2. Run the following command:

```
$ go mod init github.com/PacktPublishing/Go-Programming-Cookbook-
Second-Edition/chapter9/tools
```

You should see a file called `go.mod` that contains the following:

```
module github.com/PacktPublishing/Go-Programming-Cookbook-Second-
Edition/chapter9/tools
```

3. Create a file called `funcs.go` with the following content:

```go
package tools

import (
    "fmt"
)

func example() error {
    fmt.Println("in example")
    return nil
}

var example2 = func() int {
    fmt.Println("in example2")
    return 10
}
```

4. Create a file called `structs.go` with the following content:

```go
package tools

import (
    "errors"
    "fmt"
)

type c struct {
    Branch bool
}

func (c *c) example3() error {
    fmt.Println("in example3")
    if c.Branch {
        fmt.Println("branching code!")
        return errors.New("bad branch")
    }
```

```
        return nil
    }
```

5. Create a file called `funcs_test.go` with the following content:

```go
package tools

import (
    "testing"

    . "github.com/smartystreets/goconvey/convey"
)

func Test_example(t *testing.T) {
    tests := []struct {
        name string
    }{
        {"base-case"},
    }
    for _, tt := range tests {
        Convey(tt.name, t, func() {
            res := example()
            So(res, ShouldBeNil)
        })
    }
}

func Test_example2(t *testing.T) {
    tests := []struct {
        name string
    }{
        {"base-case"},
    }
    for _, tt := range tests {
        Convey(tt.name, t, func() {
            res := example2()
            So(res, ShouldBeGreaterThanOrEqualTo, 1)
        })
    }
}
```

6. Create a file called `structs_test.go` with the following content:

```go
package tools

import (
    "testing"
```

```
        . "github.com/smartystreets/goconvey/convey"
)

func Test_c_example3(t *testing.T) {
    type fields struct {
        Branch bool
    }
    tests := []struct {
        name string
        fields fields
        wantErr bool
    }{
        {"no branch", fields{false}, false},
        {"branch", fields{true}, true},
    }
    for _, tt := range tests {
        Convey(tt.name, t, func() {
            c := &c{
                Branch: tt.fields.Branch,
            }
            So((c.example3() != nil), ShouldEqual, tt.wantErr)
        })
    }
}
```

7. Run the gocov test | gocov report command, and you will see the following output:

```
$ gocov test | gocov report
ok github.com/PacktPublishing/Go-Programming-Cookbook-Second-
Edition/chapter9/tools 0.006s
coverage: 100.0% of statements

github.com/PacktPublishing/Go-Programming-Cookbook-Second-
Edition/chapter9/tools/struct.go
c.example3 100.00% (5/5)
github.com/PacktPublishing/Go-Programming-Cookbook-Second-
Edition/chapter9/tools/funcs.go example
100.00% (2/2)
github.com/PacktPublishing/Go-Programming-Cookbook-Second-
Edition/chapter9/tools/funcs.go @12:16
100.00% (2/2)
github.com/PacktPublishing/Go-Programming-Cookbook-Second-
Edition/chapter9/tools ----------
100.00% (9/9)

Total Coverage: 100.00% (9/9)
```

8. Run the `goconvey` command, and it will open a browser that should look like this:

9. Ensure that all the tests pass.
10. The `go.mod` file may be updated and the `go.sum` file should now be present in the top-level recipe directory.

How it works...

This recipe demonstrates how to wire the `goconvey` command into your tests. The `Convey` keyword basically replaces `t.Run` and adds additional labels in the `goconvey` web UI, but it behaves slightly differently. If you have nested `Convey` blocks, they're always re-executed in order, as follows:

```
Convey("Outer loop", t, func(){
    a := 1
    Convey("Inner loop", t, func() {
        a = 2
    })
    Convey ("Inner loop2", t, func(){
        fmt.Println(a)
    })
})
```

The preceding code, using the `goconvey` command, will print 1. If we had used the built-in `t.Run` instead, it would print 2 instead. In other words, Go `t.Run` tests are run sequentially and are never repeated. This behavior can be useful for putting the setup code into outer `Convey` blocks, but it's important to remember this distinction if you have to work with both.

When using `Convey` assertions, there are check marks on successes in the web UI and in additional stats. It can also reduce the size of checks to a single line, and it's even possible to create custom assertions.

If you leave the `goconvey` web interface up and turn on notifications, as you save your code, tests will automatically be run and you'll receive notifications on any increase or decrease in coverage, as well as when your build fails.

All three tools assertions, the test runner, and the web UI can be used independently or together.

The `gocov` tool can be useful when working toward higher test coverage. It can quickly identify functions that are lacking in coverage and help you to dive deep into your coverage report. In addition, `gocov` can be used to generate an alternate HTML report that is shipped with the Go code by using the `github.com/matm/gocov-html` package.

Behavior testing using Go

Behavior testing or integration testing is a good method of implementing end-to-end black box testing. One popular framework for this type of testing is Cucumber (`https://cucumber.io/`), which uses the Gherkin language to describe the steps to a test in English, and then implements those steps in code. Go has a Cucumber library as well (`github.com/DATA-DOG/godog`). This recipe will use the `godog` package to write behavior tests.

Getting ready

Configure your environment according to these steps:

1. Refer to the *Technical requirements* section at the beginning of this chapter.
2. Run the `go get github.com/DATA-DOG/godog/cmd/godog` command.

How to do it...

These steps cover writing and running your application:

1. From your Terminal or console application, create a new directory called `~/projects/go-programming-cookbook/chapter9/bdd`, and navigate to this directory.

2. Run the following command:

   ```
   $ go mod init github.com/PacktPublishing/Go-Programming-Cookbook-
   Second-Edition/chapter9/bdd
   ```

   You should see a file called `go.mod` that contains the following:

   ```
   module github.com/PacktPublishing/Go-Programming-Cookbook-Second-
   Edition/chapter9/bdd
   ```

3. Create a file called `handler.go` with the following content:

   ```go
   package bdd

   import (
       "encoding/json"
       "fmt"
       "net/http"
   )

   // HandlerRequest will be json decoded
   // into by Handler
   type HandlerRequest struct {
       Name string `json:"name"`
   }

   // Handler takes a request and renders a response
   func Handler(w http.ResponseWriter, r *http.Request) {
       w.Header().Set("Content-Type", "text/plain; charset=utf-8")
       if r.Method != http.MethodPost {
           w.WriteHeader(http.StatusMethodNotAllowed)
           return
       }

       dec := json.NewDecoder(r.Body)
       var req HandlerRequest
       if err := dec.Decode(&req); err != nil {
           w.WriteHeader(http.StatusBadRequest)
           return
       }
   ```

```
    w.WriteHeader(http.StatusOK)
    w.Write([]byte(fmt.Sprintf("BDD testing %s", req.Name)))
}
```

4. Create a new directory called `features`, and create a file called `features/handler.go` with the following content:

```
Feature: Bad Method
 Scenario: Good request
 Given we create a HandlerRequest payload with:
     | reader |
     | coder |
     | other |
 And we POST the HandlerRequest to /hello
 Then the response code should be 200
 And the response body should be:
     | BDD testing reader |
     | BDD testing coder |
     | BDD testing other |
```

5. Run the `godog` command, and you will see the following output:

```
$ godog
.

1 scenarios (1 undefined)
4 steps (4 undefined)
89.062µs
.
```

6. This should give you a skeleton to implement the tests that we wrote in our feature file; copy those into `handler_test.go` and implement the first two steps:

```
package bdd

import (
    "bytes"
    "encoding/json"
    "fmt"
    "net/http/httptest"

    "github.com/DATA-DOG/godog"
    "github.com/DATA-DOG/godog/gherkin"
)

var payloads []HandlerRequest
var resps []*httptest.ResponseRecorder
```

```
func weCreateAHandlerRequestPayloadWith(arg1
*gherkin.DataTable) error {
    for _, row := range arg1.Rows {
        h := HandlerRequest{
            Name: row.Cells[0].Value,
        }
        payloads = append(payloads, h)
    }
    return nil
}

func wePOSTTheHandlerRequestToHello() error {
    for _, p := range payloads {
        v, err := json.Marshal(p)
        if err != nil {
            return err
        }
        w := httptest.NewRecorder()
        r := httptest.NewRequest("POST", "/hello",
        bytes.NewBuffer(v))

        Handler(w, r)
        resps = append(resps, w)
    }
    return nil
}
```

7. Run the godog command, and you will see the following output:

```
$ godog
.

1 scenarios (1 pending)
4 steps (2 passed, 1 pending, 1 skipped)
.
```

8. Fill in the remaining two steps:

```
func theResponseCodeShouldBe(arg1 int) error {
    for _, r := range resps {
        if got, want := r.Code, arg1; got != want {
            return fmt.Errorf("got: %d; want %d", got, want)
        }
    }
    return nil
}

func theResponseBodyShouldBe(arg1 *gherkin.DataTable) error {
    for c, row := range arg1.Rows {
```

```
                    b := bytes.Buffer{}
                    b.ReadFrom(resps[c].Body)
                    if got, want := b.String(), row.Cells[0].Value;
                    got != want
                    {
                        return fmt.Errorf("got: %s; want %s", got, want)
                    }
                }
            return nil
        }

func FeatureContext(s *godog.Suite) {
    s.Step(`^we create a HandlerRequest payload with:$`,
    weCreateAHandlerRequestPayloadWith)
    s.Step(`^we POST the HandlerRequest to /hello$`,
    wePOSTTheHandlerRequestToHello)
    s.Step(`^the response code should be (d+)$`,
    theResponseCodeShouldBe)
    s.Step(`^the response body should be:$`,
    theResponseBodyShouldBe)
}
```

9. Run the `godog` command, and you will see the following output:

```
$ godog
.
1 scenarios (1 passed)
4 steps (4 passed)
552.605µs
.
```

How it works...

Cucumber frameworks work excellently for pair programming, end-to-end testing, and any sort of testing that is best communicated with written instructions and is understandable for non-technical people. Once a step has been implemented, it's generally possible to reuse it wherever it's needed. If you want to test integrations between services, tests can be written to use actual HTTP clients if you first ensure that your environment is set up to receive HTTP connections.

The datadog implementation of **behavior-driven development (BDD)** is lacking a few features that you might expect if you've used other Cucumber frameworks, including lack of examples, passing a context between functions, and a number of other keywords. However, it's a good start, and by using a few tricks in this recipe, such as globals for tracking state (and ensuring that you clean up those globals between scenarios), it's possible to build a fairly robust set of tests. The datadog testing package also uses a third-party test runner, so it's impossible to put it together with packages such as `gocov` or `go test -cover`.

10
Parallelism and Concurrency

The recipes in this chapter cover worker pools, wait groups for asynchronous operations, and the use of the `context` package. Parallelism and concurrency are some of the most advertised and promoted features of the Go language. This chapter will offer a number of useful patterns to get you started and help you understand these features.

Go provides primitives that make parallel applications possible. Goroutines allow any function to become asynchronous and concurrent. Channels allow an application to set up communication with Goroutines. One of the famous sayings in Go is, "*Do not communicate by sharing memory; instead, share memory by communicating*", and is from `https://blog.golang.org/share-memory-by-communicating`.

In this chapter, we will cover the following recipes:

- Using channels and the select statement
- Performing async operations with sync.WaitGroup
- Using atomic operations and mutex
- Using the context package
- Executing state management for channels
- Using the worker pool design pattern
- Using workers to create pipelines

Technical requirements

In order to proceed with all the recipes in this chapter, configure your environment according to these steps:

1. Download and install Go 1.12.6 or greater on your operating system from `https://golang.org/doc/install`.

2. Open a Terminal or console application, and create and navigate to a project directory such as `~/projects/go-programming-cookbook`. All the code will be run and modified from this directory.

3. Clone the latest code into `~/projects/go-programming-cookbook-original` and (optionally) work from that directory, rather than typing in the examples manually:

   ```
   $ git clone git@github.com:PacktPublishing/Go-Programming-Cookbook-
   Second-Edition.git go-programming-cookbook-original
   ```

Using channels and the select statement

Go channels, in combination with Goroutines, are first-class citizens for asynchronous communication. Channels become especially powerful when we use select statements. These statements allow a Goroutine to intelligently handle requests from multiple channels at once.

How to do it...

These steps cover writing and running your application:

1. From your Terminal or console application, create a new directory called `~/projects/go-programming-cookbook/chapter10/channels` and navigate to it.

2. Run the following command:

   ```
   $ go mod init github.com/PacktPublishing/Go-Programming-Cookbook-
   Second-Edition/chapter10/channels
   ```

   You should see a file called `go.mod` that contains the following code:

   ```
   module github.com/PacktPublishing/Go-Programming-Cookbook-Second-
   Edition/chapter10/channels
   ```

3. Copy the tests from ~/projects/go-programming-cookbook-
   original/chapter10/channels, or use this as an opportunity to write some of
   your own code!

4. Create a file called sender.go with the following content:

```
package channels

import "time"

// Sender sends "tick"" on ch until done is
// written to, then it sends "sender done."
// and exits
func Sender(ch chan string, done chan bool) {
    t := time.Tick(100 * time.Millisecond)
    for {
        select {
            case <-done:
                ch <- "sender done."
                return
            case <-t:
                ch <- "tick"
        }
    }
}
```

5. Create a file called printer.go with the following content:

```
package channels

import (
    "context"
    "fmt"
    "time"
)

// Printer will print anything sent on the ch chan
// and will print tock every 200 milliseconds
// this will repeat forever until a context is
// Done, i.e. timed out or cancelled
func Printer(ctx context.Context, ch chan string) {
    t := time.Tick(200 * time.Millisecond)
    for {
        select {
        case <-ctx.Done():
            fmt.Println("printer done.")
            return
        case res := <-ch:
```

```
                    fmt.Println(res)
                case <-t:
                    fmt.Println("tock")
            }
        }
    }
```

6. Create a new directory named `example` and navigate to it.

7. Create a file named `main.go` with the following content:

```
package main

import (
    "context"
    "time"

    "github.com/PacktPublishing/
     Go-Programming-Cookbook-Second-Edition/
     chapter10/channels"
)

func main() {
    ch := make(chan string)
    done := make(chan bool)

    ctx := context.Background()
    ctx, cancel := context.WithCancel(ctx)
    defer cancel()
    go channels.Printer(ctx, ch)
    go channels.Sender(ch, done)

    time.Sleep(2 * time.Second)
    done <- true
    cancel()
    //sleep a bit extra so channels can clean up
    time.Sleep(3 * time.Second)
}
```

8. Run `go run main.go`.

9. You may also run the following commands:

```
$ go build
$ ./example
```

You should now see the following output, but the print ordering may differ:

```
$ go run main.go
tick
tock
tick
tick
tock
tick
tick
tock
tick
.
.
.
sender done.
printer done.
```

10. The `go.mod` file may be updated and the `go.sum` file should now be present in the top-level recipe directory.
11. If you copied or wrote your own tests, go up one directory and run `go test`. Ensure that all the tests pass.

How it works...

This recipe demonstrates two ways to launch a worker process that either reads or writes to a channel, and may potentially do both. The worker will terminate when the `done` channel is written to, or when `context` is cancelled through the calling of the cancel function or by timing out. The *Using the context package* recipe will cover the `context` package in more detail.

The `main` package is used to wire together the separate functions; thanks to this, it is possible to set up multiple pairs as long as the channels are not shared. In addition to this, it's possible to have multiple Goroutines listening on the same channel, as we'll explore in the *Using the worker pool design pattern* recipe.

Lastly, due to the asynchronous nature of Goroutines, it can be tricky to establish cleanup and terminate conditions; for example, a common mistake is to do the following:

```
select{
    case <-time.Tick(200 * time.Millisecond):
    //this resets whenever any other 'lane' is chosen
}
```

By putting the `Tick` in the `select` statement, it's possible to prevent this case from ever occurring. There's also no simple way to prioritize traffic in a `select` statement.

Performing async operations with sync.WaitGroup

Sometimes, it is useful to perform a number of operations asynchronously, and then wait until they complete before moving on. For example, if an operation requires pulling information from multiple APIs and aggregating that information, it can be helpful to make those client requests asynchronously. This recipe will explore using `sync.WaitGroup` to orchestrate non-dependent tasks in parallel.

How to do it...

These steps cover writing and running your application:

1. From your Terminal or console application, create a new directory called `~/projects/go-programming-cookbook/chapter10/waitgroup` and navigate to it.

2. Run the following command:

```
$ go mod init github.com/PacktPublishing/Go-Programming-Cookbook-
Second-Edition/chapter10/waitgroup
```

You should see a file called `go.mod` that contains the following content:

```
module github.com/PacktPublishing/Go-Programming-Cookbook-Second-
Edition/chapter10/waitgroup
```

3. Copy the tests from `~/projects/go-programming-cookbook-original/chapter10/waitgroup`, or use this as an opportunity to write some of your own code!

4. Create a file called `tasks.go` with the following content:

```go
package waitgroup

import (
    "fmt"
    "log"
    "net/http"
    "strings"
    "time"
)

// GetURL gets a url, and logs the time it took
func GetURL(url string) (*http.Response, error) {
    start := time.Now()
    log.Printf("getting %s", url)
    resp, err := http.Get(url)
    log.Printf("completed getting %s in %s", url,
    time.Since(start))
    return resp, err
}

// CrawlError is our custom error type
// for aggregating errors
type CrawlError struct {
    Errors []string
}

// Add adds another error
func (c *CrawlError) Add(err error) {
    c.Errors = append(c.Errors, err.Error())
}

// Error implements the error interface
func (c *CrawlError) Error() string {
    return fmt.Sprintf("All Errors: %s", strings.Join(c.Errors,
    ","))
}

// Present can be used to determine if
// we should return this
func (c *CrawlError) Present() bool {
    return len(c.Errors) != 0
}
```

5. Create a file called `process.go` with the following content:

```go
package waitgroup

import (
    "log"
    "sync"
    "time"
)

// Crawl collects responses from a list of urls
// that are passed in. It waits for all requests
// to complete before returning.
func Crawl(sites []string) ([]int, error) {
    start := time.Now()
    log.Printf("starting crawling")
    wg := &sync.WaitGroup{}

    var resps []int
    cerr := &CrawlError{}
    for _, v := range sites {
        wg.Add(1)
        go func(v string) {
            defer wg.Done()
            resp, err := GetURL(v)
            if err != nil {
                cerr.Add(err)
                return
            }
            resps = append(resps, resp.StatusCode)
        }(v)
    }
    wg.Wait()
    // we encountered a crawl error
    if cerr.Present() {
        return resps, cerr
    }
    log.Printf("completed crawling in %s", time.Since(start))
    return resps, nil
}
```

6. Create a new directory named `example` and navigate to it.

7. Create a file named `main.go` with the following content:

```go
package main

import (
    "fmt"
```

```
        "github.com/PacktPublishing/
        Go-Programming-Cookbook-Second-Edition/
        chapter10/waitgroup"
    )

    func main() {
        sites := []string{
            "https://golang.org",
            "https://godoc.org",
            "https://www.google.com/search?q=golang",
        }

        resps, err := waitgroup.Crawl(sites)
        if err != nil {
            panic(err)
        }
        fmt.Println("Resps received:", resps)
    }
```

8. Run `go run main.go`.

9. You may also run the following commands:

```
$ go build
$ ./example
```

You should see the following output:

```
$ go run main.go
2017/04/05 19:45:07 starting crawling
2017/04/05 19:45:07 getting https://www.google.com/search?
q=golang
2017/04/05 19:45:07 getting https://golang.org
2017/04/05 19:45:07 getting https://godoc.org
2017/04/05 19:45:07 completed getting https://golang.org in
178.22407ms
2017/04/05 19:45:07 completed getting https://godoc.org in
181.400873ms
2017/04/05 19:45:07 completed getting
https://www.google.com/search?q=golang in 238.019327ms
2017/04/05 19:45:07 completed crawling in 238.191791ms
Resps received: [200 200 200]
```

10. The `go.mod` file may be updated and the `go.sum` file should now be present in the top-level recipe directory.

11. If you copied or wrote your own tests, go up one directory and run `go test`. Ensure that all the tests pass.

How it works...

This recipe shows you how to use `waitgroups` as a synchronization mechanism when waiting for work. In essence, `waitgroup.Wait()` will wait until its internal counter has reached 0. The `waitgroup.Add(int)` method will increment the counter by the amount that's entered, and `waitgroup.Done()` will decrement the counter by 1. Because of this, it is necessary to asynchronously `Wait()` while the various Goroutines mark `waitgroup` as `Done()`.

In this recipe, we increment before dispatching each HTTP request and then call a defer `wg.Done()` method so that we can decrement whenever the Goroutine terminates. We then wait for all Goroutines to finish before returning our aggregated results.

In practice, it's better to use channels for passing the errors and responses around.

When performing operations asynchronously like this, you should consider thread safety for things such as modifying a shared map. If you keep this in mind, `waitgroups` are a useful feature for waiting on any kind of asynchronous operation.

Using atomic operations and mutex

In a language such as Go, where you can build in asynchronous operations and parallelism, it becomes important to consider things such as thread safety. For example, it is dangerous to access a map from multiple Goroutines simultaneously. Go provides a number of helpers in the `sync` and `sync/atomic` packages to make sure that certain events occur only once, or that Goroutines can serialize on an operation.

This recipe will demonstrate the use of these packages to safely modify a map with various Goroutines and to keep a global ordinal value that can be safely accessed by numerous Goroutines. It will also showcase the `Once.Do` method, which can be used to ensure that something is only done by a Go application once, such as reading a configuration file or initializing a variable.

How to do it...

These steps cover writing and running your application:

1. From your Terminal or console application, create a new directory called `~/projects/go-programming-cookbook/chapter10/atomic` and navigate to it.

2. Run the following command:

   ```
   $ go mod init github.com/PacktPublishing/Go-Programming-Cookbook-
   Second-Edition/chapter10/atomic
   ```

   You should see a file called `go.mod` that contains the following content:

   ```
   module github.com/PacktPublishing/Go-Programming-Cookbook-Second-
   Edition/chapter10/atomic
   ```

3. Copy the tests from `~/projects/go-programming-cookbook-original/chapter10/atomic`, or use this as an opportunity to write some of your own code!

4. Create a file called `map.go` with the following content:

   ```go
   package atomic

   import (
       "errors"
       "sync"
   )

   // SafeMap uses a mutex to allow
   // getting and setting in a thread-safe way
   type SafeMap struct {
       m map[string]string
       mu *sync.RWMutex
   }

   // NewSafeMap creates a SafeMap
   func NewSafeMap() SafeMap {
       return SafeMap{m: make(map[string]string), mu:
       &sync.RWMutex{}}
   }

   // Set uses a write lock and sets the value given
   // a key
   func (t *SafeMap) Set(key, value string) {
       t.mu.Lock()
   ```

```
        defer t.mu.Unlock()

        t.m[key] = value
    }

    // Get uses a RW lock and gets the value if it exists,
    // otherwise an error is returned
    func (t *SafeMap) Get(key string) (string, error) {
        t.mu.RLock()
        defer t.mu.RUnlock()

        if v, ok := t.m[key]; ok {
            return v, nil
        }

        return "", errors.New("key not found")
    }
```

5. Create a file called `ordinal.go` with the following content:

```
package atomic

import (
    "sync"
    "sync/atomic"
)

// Ordinal holds a global a value
// and can only be initialized once
type Ordinal struct {
    ordinal uint64
    once *sync.Once
}

// NewOrdinal returns ordinal with once
// setup
func NewOrdinal() *Ordinal {
    return &Ordinal{once: &sync.Once{}}
}

// Init sets the ordinal value
// can only be done once
func (o *Ordinal) Init(val uint64) {
    o.once.Do(func() {
        atomic.StoreUint64(&o.ordinal, val)
    })
}
```

```
    // GetOrdinal will return the current
    // ordinal
    func (o *Ordinal) GetOrdinal() uint64 {
        return atomic.LoadUint64(&o.ordinal)
    }

    // Increment will increment the current
    // ordinal
    func (o *Ordinal) Increment() {
        atomic.AddUint64(&o.ordinal, 1)
    }
```

6. Create a new directory named `example` and navigate to it.

7. Create a file named `main.go` with the following content:

```
package main

import (
    "fmt"
    "sync"

    "github.com/PacktPublishing/
    Go-Programming-Cookbook-Second-Edition/
    chapter10/atomic"
)

func main() {
    o := atomic.NewOrdinal()
    m := atomic.NewSafeMap()
    o.Init(1123)
    fmt.Println("initial ordinal is:", o.GetOrdinal())
    wg := sync.WaitGroup{}
    for i := 0; i < 10; i++ {
        wg.Add(1)
        go func(i int) {
            defer wg.Done()
            m.Set(fmt.Sprint(i), "success")
            o.Increment()
        }(i)
    }

    wg.Wait()
    for i := 0; i < 10; i++ {
        v, err := m.Get(fmt.Sprint(i))
        if err != nil || v != "success" {
            panic(err)
        }
    }
}
```

```
                 fmt.Println("final ordinal is:", o.GetOrdinal())
                 fmt.Println("all keys found and marked as: 'success'")
        }
```

8. Run `go run main.go`.

9. You may also run the following commands:

   ```
   $ go build
   $ ./example
   ```

   You should now see the following output:

   ```
   $ go run main.go
   initial ordinal is: 1123
   final ordinal is: 1133
   all keys found and marked as: 'success'
   ```

10. The `go.mod` file may be updated and the `go.sum` file should now be present in the top-level recipe directory.

11. If you copied or wrote your own tests, go up one directory and run `go test`. Ensure that all the tests pass.

How it works...

For our map recipe, we used a `ReadWrite` mutex. The idea behind this mutex is that any number of readers can acquire a read lock, but only one writer can acquire a write lock. Additionally, a writer cannot acquire a lock when anyone else (a reader or a writer) has one. This is useful because reads are very fast and non-blocking, compared to a standard mutex. Whenever we want to set data, we use the `Lock()` object, and whenever we want to read data, we use `RLock()`. It is critical that you use `Unlock()` or `RUnlock()` eventually so that you don't deadlock your application. A deferred `Unlock()` object can be useful, but may be slower than calling `Unlock()` manually.

This pattern may not be flexible enough when you want to group additional actions with the locked value. For example, in some cases, you may want to lock, do some additional processing, and only after you've completed this will you unlock. It's important to consider this for your designs.

The `sync/atmoic` package is used by `Ordinal` to get and set values. There are also atomic comparison operations, such as `atomic.CompareAndSwapUInt64()`, which are extremely valuable. This recipe allows `Init` to be called on an `Ordinal` object only once; otherwise, it can only be incremented and does so atomically.

We loop and create 10 Goroutines (synchronizing with `sync.Waitgroup`) and show that the ordinal correctly incremented 10 times and that every key in our map was appropriately set.

Using the context package

Several recipes throughout this book make use of the `context` package. This recipe will explore the basics of creating and managing contexts. A good reference for understanding context is `https://blog.golang.org/context`. Since this blog post was written, context moved from `net/context` to a package called `context`. This still occasionally causes problems when interacting with third-party libraries such as GRPC.

This recipe will explore setting and getting values for contexts, cancellation, and timeouts.

How to do it...

These steps cover writing and running your application:

1. From your Terminal or console application, create a new directory called `~/projects/go-programming-cookbook/chapter10/context` and navigate to it.
2. Run the following command:

    ```
    $ go mod init github.com/PacktPublishing/Go-Programming-Cookbook-
    Second-Edition/chapter10/context
    ```

    You should see a file called `go.mod` that contains the following content:

    ```
    module github.com/PacktPublishing/Go-Programming-Cookbook-Second-
    Edition/chapter10/context
    ```

3. Copy the tests from `~/projects/go-programming-cookbook-original/chapter10/context`, or use this as an exercise to write some of your own code!
4. Create a file called `values.go` with the following content:

    ```
    package context

    import "context"

    type key string
    ```

```go
const (
    timeoutKey key = "TimeoutKey"
    deadlineKey key = "DeadlineKey"
)

// Setup sets some values
func Setup(ctx context.Context) context.Context {

    ctx = context.WithValue(ctx, timeoutKey,
    "timeout exceeded")
    ctx = context.WithValue(ctx, deadlineKey,
    "deadline exceeded")

    return ctx
}

// GetValue grabs a value given a key and
// returns a string representation of the
// value
func GetValue(ctx context.Context, k key) string {

    if val, ok := ctx.Value(k).(string); ok {
        return val
    }
    return ""

}
```

5. Create a file called `exec.go` with the following content:

```go
package context

import (
    "context"
    "fmt"
    "math/rand"
    "time"
)

// Exec sets two random timers and prints
// a different context value for whichever
// fires first
func Exec() {
    // a base context
    ctx := context.Background()
    ctx = Setup(ctx)

    rand.Seed(time.Now().UnixNano())
```

```
timeoutCtx, cancel := context.WithTimeout(ctx,
(time.Duration(rand.Intn(2)) * time.Millisecond))
defer cancel()

deadlineCtx, cancel := context.WithDeadline(ctx,
time.Now().Add(time.Duration(rand.Intn(2))
*time.Millisecond))
defer cancel()

for {
    select {
        case <-timeoutCtx.Done():
        fmt.Println(GetValue(ctx, timeoutKey))
        return
        case <-deadlineCtx.Done():
            fmt.Println(GetValue(ctx, deadlineKey))
            return

    }

}

}
```

6. Create a new directory named `example` and navigate to it.

7. Create a file named `main.go` with the following content:

```
package main

    import "github.com/PacktPublishing/
            Go-Programming-Cookbook-Second-Edition/
            chapter10/context"

func main() {
    context.Exec()
}
```

8. Run `go run main.go`.

9. You may also run the following commands:

```
$ go build
$ ./example
```

You should now see the following output:

```
$ go run main.go
timeout exceeded
        OR
$ go run main.go
deadline exceeded
```

10. The `go.mod` file may be updated and the `go.sum` file should now be present in the top-level recipe directory.

11. If you copied or wrote your own tests, go up one directory and run `go test`. Ensure that all the tests pass.

How it works...

When working with context values, it's good to create a new type to represent the key. In this case, we created a `key` type, then declared some corresponding `const` values to represent all of our possible keys.

In this case, we initialize all our key/value pairs at the same time using the `Setup()` function. When modifying contexts, functions generally take a `context` argument and return a `context` value. So, the signature often looks like this:

```
func ModifyContext(ctx context.Context) context.Context
```

Sometimes, these methods also return an error or the `cancel()` function, such as in the cases of `context.WithCancel`, `context.WithTimeout`, and `context.WithDeadline`. All child contexts inherit the attributes of the parent.

In this recipe, we created two child contexts, one with a deadline and one with a timeout. We set these to timeout to be random ranges, then terminated when either is received. Lastly, we extracted a value given a set key and printed it.

Executing state management for channels

Channels can be any type in Go. A channel of structs allows you to pass a lot of state with a single message. This recipe will explore the use of channels to pass around complex request structures and return their results in complex response structs.

In the next recipe, *Using the worker pool design pattern*, the value of this becomes even more apparent as you can create general purpose workers capable of performing a variety of tasks.

How to do it...

These steps cover writing and running your application:

1. From your Terminal or console application, create a new directory
   called ~/projects/go-programming-cookbook/chapter10/state and
   navigate to it.
2. Run the following command:

   ```
   $ go mod init github.com/PacktPublishing/Go-Programming-Cookbook-
   Second-Edition/chapter10/state
   ```

   You should see a file called go.mod that contains the following content:

   ```
   module github.com/PacktPublishing/Go-Programming-Cookbook-Second-
   Edition/chapter10/state
   ```

3. Copy the tests from ~/projects/go-programming-cookbook-
   original/chapter10/state, or use this as an opportunity to write some of
   your own code!
4. Create a file called state.go with the following content:

   ```go
   package state

   type op string

   const (
       // Add values
       Add op = "add"
       // Subtract values
       Subtract = "sub"
       // Multiply values
       Multiply = "mult"
       // Divide values
       Divide = "div"
   )

   // WorkRequest perform an op
   // on two values
   type WorkRequest struct {
       Operation op
       Value1 int64
       Value2 int64
   }

   // WorkResponse returns the result
   ```

```
    // and any errors
    type WorkResponse struct {
        Wr *WorkRequest
        Result int64
        Err error
    }
```

5. Create a file called `processor.go` with the following content:

```
package state

import "context"

// Processor routes work to Process
func Processor(ctx context.Context, in chan *WorkRequest, out
chan *WorkResponse) {
    for {
        select {
            case <-ctx.Done():
                return
            case wr := <-in:
                out <- Process(wr)
        }
    }
}
```

6. Create a file called `process.go` with the following content:

```
package state

import "errors"

// Process switches on operation type
// Then does work
func Process(wr *WorkRequest) *WorkResponse {
    resp := WorkResponse{Wr: wr}

    switch wr.Operation {
        case Add:
            resp.Result = wr.Value1 + wr.Value2
        case Subtract:
            resp.Result = wr.Value1 - wr.Value2
        case Multiply:
            resp.Result = wr.Value1 * wr.Value2
        case Divide:
            if wr.Value2 == 0 {
                resp.Err = errors.New("divide by 0")
                break
```

```
                    }
                    resp.Result = wr.Value1 / wr.Value2
                    default:
                        resp.Err = errors.New("unsupported operation")
            }
            return &resp
    }
```

7. Create a new directory named `example` and navigate to it.

8. Create a file named `main.go` with the following content:

```go
package main

import (
    "context"
    "fmt"

    "github.com/PacktPublishing/
     Go-Programming-Cookbook-Second-Edition/
     chapter10/state"
)

func main() {
    in := make(chan *state.WorkRequest, 10)
    out := make(chan *state.WorkResponse, 10)
    ctx := context.Background()
    ctx, cancel := context.WithCancel(ctx)
    defer cancel()

    go state.Processor(ctx, in, out)
    req := state.WorkRequest{state.Add, 3, 4}
    in <- &req

    req2 := state.WorkRequest{state.Subtract, 5, 2}
    in <- &req2

    req3 := state.WorkRequest{state.Multiply, 9, 9}
    in <- &req3

    req4 := state.WorkRequest{state.Divide, 8, 2}
    in <- &req4

    req5 := state.WorkRequest{state.Divide, 8, 0}
    in <- &req5

    for i := 0; i < 5; i++ {
        resp := <-out
        fmt.Printf("Request: %v; Result: %v, Error: %vn",
```

```
                    resp.Wr, resp.Result, resp.Err)
            }
        }
```

9. Run `go run main.go`.

10. You may also run the following commands:

    ```
    $ go build
    $ ./example
    ```

    You should now see the following output:

    ```
    $ go run main.go
    Request: &{add 3 4}; Result: 7, Error: <nil>
    Request: &{sub 5 2}; Result: 3, Error: <nil>
    Request: &{mult 9 9}; Result: 81, Error: <nil>
    Request: &{div 8 2}; Result: 4, Error: <nil>
    Request: &{div 8 0}; Result: 0, Error: divide by 0
    ```

11. The `go.mod` file may be updated and the `go.sum` file should now be present in the top-level recipe directory.

12. If you copied or wrote your own tests, go up one directory and run `go test`. Ensure that all the tests pass.

How it works...

The `Processor()` function in this recipe is a function that loops forever until its context is canceled, either through explicit calls to cancel or via timeout. It dispatches all work to `Process()`, which can handle different functions when given various operations. It would also be possible to have each of these cases dispatch another function for even more modular code.

Ultimately, the response is returned to a response channel, and we loop over and print all the results at the very end. We also demonstrate an error case in the `divide by 0` example.

Using the worker pool design pattern

The worker pool design pattern is one where you dispatch long-running Goroutines as workers. These workers can process a variety of work either using multiple channels, or by using a stateful request structure that specifies the type, as described in the preceding recipe. This recipe will create stateful workers and demonstrate how to coordinate and spin up multiple workers who are all handling requests concurrently on the same channel. These workers will be `crypto` workers, as in a web authentication application. Their purpose will be to hash plaintext strings using the `bcrypt` package and compare a text password against a hash.

How to do it...

These steps cover writing and running your application:

1. From your Terminal or console application, create a new directory called `~/projects/go-programming-cookbook/chapter10/pool` and navigate to it.

2. Run the following command:

    ```
    $ go mod init github.com/PacktPublishing/Go-Programming-Cookbook-
    Second-Edition/chapter10/pool
    ```

    You should see a file called `go.mod` that contains the following content:

    ```
    module github.com/PacktPublishing/Go-Programming-Cookbook-Second-
    Edition/chapter10/pool
    ```

3. Copy the tests from `~/projects/go-programming-cookbook-original/chapter10/pool`, or use this as an opportunity to write some of your own code!

4. Create a file called `worker.go` with the following content:

    ```go
    package pool

    import (
        "context"
        "fmt"
    )

    // Dispatch creates numWorker workers, returns a cancel
    // function channels for adding work and responses,
    // cancel must be called
    ```

```go
func Dispatch(numWorker int) (context.CancelFunc, chan
WorkRequest, chan WorkResponse) {
    ctx := context.Background()
    ctx, cancel := context.WithCancel(ctx)
    in := make(chan WorkRequest, 10)
    out := make(chan WorkResponse, 10)

    for i := 0; i < numWorker; i++ {
        go Worker(ctx, i, in, out)
    }
    return cancel, in, out
}

// Worker loops forever and is part of the worker pool
func Worker(ctx context.Context, id int, in chan WorkRequest,
out chan WorkResponse) {
    for {
        select {
            case <-ctx.Done():
                return
            case wr := <-in:
                fmt.Printf("worker id: %d, performing %s
                workn", id, wr.Op)
                out <- Process(wr)
        }
    }
}
```

5. Create a file called `work.go` with the following content:

```go
package pool

import "errors"

type op string

const (
    // Hash is the bcrypt work type
    Hash op = "encrypt"
    // Compare is bcrypt compare work
    Compare = "decrypt"
)

// WorkRequest is a worker req
type WorkRequest struct {
    Op op
    Text []byte
    Compare []byte // optional
```

```
    }

    // WorkResponse is a worker resp
    type WorkResponse struct {
        Wr WorkRequest
        Result []byte
        Matched bool
        Err error
    }

    // Process dispatches work to the worker pool channel
    func Process(wr WorkRequest) WorkResponse {
        switch wr.Op {
        case Hash:
            return hashWork(wr)
        case Compare:
            return compareWork(wr)
        default:
            return WorkResponse{Err: errors.New("unsupported
            operation")}
        }
    }
```

6. Create a file called `crypto.go` with the following content:

```
    package pool

    import "golang.org/x/crypto/bcrypt"

    func hashWork(wr WorkRequest) WorkResponse {
        val, err := bcrypt.GenerateFromPassword(wr.Text,
        bcrypt.DefaultCost)
        return WorkResponse{
            Result: val,
            Err: err,
            Wr: wr,
        }
    }

    func compareWork(wr WorkRequest) WorkResponse {
        var matched bool
        err := bcrypt.CompareHashAndPassword(wr.Compare, wr.Text)
        if err == nil {
            matched = true
        }
        return WorkResponse{
            Matched: matched,
            Err: err,
```

```
            Wr: wr,
        }
    }
```

7. Create a new directory named `example` and navigate to it.

8. Create a file named `main.go` with the following content:

```go
package main

import (
    "fmt"

    "github.com/PacktPublishing/
    Go-Programming-Cookbook-Second-Edition/
    chapter10/pool"
)

func main() {
    cancel, in, out := pool.Dispatch(10)
    defer cancel()

    for i := 0; i < 10; i++ {
        in <- pool.WorkRequest{Op: pool.Hash, Text:
        []byte(fmt.Sprintf("messages %d", i))}
    }

    for i := 0; i < 10; i++ {
        res := <-out
        if res.Err != nil {
            panic(res.Err)
        }
        in <- pool.WorkRequest{Op: pool.Compare, Text:
        res.Wr.Text, Compare: res.Result}
    }

    for i := 0; i < 10; i++ {
        res := <-out
        if res.Err != nil {
            panic(res.Err)
        }
        fmt.Printf("string: "%s"; matched: %vn",
        string(res.Wr.Text), res.Matched)
    }
}
```

9. Run `go run main.go`.

10. You may also run the following commands:

```
$ go build
$ ./example
```

You should now see the following output:

```
$ go run main.go
worker id: 9, performing encrypt work
worker id: 5, performing encrypt work
worker id: 2, performing encrypt work
worker id: 8, performing encrypt work
worker id: 6, performing encrypt work
worker id: 1, performing encrypt work
worker id: 0, performing encrypt work
worker id: 4, performing encrypt work
worker id: 3, performing encrypt work
worker id: 7, performing encrypt work
worker id: 2, performing decrypt work
worker id: 6, performing decrypt work
worker id: 8, performing decrypt work
worker id: 1, performing decrypt work
worker id: 0, performing decrypt work
worker id: 9, performing decrypt work
worker id: 3, performing decrypt work
worker id: 4, performing decrypt work
worker id: 7, performing decrypt work
worker id: 5, performing decrypt work
string: "messages 9"; matched: true
string: "messages 3"; matched: true
string: "messages 4"; matched: true
string: "messages 0"; matched: true
string: "messages 1"; matched: true
string: "messages 8"; matched: true
string: "messages 5"; matched: true
string: "messages 7"; matched: true
string: "messages 2"; matched: true
string: "messages 6"; matched: true
```

11. The `go.mod` file may be updated and the `go.sum` file should now be present in the top-level recipe directory.

12. If you copied or wrote your own tests, go up one directory and run `go test`. Ensure that all the tests pass.

How it works...

This recipe uses the `Dispatch()` method to create a number of workers on a single input channel, output channel, and those attached to a single `cancel()` function. This can be used if you want to make different pools for different purposes. For example, you can create 10 `crypto` and 20 `compare` workers by using separate pools. For this recipe, we use a single pool, send hash requests to the workers, retrieve the responses, and then send `compare` requests to the same pool. Because of this, the worker performing the work will be different each time, but they're all capable of performing either type of work.

The advantage of this approach is that both requests allow for parallelism and can also control the maximum concurrency. Bounding the maximum number of Goroutines can also be important for limiting memory. I chose `crypto` for this recipe because `crypto` is a good example of code that can overwhelm your CPU or memory if you spin up a new Goroutine for every new request; for example, in a web service.

Using workers to create pipelines

This recipe demonstrates creating groups of worker pools and connecting them together to form a pipeline. For this recipe, we link together two pools, but the pattern can be used for much more complex operations, similar to middleware.

Worker pools can be useful for keeping workers relatively simple and to also further control concurrency. For example, it may be useful to serialize logging while parallelizing other operations. It may also be useful to have a smaller pool for more expensive operations so that you don't overload machine resources.

How to do it...

These steps cover writing and running your application:

1. From your Terminal or console application, create a new directory called `~/projects/go-programming-cookbook/chapter10/pipeline` and navigate to it.
2. Run the following command:

```
$ go mod init github.com/PacktPublishing/Go-Programming-Cookbook-
Second-Edition/chapter10/pipeline
```

You should see a file called `go.mod` that contains the following content:

```
module github.com/PacktPublishing/Go-Programming-Cookbook-Second-
Edition/chapter10/pipeline
```

3. Copy the tests from `~/projects/go-programming-cookbook-original/chapter10/pipeline`, or use this as an opportunity to write some of your own code!

4. Create a file called `worker.go` with the following content:

```go
package pipeline

import "context"

// Worker have one role
// that is determined when
// Work is called
type Worker struct {
    in chan string
    out chan string
}

// Job is a job a worker can do
type Job string

const (
    // Print echo's all input to
    // stdout
    Print Job = "print"
    // Encode base64 encodes input
    Encode Job = "encode"
)

// Work is how to dispatch a worker, they are assigned
// a job here
func (w *Worker) Work(ctx context.Context, j Job) {
    switch j {
        case Print:
            w.Print(ctx)
        case Encode:
            w.Encode(ctx)
        default:
            return
    }
}
```

5. Create a file called `print.go` with the following content:

```go
package pipeline

import (
    "context"
    "fmt"
)

// Print prints w.in and repalys it
// on w.out
func (w *Worker) Print(ctx context.Context) {
    for {
        select {
        case <-ctx.Done():
            return
        case val := <-w.in:
            fmt.Println(val)
            w.out <- val
        }
    }
}
```

6. Create a file called `encode.go` with the following content:

```go
package pipeline

import (
    "context"
    "encoding/base64"
    "fmt"
)

// Encode takes plain text as int
// and returns "string => <base64 string encoding>
// as out
func (w *Worker) Encode(ctx context.Context) {
    for {
        select {
        case <-ctx.Done():
            return
        case val := <-w.in:
            w.out <- fmt.Sprintf("%s => %s", val,
                base64.StdEncoding.EncodeToString([]byte(val)))
        }
    }
}
```

7. Create a file called `pipeline.go` with the following content:

```go
package pipeline

import "context"

// NewPipeline initializes the workers and
// connects them, it returns the input of the pipeline
// and the final output
func NewPipeline(ctx context.Context, numEncoders, numPrinters
int) (chan string, chan string) {
    inEncode := make(chan string, numEncoders)
    inPrint := make(chan string, numPrinters)
    outPrint := make(chan string, numPrinters)
    for i := 0; i < numEncoders; i++ {
        w := Worker{
            in: inEncode,
            out: inPrint,
        }
        go w.Work(ctx, Encode)
    }

    for i := 0; i < numPrinters; i++ {
        w := Worker{
            in: inPrint,
            out: outPrint,
        }
        go w.Work(ctx, Print)
    }
    return inEncode, outPrint
}
```

8. Create a new directory named `example` and navigate to it.

9. Create a file named `main.go` with the following content:

```go
package main

import (
    "context"
    "fmt"

    "github.com/PacktPublishing/
    Go-Programming-Cookbook-Second-Edition/
    chapter10/pipeline"
)

func main() {
    ctx := context.Background()
```

```
        ctx, cancel := context.WithCancel(ctx)
        defer cancel()

        in, out := pipeline.NewPipeline(ctx, 10, 2)

        go func() {
            for i := 0; i < 20; i++ {
                in <- fmt.Sprint("Message", i)
            }
        }()

        for i := 0; i < 20; i++ {
            <-out
        }
    }
```

10. Run `go run main.go`.

11. You may also run the following commands:

    ```
    $ go build
    $ ./example
    ```

    You should now see the following output:

    ```
    $ go run main.go
    Message3 => TWVzc2FnZTM=
    Message7 => TWVzc2FnZTc=
    Message8 => TWVzc2FnZTg=
    Message9 => TWVzc2FnZTk=
    Message5 => TWVzc2FnZTU=
    Message11 => TWVzc2FnZTEx
    Message10 => TWVzc2FnZTEw
    Message4 => TWVzc2FnZTQ=
    Message12 => TWVzc2FnZTEy
    Message6 => TWVzc2FnZTY=
    Message14 => TWVzc2FnZTE0
    Message13 => TWVzc2FnZTEz
    Message0 => TWVzc2FnZTA=
    Message15 => TWVzc2FnZTE1
    Message1 => TWVzc2FnZTE=
    Message17 => TWVzc2FnZTE3
    Message16 => TWVzc2FnZTE2
    Message19 => TWVzc2FnZTE5
    Message18 => TWVzc2FnZTE4
    Message2 => TWVzc2FnZTI=
    ```

12. The `go.mod` file may be updated and the `go.sum` file should now be present in the top-level recipe directory.
13. If you copied or wrote your own tests, go up one directory and run `go test`. Ensure that all the tests pass.

How it works...

The `main` package creates a pipeline consisting of 10 encoders and 2 printers. It enqueues 20 strings on the in channel and waits for 20 responses on the out channel. If messages reach the out channel, it indicates that they've gone through the entire pipeline successfully.

The `NewPipeline` function is used to wire up the pools. It ensures that the channels are created with the properly buffered sizes and that the output channels of some pools are connected to the appropriate input channels of other pools. It's also possible to fan out the pipeline by using an array of in channels and an array of out channels on each worker, multiple named channels, or maps of channels. This would allow for things such as sending messages to a logger at each step.

11
Distributed Systems

Sometimes, application-level parallelism is not enough, and things that seem simple in development can become complex during deployment. Distributed systems provide a number of challenges that aren't found when developing on a single machine. These applications have added complexity for things such as monitoring, writing applications that require strong consistency guarantees, and service discovery. In addition, you must always be mindful of single points of failure, such as a database, otherwise your distributed applications can fail when this single component fails.

This chapter will explore methods of managing distributed data, orchestration, containerization, metrics, and monitoring. These will become part of your toolbox for writing and maintaining microservices and large distributed applications.

In this chapter, we will cover the following recipes:

- Using service discovery with Consul
- Implementing basic consensus using Raft
- Using containerization with Docker
- Orchestration and deployment strategies
- Monitoring applications
- Collecting metrics

Technical requirements

To follow all the recipes in this chapter, configure your environment according to these steps:

1. Download and install Go 1.12.6 or above on your operating system from `https:/ /golang.org/doc/install`.
2. Install Consul from `https://www.consul.io/intro/getting-started/install. html`.

3. Open a Terminal or console application and create and navigate to a project directory such as `~/projects/go-programming-cookbook`. All the code will be run and modified from this directory.

4. Clone the latest code into `~/projects/go-programming-cookbook-original` and (optionally) work from that directory rather than typing in the examples manually:

```
$ git clone git@github.com:PacktPublishing/Go-Programming-Cookbook-Second-Edition.git go-programming-cookbook-original
```

Using service discovery with Consul

When using the microservice approach to applications, you end up with a lot of servers listening on a variety of IPs, domains, and ports. These IP addresses will vary by environment (staging versus production), and it can be tricky to keep them static for configuration between services. You also want to know when a machine or service is down or unreachable due to a network partition. A network partition occurs when two parts of the network cannot reach each other. For example, if a switch fails between two data centers, then the services within one datacenter cannot reach services in the other datacenter. Consul is a tool that provides a lot of functionality, but here, we'll explore registering services with Consul and querying them from our other services.

How to do it...

These steps cover writing and running your application:

1. From your Terminal or console application, create a new directory called `~/projects/go-programming-cookbook/chapter11/discovery` and navigate to it.

2. Run the following command:

```
$ go mod init github.com/PacktPublishing/Go-Programming-Cookbook-Second-Edition/chapter11/discovery
```

You should see a file called `go.mod` that contains the following content:

```
module github.com/PacktPublishing/Go-Programming-Cookbook-Second-Edition/chapter11/discovery
```

3. Copy the tests from `~/projects/go-programming-cookbook-original/chapter11/discovery`, or use this as an opportunity to write some of your own code!

4. Create a file called `client.go` with the following content:

```go
package discovery

import "github.com/hashicorp/consul/api"

// Client exposes api methods we care
// about
type Client interface {
    Register(tags []string) error
    Service(service, tag string) ([]*api.ServiceEntry,
    *api.QueryMeta, error)
}

type client struct {
    client *api.Client
    address string
    name string
    port int
}

//NewClient iniitalizes a consul client
func NewClient(config *api.Config, address, name string, port
int) (Client, error) {
    c, err := api.NewClient(config)
    if err != nil {
        return nil, err
    }
    cli := &client{
        client: c,
        name: name,
        address: address,
        port: port,
    }
    return cli, nil
}
```

5. Create a file called `operations.go` with the following content:

```go
package discovery

import "github.com/hashicorp/consul/api"

// Register adds our service to consul
```

```
func (c *client) Register(tags []string) error {
    reg := &api.AgentServiceRegistration{
        ID: c.name,
        Name: c.name,
        Port: c.port,
        Address: c.address,
        Tags: tags,
    }
    return c.client.Agent().ServiceRegister(reg)
}

// Service return a service
func (c *client) Service(service, tag string)
([]*api.ServiceEntry, *api.QueryMeta, error) {
    return c.client.Health().Service(service, tag, false,
    nil)
}
```

6. Create a file called `exec.go` with the following content:

```
package discovery

import "fmt"

// Exec creates a consul entry then queries it
func Exec(cli Client) error {
    if err := cli.Register([]string{"Go", "Awesome"}); err != nil {
        return err
    }

    entries, _, err := cli.Service("discovery", "Go")
    if err != nil {
        return err
    }
    for _, entry := range entries {
        fmt.Printf("%#v\n", entry.Service)
    }

    return nil
}
```

7. Create a new directory named `example` and navigate to it.
8. Create a file named `main.go` with the following content:

```
package main

import "github.com/PacktPublishing/
        Go-Programming-Cookbook-Second-Edition/
```

```
            chapter11/discovery"

    func main() {
        if err := discovery.Exec(); err != nil {
            panic(err)
        }
    }
```

9. Start Consul in a separate Terminal using the `consul agent -dev -node=localhost` command.

10. Run the `go run main.go` command.

11. You may also run the following commands:

```
$ go build
$ ./example
```

You should see the following output:

```
$ go run main.go
&api.AgentService{ID:"discovery", Service:"discovery", Tags:
[]string{"Go", "Awesome"}, Port:8080, Address:"localhost",
EnableTagOverride:false, CreateIndex:0x23, ModifyIndex:0x23}
```

12. The `go.mod` file may be updated and the `go.sum` file should now be present in the top-level recipe directory.

13. If you copied or wrote your own tests, go up one directory and run `go test`. Ensure that all the tests pass.

How it works...

Consul provides a robust Go API library. It can feel daunting when you're starting for the first time, but this recipe shows how you might approach wrapping it. Configuring Consul further is beyond the scope of this recipe; this shows the basics of registering a service and querying for other services when given a key and tag.

It would be possible to use this to register new microservices at startup time, query for all dependent services, and deregister at shutdown. You may also want to cache this information so that you're not hitting Consul for every request, but this recipe provides the basic tools that you can expand upon. The Consul agent also makes these repeated requests fast and efficient (https://www.consul.io/intro/getting-started/agent.html). Once you've s

Implementing basic consensus using Raft

Raft is a consensus algorithm. It allows distributed systems to keep a shared and managed state (`https://raft.github.io/`). Setting up a Raft system is complex in many ways – for one, you need consensus for an election to occur and succeed. This can be difficult to bootstrap when you're working with multiple nodes and can be difficult to get started. It is possible to run a basic cluster on a single node/leader. However, if you want redundancy, at least three nodes are needed to prevent data loss in the case of a single node failure. This concept is known as quorum, where you must maintain ($n/2$)+1 available nodes to ensure new logs can be committed to the Raft cluster. Basically, if you can maintain quorum, the cluster remains healthy and usable.

This recipe implements a basic in-memory Raft cluster, constructs a state machine that can transition between certain allowed states, and connects the distributed state machine to a web handler that can trigger the transition. This can be useful when you're implementing the base finite state machine interface that Raft requires, or when testing. This recipe uses `https://github.com/hashicorp/raft` for the base Raft implementation.

How to do it...

The following steps cover writing and running your application:

1. From your Terminal or console application, create a new directory called `~/projects/go-programming-cookbook/chapter11/consensus` and navigate to it.
2. Run the following command:

```
$ go mod init github.com/PacktPublishing/Go-Programming-Cookbook-
Second-Edition/chapter11/consensus
```

You should see a file called `go.mod` that contains the following content:

```
module github.com/PacktPublishing/Go-Programming-Cookbook-Second-
Edition/chapter11/consensus
```

3. Copy the tests from ~/projects/go-programming-cookbook-
   original/chapter11/consensus, or use this as an opportunity to write some
   of your own code!

4. Create a file called state.go with the following content:

```go
package consensus

type state string

const (
    first state = "first"
    second = "second"
    third = "third"
)

var allowedState map[state][]state

func init() {
    // setup valid states
    allowedState = make(map[state][]state)
    allowedState[first] = []state{second, third}
    allowedState[second] = []state{third}
    allowedState[third] = []state{first}
}

// CanTransition checks if a new state is valid
func (s *state) CanTransition(next state) bool {
    for _, n := range allowedState[*s] {
        if n == next {
            return true
        }
    }
    return false
}

// Transition will move a state to the next
// state if able
func (s *state) Transition(next state) {
    if s.CanTransition(next) {
        *s = next
    }
}
```

5. Create a file called `raftset.go` with the following content:

```go
package consensus

import (
  "fmt"

  "github.com/hashicorp/raft"
)

// keep a map of rafts for later
var rafts map[raft.ServerAddress]*raft.Raft

func init() {
  rafts = make(map[raft.ServerAddress]*raft.Raft)
}

// raftSet stores all the setup material we need
type raftSet struct {
  Config *raft.Config
  Store *raft.InmemStore
  SnapShotStore raft.SnapshotStore
  FSM *FSM
  Transport raft.LoopbackTransport
  Configuration raft.Configuration
}

// generate n raft sets to bootstrap the raft cluster
func getRaftSet(num int) []*raftSet {
  rs := make([]*raftSet, num)
  servers := make([]raft.Server, num)
  for i := 0; i < num; i++ {
    addr := raft.ServerAddress(fmt.Sprint(i))
    _, transport := raft.NewInmemTransport(addr)
    servers[i] = raft.Server{
      Suffrage: raft.Voter,
      ID: raft.ServerID(addr),
      Address: addr,
    }
    config := raft.DefaultConfig()
    config.LocalID = raft.ServerID(addr)

    rs[i] = &raftSet{
      Config: config,
      Store: raft.NewInmemStore(),
      SnapShotStore: raft.NewInmemSnapshotStore(),
      FSM: NewFSM(),
      Transport: transport,
```

```
      }
    }

    // configuration needs to be consistent between
    // services and so we need the full serverlist in this
    // case
    for _, r := range rs {
      r.Configuration = raft.Configuration{Servers: servers}
    }

    return rs
}
```

6. Create a file called `config.go` with the following content:

```
package consensus

import (
  "github.com/hashicorp/raft"
)

// Config creates num in-memory raft
// nodes and connects them
func Config(num int) {

  // create n "raft-sets" consisting of
  // everything needed to represent a node
  rs := getRaftSet(num)

  //connect all of the transports
  for _, r1 := range rs {
    for _, r2 := range rs {
      r1.Transport.Connect(r2.Transport.LocalAddr(), r2.Transport)
    }
  }

  // for each node, bootstrap then connect
  for _, r := range rs {
    if err := raft.BootstrapCluster(r.Config, r.Store, r.Store,
r.SnapShotStore, r.Transport, r.Configuration); err != nil {
      panic(err)
    }
    raft, err := raft.NewRaft(r.Config, r.FSM, r.Store, r.Store,
r.SnapShotStore, r.Transport)
    if err != nil {
      panic(err)
    }
    rafts[r.Transport.LocalAddr()] = raft
```

```
        }
    }
```

7. Create a file called `fsm.go` with the following content:

```go
package consensus

import (
    "io"

    "github.com/hashicorp/raft"
)

// FSM implements the raft FSM interface
// and holds a state
type FSM struct {
    state state
}

// NewFSM creates a new FSM with
// start state of "first"
func NewFSM() *FSM {
    return &FSM{state: first}
}

// Apply updates our FSM
func (f *FSM) Apply(r *raft.Log) interface{} {
    f.state.Transition(state(r.Data))
    return string(f.state)
}

// Snapshot needed to satisfy the raft FSM interface
func (f *FSM) Snapshot() (raft.FSMSnapshot, error) {
    return nil, nil
}

// Restore needed to satisfy the raft FSM interface
func (f *FSM) Restore(io.ReadCloser) error {
    return nil
}
```

8. Create a file called `handler.go` with the following content:

```go
package consensus

import (
    "net/http"
    "time"
```

```
)

// Handler grabs the get param ?next= and tries
// to transition to the state contained there
func Handler(w http.ResponseWriter, r *http.Request) {
  r.ParseForm()
  state := r.FormValue("next")
  for address, raft := range rafts {
    if address != raft.Leader() {
      continue
    }
    result := raft.Apply([]byte(state), 1*time.Second)
    if result.Error() != nil {
      w.WriteHeader(http.StatusBadRequest)
      return
    }
    newState, ok := result.Response().(string)
    if !ok {
      w.WriteHeader(http.StatusInternalServerError)
      return
    }

    if newState != state {
      w.WriteHeader(http.StatusBadRequest)
      w.Write([]byte("invalid transition"))
      return
    }
    w.WriteHeader(http.StatusOK)
    w.Write([]byte(newState))
    return
  }
}
```

9. Create a new directory named `example` and navigate to it.

10. Create a file named `main.go` with the following content:

```
package main

import (
    "net/http"

    "github.com/PacktPublishing/
    Go-Programming-Cookbook-Second-Edition/
    chapter11/consensus"
)

func main() {
    consensus.Config(3)
```

```
http.HandleFunc("/", consensus.Handler)
err := http.ListenAndServe(":3333", nil)
panic(err)
}
```

11. Run the `go run main.go` command. Alternatively, you may also run the following commands:

```
$ go build
$ ./example
```

You should now see the following output:

```
$ go run main.go
2019/05/04 21:06:46 [INFO] raft: Initial configuration (index=1):
[{Suffrage:Voter ID:0 Address:0} {Suffrage:Voter ID:1 Address:1}
{Suffrage:Voter ID:2 Address:2}]
2019/05/04 21:06:46 [INFO] raft: Initial configuration (index=1):
[{Suffrage:Voter ID:0 Address:0} {Suffrage:Voter ID:1 Address:1}
{Suffrage:Voter ID:2 Address:2}]
2019/05/04 21:06:46 [INFO] raft: Node at 0 [Follower] entering
Follower state (Leader: "")
2019/05/04 21:06:46 [INFO] raft: Node at 1 [Follower] entering
Follower state (Leader: "")
2019/05/04 21:06:46 [INFO] raft: Initial configuration (index=1):
[{Suffrage:Voter ID:0 Address:0} {Suffrage:Voter ID:1 Address:1}
{Suffrage:Voter ID:2 Address:2}]
2019/05/04 21:06:46 [INFO] raft: Node at 2 [Follower] entering
Follower state (Leader: "")
2019/05/04 21:06:47 [WARN] raft: Heartbeat timeout from "" reached,
starting election
2019/05/04 21:06:47 [INFO] raft: Node at 0 [Candidate] entering
Candidate state in term 2
2019/05/04 21:06:47 [DEBUG] raft: Votes needed: 2
2019/05/04 21:06:47 [DEBUG] raft: Vote granted from 0 in term 2.
Tally: 1
2019/05/04 21:06:47 [DEBUG] raft: Vote granted from 1 in term 2.
Tally: 2
2019/05/04 21:06:47 [INFO] raft: Election won. Tally: 2
2019/05/04 21:06:47 [INFO] raft: Node at 0 [Leader] entering Leader
state
2019/05/04 21:06:47 [INFO] raft: Added peer 1, starting replication
2019/05/04 21:06:47 [INFO] raft: Added peer 2, starting replication
2019/05/04 21:06:47 [INFO] raft: pipelining replication to peer
{Voter 1 1}
2019/05/04 21:06:47 [INFO] raft: pipelining replication to peer
{Voter 2 2}
```

12. In a separate Terminal, run the following command:

```
$ curl "http://localhost:3333/?next=second"
second

$ curl "http://localhost:3333/?next=third"
third

$ curl "http://localhost:3333/?next=second"
invalid transition

$ curl "http://localhost:3333/?next=first"
first
```

13. The `go.mod` file may be updated and the `go.sum` file should now be present in the top-level recipe directory.

14. If you copied or wrote your own tests, go up one directory and run `go test`. Ensure that all the tests pass.

How it works...

When the application starts, we initialize multiple Raft objects. These each have their own address and transport. The `InmemTransport{}` function also provides a method for connecting the other transports, and is called `Connect()`. Once these connections are established, the Raft cluster holds an election. When communicating in a Raft cluster, clients must communicate with the leader. In our case, one handler can talk to all of the nodes, so the handler is responsible for having the `Raft` leader's `call Apply()` object. This in turn runs `apply()` on all of the other nodes.

The `InmemTransport{}` function simplifies the election and bootstrapping process by allowing everything to reside in memory. In practice, this isn't very helpful, except for testing and proof of concepts, since Goroutines can freely access shared memory. A more production-minded implementation would use something like an HTTP Transport such that service instances can communicate across machines. This may require some additional bookkeeping or service discovery as the service instances have to listen and serve as well as have the ability discover and establish connections with one another.

Using containerization with Docker

Docker is a container technology for packaging and shipping applications. Other advantages include portability, since a container will run the same way regardless of the host OS. It provides a lot of the advantages of a virtual machine, but in a more lightweight container. It's possible to limit the resource consumption of individual containers and sandbox your environment. It can be extremely useful to have a common environment for your applications locally and when you ship your code to production. Docker is written in Go and is open source, so it's simple to take advantage of the client and libraries. This recipe will set up a Docker container for a basic Go application, store some version information about the container, and demonstrate hitting a handler from a Docker endpoint.

Getting ready

Configure your environment according to these steps:

1. Refer to the *Technical requirements* section in this chapter for steps to configure your environment.
2. Install Docker from `https://docs.docker.com/install`. This will also include Docker Compose.

How to do it...

These steps cover writing and running your application:

1. From your Terminal or console application, create a new directory called `~/projects/go-programming-cookbook/chapter11/docker` and navigate to it.
2. Run the following command:

```
$ go mod init github.com/PacktPublishing/Go-Programming-Cookbook-
Second-Edition/chapter11/docker
```

You should see a file called `go.mod` that contains the following content:

```
module github.com/PacktPublishing/Go-Programming-Cookbook-Second-
Edition/chapter11/docker
```

3. Copy the tests from `~/projects/go-programming-cookbook-original/chapter11/docker`, or use this as an opportunity to write some of your own code!

4. Create a file called `dockerfile` with the following content:

```
FROM alpine

ADD ./example/example /example
EXPOSE 8000
ENTRYPOINT /example
```

5. Create a file called `setup.sh` with the following content:

```
#!/usr/bin/env bash

pushd example
env GOOS=linux go build -ldflags "-X main.version=1.0 -X
main.builddate=$(date +%s)"
popd
docker build . -t example
docker run -d -p 8000:8000 example
```

6. Create a file called `version.go` with the following content:

```go
package docker

import (
    "encoding/json"
    "net/http"
    "time"
)

// VersionInfo holds artifacts passed in
// at build time
type VersionInfo struct {
    Version   string
    BuildDate time.Time
    Uptime    time.Duration
}

// VersionHandler writes the latest version info
func VersionHandler(v *VersionInfo) http.HandlerFunc {
```

```
        t := time.Now()
        return func(w http.ResponseWriter, r *http.Request) {
            v.Uptime = time.Since(t)
            vers, err := json.Marshal(v)
                if err != nil {
                    w.WriteHeader
                    (http.StatusInternalServerError)
                    return
                }
                w.WriteHeader(http.StatusOK)
                w.Write(vers)
        }
    }
```

7. Create a new directory named example and navigate to it.

8. Create a main.go file with the following content:

```
    package main

    import (
        "fmt"
        "net/http"
        "strconv"
        "time"

        "github.com/PacktPublishing/
        Go-Programming-Cookbook-Second-Edition/
        chapter11/docker"
    )

    // these are set at build time
    var (
        version string
        builddate string
        )

        var versioninfo docker.VersionInfo

        func init() {
            // parse buildtime variables
            versioninfo.Version = version
            i, err := strconv.ParseInt(builddate, 10, 64)
                if err != nil {
                    panic(err)
                }
                tm := time.Unix(i, 0)
                versioninfo.BuildDate = tm
        }
```

```
func main() {
    http.HandleFunc("/version",
    docker.VersionHandler(&versioninfo))
    fmt.Printf("version %s listening on :8000\n",
    versioninfo.Version)
    panic(http.ListenAndServe(":8000", nil))
}
```

9. Navigate back to the starting directory.

10. Run the following command:

```
$ bash setup.sh
```

You should now see the following output:

```
$ bash setup.sh
~/go/src/github.com/PacktPublishing/Go-Programming-Cookbook-
Second-Edition/chapter11/docker/example
~/go/src/github.com/PacktPublishing/Go-Programming-Cookbook-
Second-Edition/chapter11/docker
~/go/src/github.com/PacktPublishing/Go-Programming-Cookbook-
Second-Edition/chapter11/docker
Sending build context to Docker daemon 6.031 MB
Step 1/4 : FROM alpine
 ---> 4a415e366388
Step 2/4 : ADD ./example/example /example
 ---> de34c3c5451e
Removing intermediate container bdcd9c4f4381
Step 3/4 : EXPOSE 8000
 ---> Running in 188f450d4e7b
 ---> 35d1a2652b43
Removing intermediate container 188f450d4e7b
Step 4/4 : ENTRYPOINT /example
 ---> Running in cf0af4f48c3a
 ---> 3d737fc4e6e2
Removing intermediate container cf0af4f48c3a
Successfully built 3d737fc4e6e2
b390ef429fbd6e7ff87058dc82e15c3e7a8b2e
69a601892700d1d434e9e8e43b
```

11. Run the following commands:

```
$ docker ps
CONTAINER ID IMAGE COMMAND CREATED STATUS PORTS NAMES
b390ef429fbd example "/bin/sh -c /example" 22 seconds ago Up 23
seconds 0.0.0.0:8000->8000/tcp optimistic_wescoff

$ curl localhost:8000/version
```

```
{"Version":"1.0","BuildDate":"2017-04-
30T21:55:56Z","Uptime":48132111264}

$docker kill optimistic_wescoff # grab from first output
optimistic_wescoff
```

12. The `go.mod` file may be updated and the `go.sum` file should now be present in the top-level recipe directory.
13. If you copied or wrote your own tests, go up one directory and run `go test`. Ensure that all the tests pass.

How it works...

This recipe created a script that compiles the Go binary for the Linux architecture and sets a variety of private variables in `main.go`. These variables are used to return version information on a version endpoint. Once the binary is compiled, a Docker container is created that contains the binary. This allows us to use very small container images since the Go runtime is self-contained in the binary. We then run the container while exposing the port on which the container is listening for HTTP traffic. Lastly, we `curl` the port on localhost and see our version information returned.

Orchestration and deployment strategies

Docker makes orchestration and deployment much simpler. In this recipe, we'll set up a connection to MongoDB and then insert a document and query it all from Docker containers. This recipe will set up the same environment as the *Using NoSQL with MongoDB and mgo* recipe from Chapter 6, *All about Databases and Storage*, but will run the application and environment inside of containers and will use Docker Compose to orchestrate and connect to them.

This can later be used in conjunction with Docker Swarm, an integrated Docker tool that allows you to manage a cluster, create and deploy nodes that can be scaled up or down easily, and manage load balancing (https://docs.docker.com/engine/swarm/). Another good example of container orchestration is Kubernetes (https://kubernetes.io/), a container orchestration framework written by Google using the Go programming language.

How to do it...

The following steps cover writing and running your application:

1. From your Terminal or console application, create a new directory called `~/projects/go-programming-cookbook/chapter11/orchestrate` and navigate to it.

2. Run the following command:

   $ go mod init github.com/PacktPublishing/Go-Programming-Cookbook-Second-Edition/chapter11/orchestrate

   You should see a file called `go.mod` that contains the following content:

   ```
   module github.com/PacktPublishing/Go-Programming-Cookbook-Second-
   Edition/chapter11/orchestrate
   ```

3. Copy the tests from `~/projects/go-programming-cookbook-original/chapter11/orchestrate`, or use this as an opportunity to write some of your own code!

4. Create a file called `Dockerfile` with the following content:

   ```
   FROM golang:1.12.4-alpine3.9

   ENV GOPATH /code/
   ADD . /code/src/github.com/PacktPublishing/Go-Programming-Cookbook-
   Second-Edition/chapter11/docker
   WORKDIR /code/src/github.com/PacktPublishing/Go-Programming-
   Cookbook-Second-Edition/chapter11/docker/example
   RUN GO111MODULE=on GOPROXY=off go build -mod=vendor

   ENTRYPOINT /code/src/github.com/PacktPublishing/Go-Programming-
   Cookbook-Second-Edition/chapter11/docker/example/example
   ```

5. Create a file called `docker-compose.yml` with the following content:

   ```
   version: '2'
   services:
    app:
    build: .
    mongodb:
    image: "mongo:latest"
   ```

6. Create a file called `config.go` with the following content:

```go
package mongodb

import (
  "context"
  "fmt"
  "time"

  "github.com/mongodb/mongo-go-driver/mongo"
  "go.mongodb.org/mongo-driver/mongo/options"
)

// Setup initializes a mongo client
func Setup(ctx context.Context, address string) (*mongo.Client,
error) {
  ctx, cancel := context.WithTimeout(ctx, 1*time.Second)
  defer cancel()

  fmt.Println(address)
  client, err :=
mongo.NewClient(options.Client().ApplyURI(address))
  if err != nil {
    return nil, err
  }

  if err := client.Connect(ctx); err != nil {
    return nil, err
  }
  return client, nil
}
```

7. Create a file called `exec.go` with the following content:

```go
package mongodb

import (
  "context"
  "fmt"

  "github.com/mongodb/mongo-go-driver/bson"
)

// State is our data model
type State struct {
  Name string `bson:"name"`
  Population int `bson:"pop"`
}
```

```
// Exec creates then queries an Example
func Exec(address string) error {
  ctx := context.Background()
  db, err := Setup(ctx, address)
  if err != nil {
    return err
  }

  conn := db.Database("gocookbook").Collection("example")

  vals := []interface{}{&State{"Washington", 7062000},
&State{"Oregon", 3970000}}

  // we can inserts many rows at once
  if _, err := conn.InsertMany(ctx, vals); err != nil {
    return err
  }

  var s State
  if err := conn.FindOne(ctx, bson.M{"name":
"Washington"}).Decode(&s); err != nil {
    return err
  }

  if err := conn.Drop(ctx); err != nil {
    return err
  }

  fmt.Printf("State: %#v\n", s)
  return nil
}
```

8. Create a new directory named `example` and navigate to it.
9. Create a `main.go` file with the following content:

```
package main

import mongodb "github.com/PacktPublishing/Go-Programming-Cookbook-
Second-Edition/chapter11/orchestrate"

func main() {
  if err := mongodb.Exec("mongodb://mongodb:27017"); err != nil {
    panic(err)
  }
}
```

10. Navigate back to the starting directory.
11. Run the `go mod vendor` command.
12. Run the `docker-compose up -d` command.
13. Run the `docker logs orchestrate_app_1` command. You should now see the following output:

```
$ docker logs orchestrate_app_1
State: docker.State{Name:"Washington", Population:7062000}
```

14. The `go.mod` file may be updated and the `go.sum` file should now be present in the top-level recipe directory.
15. If you copied or wrote your own tests, go up one directory and run `go test`. Ensure that all the tests pass.

How it works...

This configuration is good for local development. Once the `docker-compose up` command is run, the local directory is rebuilt, Docker establishes a connection to a MongoDB instance using the latest version, and begins operating against it. This recipe uses the go mod vendor for dependency management. As a result, we disable the `go mod cache` and tell the `go build` command to use the vendor directory we created.

This can provide a good baseline when starting on apps that require connections to external services; all of the recipes in `Chapter 6`, *All about Databases and Storage*, can make use of this approach rather than creating a local instance of the database. For production, you probably won't want to run your data storage behind a Docker container, but you'll also generally have static host names for configuration.

Monitoring applications

There are a variety of ways to monitor Go applications. One of the easiest ways is to set up Prometheus, a monitoring application written in Go (`https://prometheus.io`). This is an application that polls an endpoint based on your configuration file and collects a lot of information about your app, including the number of Goroutines, memory usage, and much more. This app will use the techniques from the previous recipe to set up a Docker environment to host Prometheus and connect to it.

How to do it...

The following steps cover writing and running your application:

1. From your Terminal or console application, create a new directory called `~/projects/go-programming-cookbook/chapter11/monitoring` and navigate to it.

2. Run the following command:

   $ go mod init github.com/PacktPublishing/Go-Programming-Cookbook-Second-Edition/chapter11/monitoring

   You should see a file called `go.mod` that contains the following content:

   ```
   module github.com/PacktPublishing/Go-Programming-Cookbook-Second-Edition/chapter11/monitoring
   ```

3. Copy the tests from `~/projects/go-programming-cookbook-original/chapter11/monitoring`, or use this as an opportunity to write some of your own code!

4. Create a file called `Dockerfile` with the following content:

   ```
   FROM golang:1.12.4-alpine3.9

   ENV GOPATH /code/
   ADD . /code/src/github.com/agtorre/go-cookbook/chapter11/monitoring
   WORKDIR /code/src/github.com/agtorre/go-cookbook/chapter11/monitoring
   RUN GO111MODULE=on GOPROXY=off go build -mod=vendor

   ENTRYPOINT /code/src/github.com/agtorre/go-cookbook/chapter11/monitoring/monitoring
   ```

5. Create a file called `docker-compose.yml` with the following content:

   ```
   version: '2'
   services:
    app:
    build: .
    prometheus:
    ports:
    - 9090:9090
    volumes:
    - ./prometheus.yml:/etc/prometheus/prometheus.yml
    image: "prom/prometheus"
   ```

6. Create a file called `main.go` with the following content:

```
package main

import (
    "net/http"

    "github.com/prometheus/client_golang/prometheus/promhttp"
)

func main() {
    http.Handle("/metrics", promhttp.Handler())
    panic(http.ListenAndServe(":80", nil))
}
```

7. Create a file called `prometheus.yml` with the following content:

```
global:
 scrape_interval: 15s # By default, scrape targets every 15
 seconds.

# A scrape configuration containing exactly one endpoint to
scrape:
# Here it's Prometheus itself.
scrape_configs:
 # The job name is added as a label `job=<job_name>` to any
 timeseries scraped from this config.
 - job_name: 'app'

 # Override the global default and scrape targets from this job
 every 5 seconds.
 scrape_interval: 5s

 static_configs:
 - targets: ['app:80']
```

8. Run the `go mod vendor` command.

9. Run the `docker-compose up` command. You should now see the following output:

```
$ docker-compose up
Starting monitoring_prometheus_1 ... done
Starting monitoring_app_1 ... done
Attaching to monitoring_app_1, monitoring_prometheus_1
prometheus_1 | time="2019-05-05T03:10:25Z" level=info msg="Starting
prometheus (version=1.6.1, branch=master,
revision=4666df502c0e239ed4aa1d80abbbfb54f61b23c3)"
```

```
source="main.go:88"
prometheus_1 | time="2019-05-05T03:10:25Z" level=info msg="Build
context (go=go1.8.1, user=root@7e45fa0366a7,
date=20170419-14:32:22)" source="main.go:89"
prometheus_1 | time="2019-05-05T03:10:25Z" level=info msg="Loading
configuration file /etc/prometheus/prometheus.yml"
source="main.go:251"
prometheus_1 | time="2019-05-05T03:10:25Z" level=info msg="Loading
series map and head chunks..." source="storage.go:421"
prometheus_1 | time="2019-05-05T03:10:25Z" level=warning
msg="Persistence layer appears dirty." source="persistence.go:846"
prometheus_1 | time="2019-05-05T03:10:25Z" level=warning
msg="Starting crash recovery. Prometheus is inoperational until
complete." source="crashrecovery.go:40"
prometheus_1 | time="2019-05-05T03:10:25Z" level=warning msg="To
avoid crash recovery in the future, shut down Prometheus with
SIGTERM or a HTTP POST to /-/quit." source="crashrecovery.go:41"
prometheus_1 | time="2019-05-05T03:10:25Z" level=info msg="Scanning
files." source="crashrecovery.go:55"
prometheus_1 | time="2019-05-05T03:10:25Z" level=info msg="File
scan complete. 43 series found." source="crashrecovery.go:83"
prometheus_1 | time="2019-05-05T03:10:25Z" level=info msg="Checking
for series without series file." source="crashrecovery.go:85"
prometheus_1 | time="2019-05-05T03:10:25Z" level=info msg="Check
for series without series file complete."
source="crashrecovery.go:131"
prometheus_1 | time="2019-05-05T03:10:25Z" level=info msg="Cleaning
up archive indexes." source="crashrecovery.go:411"
prometheus_1 | time="2019-05-05T03:10:25Z" level=info msg="Clean-up
of archive indexes complete." source="crashrecovery.go:504"
prometheus_1 | time="2019-05-05T03:10:25Z" level=info
msg="Rebuilding label indexes." source="crashrecovery.go:512"
prometheus_1 | time="2019-05-05T03:10:25Z" level=info msg="Indexing
metrics in memory." source="crashrecovery.go:513"
prometheus_1 | time="2019-05-05T03:10:25Z" level=info msg="Indexing
archived metrics." source="crashrecovery.go:521"
prometheus_1 | time="2019-05-05T03:10:25Z" level=info msg="All
requests for rebuilding the label indexes queued. (Actual
processing may lag behind.)" source="crashrecovery.go:540"
prometheus_1 | time="2019-05-05T03:10:25Z" level=warning msg="Crash
recovery complete." source="crashrecovery.go:153"
prometheus_1 | time="2019-05-05T03:10:25Z" level=info msg="43
series loaded." source="storage.go:432"
prometheus_1 | time="2019-05-05T03:10:25Z" level=info msg="Starting
target manager..." source="targetmanager.go:61"
prometheus_1 | time="2019-05-05T03:10:25Z" level=info
msg="Listening on :9090" source="web.go:259"
```

10. The `go.mod` file may be updated and the `go.sum` file should now be present in the top-level recipe directory.

11. Navigate your browser to `http://localhost:9090/`. You should see a variety of metrics related to your app!

How it works...

This recipe creates a simple handler in Go that exports stats about the running application to prometheus using the prometheus go client. We connect our application to a prometheus server that is running in docker and handle the network connection and startup using docker-compose. Settings for how often to collect data, which port the application is serving on, and the name of the app are all specified in the `prometheus.yml` file. Once both containers start, the prometheus server begins harvesting and monitoring the app on the specified port. It also exposes a web interface which we visit in the browser to see more information about our app.

The Prometheus client handler will return a variety of stats about your application to a Prometheus server. This allows you to point multiple Prometheus servers at an app, without the need to reconfigure or deploy the app. Most of these stats are generic and beneficial for things such as detecting memory leaks. A lot of other solutions require you to periodically send information to a server instead. The next recipe, *Collecting metrics*, will demonstrate how to ship custom metrics to the Prometheus server.

Collecting metrics

In addition to general information about your app, it can be helpful to emit metrics that are app-specific. For example, we might want to collect timing data or keep track of the number of times an event occurs.

This recipe will use the `github.com/rcrowley/go-metrics` package to collect metrics and expose them via an endpoint. There are various exporter tools that you can use to export metrics to places such as Prometheus and InfluxDB, which are also written in Go.

Getting ready

Configure your environment according to these steps:

1. Refer to the *Technical requirements* section in this chapter for steps to configure your environment.
2. Run the `go get github.com/rcrowley/go-metrics` command.

How to do it...

These steps cover writing and running your application:

1. From your Terminal or console application, create a new directory called `~/projects/go-programming-cookbook/chapter11/metrics` and navigate to it.
2. Run the following command:

   $ go mod init github.com/PacktPublishing/Go-Programming-Cookbook-Second-Edition/chapter11/metrics

   You should see a file called `go.mod` that contains the following content:

   ```
   module github.com/PacktPublishing/Go-Programming-Cookbook-Second-Edition/chapter11/metrics
   ```

3. Copy the tests from `~/projects/go-programming-cookbook-original/chapter11/metrics`, or use this as an opportunity to write some of your own code!
4. Create a file called `handler.go` with the following content:

   ```
   package metrics

   import (
       "net/http"
       "time"

       metrics "github.com/rcrowley/go-metrics"
   )

   // CounterHandler will update a counter each time it's called
   func CounterHandler(w http.ResponseWriter, r *http.Request) {
       c := metrics.GetOrRegisterCounter("counterhandler.counter",
       nil)
       c.Inc(1)
   ```

```
        w.WriteHeader(http.StatusOK)
        w.Write([]byte("success"))
}

// TimerHandler records the duration required to compelete
func TimerHandler(w http.ResponseWriter, r *http.Request) {
        currt := time.Now()
        t := metrics.GetOrRegisterTimer("timerhandler.timer", nil)

        w.WriteHeader(http.StatusOK)
        w.Write([]byte("success"))
        t.UpdateSince(currt)
}
```

5. Create a file called `report.go` with the following content:

```
package metrics

import (
    "net/http"

    gometrics "github.com/rcrowley/go-metrics"
)

// ReportHandler will emit the current metrics in json format
func ReportHandler(w http.ResponseWriter, r *http.Request) {

        w.WriteHeader(http.StatusOK)

        t := gometrics.GetOrRegisterTimer(
        "reporthandler.writemetrics", nil)
        t.Time(func() {
            gometrics.WriteJSONOnce(gometrics.DefaultRegistry, w)
        })
}
```

6. Create a new directory named `example` and navigate to it.

7. Create a file named `main.go` :

```
package main

import (
    "net/http"

    "github.com/PacktPublishing/
    Go-Programming-Cookbook-Second-Edition/
    chapter11/metrics"
)
```

```
func main() {
    // handler to populate metrics
    http.HandleFunc("/counter", metrics.CounterHandler)
    http.HandleFunc("/timer", metrics.TimerHandler)
    http.HandleFunc("/report", metrics.ReportHandler)
    fmt.Println("listening on :8080")
    panic(http.ListenAndServe(":8080", nil))
}
```

8. Run `go run main.go`. Alternatively, you may also run the following command:

```
$ go build
$ ./example
```

You should now see the following output:

```
$ go run main.go
listening on :8080
```

9. Run the following commands from a separate shell:

```
$ curl localhost:8080/counter
success

$ curl localhost:8080/timer
success

$ curl localhost:8080/report
{"counterhandler.counter":{"count":1},
"reporthandler.writemetrics":
{"15m.rate":0,"1m.rate":0,"5m.rate":0,"75%":0,"95%":0,"99%":0,"99.9
%":0,"count":0,"max":0,"mean":0,"mean.rate":0,"median":0,"min":0,"s
tddev":0},"timerhandler.timer":{"15m.rate":0.0011080303990206543,"1
m.rate":0.015991117074135343,"5m.rate":0.0033057092356765017,"75%":
60485,"95%":60485,"99%":60485,"99.9%":60485,"count":1,"max":60485,"
mean":60485,"mean.rate":1.1334543719787356,"median":60485,"min":604
85,"stddev":0}}
```

10. Try hitting all the endpoints a few more times to see how they change.
11. The `go.mod` file may be updated and the `go.sum` file should now be present in the top-level recipe directory.
12. If you copied or wrote your own tests, go up one directory and run `go test`. Ensure that all the tests pass.

How it works...

The gometrics keeps all of your metrics in a registry. Once it's set up, you can use any of the metric emit options, such as counter or timer, and it will store this update in the registry. There are multiple exporters that will export metrics to third-party tools. In our case, we set up a handler that emits all the metrics in JSON format.

We set up three handlers—one that increments a counter, one that records the time to exit the handler, and one that prints a report (while also incrementing an additional counter). The GetOrRegister functions are useful for atomically getting or creating a metric emitter if it doesn't currently exist in a thread-safe way. Alternatively, you can register everything once in advance.

12
Reactive Programming and Data Streams

In this chapter, we will discuss reactive programming design patterns in Go. Reactive programming is a programming concept that focuses on data streams and the propagation of change. Technologies such as Kafka allow you to quickly produce or consume a stream of data. As a result, these technologies are a natural fit for one another. In the *Connecting Kafka to Goflow* recipe, we'll explore combining a `kafka` message queue with `goflow` to show a practical example of using these technologies. This chapter will also explore various ways to connect with Kafka and use it to process messages. Lastly, this chapter will demonstrate how to create a basic `graphql` server in Go.

In this chapter, we will cover the following recipes:

- Using Goflow for data flow programming
- Using Kafka with Sarama
- Using async producers with Kafka
- Connecting Kafka to Goflow
- Writing a GraphQL server in Go

Technical requirements

In order to proceed with all the recipes in this chapter, configure your environment according to these steps:

1. Download and install Go 1.12.6 or greater on your operating system from `https://golang.org/doc/install`.
2. Open a Terminal or console application, and create and navigate to a project directory such as `~/projects/go-programming-cookbook`. All code will be run and modified from this directory.

3. Clone the latest code into ~/projects/go-programming-cookbook-original and optionally work from that directory, rather than typing the examples manually:

```
$ git clone git@github.com:PacktPublishing/Go-Programming-Cookbook-Second-Edition.git go-programming-cookbook-original
```

Using Goflow for data flow programming

The github.com/trustmaster/goflow package is useful for creating data flow-based applications. It tries to abstract the concepts so that you can write components and connect them together using a custom network. This recipe will recreate the application discussed in Chapter 9, *Testing Go Code*, but will do so using the goflow package.

How to do it...

These steps cover writing and running your application:

1. From your Terminal or console application, create a new directory called ~/projects/go-programming-cookbook/chapter12/goflow and navigate to this directory.
2. Run the following command:

```
$ go mod init github.com/PacktPublishing/Go-Programming-Cookbook-Second-Edition/chapter12/goflow
```

You should see a file called go.mod that contains the following:

```
module github.com/PacktPublishing/Go-Programming-Cookbook-Second-Edition/chapter12/goflow
```

3. Copy the tests from ~/projects/go-programming-cookbook-original/chapter12/goflow, or use this as an exercise to write some of your own code!
4. Create a file called components.go with the following content:

```
package goflow

import (
  "encoding/base64"
  "fmt"
)
```

```go
// Encoder base64 encodes all input
type Encoder struct {
  Val <-chan string
  Res chan<- string
}

// Process does the encoding then pushes the result onto Res
func (e *Encoder) Process() {
  for val := range e.Val {
    encoded := base64.StdEncoding.EncodeToString([]byte(val))
    e.Res <- fmt.Sprintf("%s => %s", val, encoded)
  }
}

// Printer is a component for printing to stdout
type Printer struct {
  Line <-chan string
}

// Process Prints the current line received
func (p *Printer) Process() {
  for line := range p.Line {
    fmt.Println(line)
  }
}
```

5. Create a file called `network.go` with the following content:

```go
package goflow

import (
  "github.com/trustmaster/goflow"
)

// NewEncodingApp wires together the components
func NewEncodingApp() *goflow.Graph {
  e := goflow.NewGraph()

  // define component types
  e.Add("encoder", new(Encoder))
  e.Add("printer", new(Printer))

  // connect the components using channels
  e.Connect("encoder", "Res", "printer", "Line")

  // map the in channel to Val, which is
  // tied to OnVal function
  e.MapInPort("In", "encoder", "Val")
```

```
      return e
    }
```

6. Create a new directory named `example` and navigate to it.

7. Create a file named `main.go` with the following content:

```go
package main

import (
  "fmt"

  "github.com/PacktPublishing/
   Go-Programming-Cookbook-Second-Edition/chapter12/goflow"
  flow "github.com/trustmaster/goflow"
)

func main() {

  net := goflow.NewEncodingApp()

  in := make(chan string)
  net.SetInPort("In", in)

  wait := flow.Run(net)

  for i := 0; i < 20; i++ {
    in <- fmt.Sprint("Message", i)
  }

  close(in)
  <-wait
}
```

8. Run `go run main.go`.

9. You may also run the following commands:

```
$ go build
$ ./example
```

You should now see the following output:

```
$ go run main.go
Message6 => TWVzc2FnZTY=
Message5 => TWVzc2FnZTU=
Message1 => TWVzc2FnZTE=
Message0 => TWVzc2FnZTA=
Message4 => TWVzc2FnZTQ=
Message8 => TWVzc2FnZTg=
```

```
Message2 => TWVzc2FnZTI=
Message3 => TWVzc2FnZTM=
Message7 => TWVzc2FnZTc=
Message10 => TWVzc2FnZTEw
Message9 => TWVzc2FnZTk=
Message12 => TWVzc2FnZTEy
Message11 => TWVzc2FnZTEx
Message14 => TWVzc2FnZTE0
Message13 => TWVzc2FnZTEz
Message16 => TWVzc2FnZTE2
Message15 => TWVzc2FnZTE1
Message18 => TWVzc2FnZTE4
Message17 => TWVzc2FnZTE3
Message19 => TWVzc2FnZTE5
```

10. The `go.mod` file may be updated, and the `go.sum` file should now be present in the top-level recipe directory.
11. If you have copied or written your own tests, go up one directory and run the `go test` command. Ensure that all the tests pass.

How it works...

The `github.com/trustmaster/goflow` package works by defining a network/graph, registering some components, and then wiring them together. This can feel a bit error-prone since components are described using strings, but usually this will fail early in runtime until the application is set up and functioning correctly.

In this recipe, we set up two components, one that Base64-encodes an incoming string, and one that prints anything passed to it. We connect it to an in channel that is initialized in `main.go`, and anything passed onto that channel will flow through our pipeline.

A lot of the emphasis of this approach is on ignoring the internals of what's going on. We treat everything like a connected black box and let `goflow` do the rest. You can see, in this recipe, how small the code is to accomplish this pipeline of tasks and that we have fewer knobs to control the number of workers, among other things.

Using Kafka with Sarama

Kafka is a popular distributed message queue with a lot of advanced functions for building distributed systems. This recipe will show how to write to a Kafka topic using a synchronous producer, and how to consume the same topic using a partition consumer. This recipe will not explore different configurations of Kafka, as that is a much wider topic beyond the scope of this book, but I suggest beginning at `https://kafka.apache.org/intro`.

Getting ready

Configure your environment according to these steps:

1. Refer to the *Technical requirements* section at the beginning of this chapter.
2. Install Kafka using the steps mentioned at `https://www.tutorialspoint.com/apache_kafka/apache_kafka_installation_steps.htm`.
3. Alternatively, you can also access `https://github.com/spotify/docker-kafka`.

How to do it...

These steps cover writing and running your application:

1. From your Terminal or console application, create a new directory called `~/projects/go-programming-cookbook/chapter12/synckafka` and navigate to this directory.
2. Run this command:

   ```
   $ go mod init github.com/PacktPublishing/Go-Programming-Cookbook-
   Second-Edition/chapter12/synckafka
   ```

   You should see a file called `go.mod` that contains the following:

   ```
   module github.com/PacktPublishing/Go-Programming-Cookbook-Second-
   Edition/chapter12/synckafka
   ```

3. Copy the tests from `~/projects/go-programming-cookbook-original/chapter12/synckafka`, or use this as an exercise to write some of your own code!

4. Ensure that Kafka is up and running on `localhost:9092`.

5. Create a file called `main.go` in a directory named `consumer` with the following content:

```go
package main

import (
    "log"

    sarama "github.com/Shopify/sarama"
)

func main() {
    consumer, err :=
    sarama.NewConsumer([]string{"localhost:9092"}, nil)
    if err != nil {
        panic(err)
    }
    defer consumer.Close()

    partitionConsumer, err :=

    consumer.ConsumePartition("example", 0,
    sarama.OffsetNewest)
    if err != nil {
        panic(err)
    }
    defer partitionConsumer.Close()

    for {
        msg := <-partitionConsumer.Messages()
        log.Printf("Consumed message: \"%s\" at offset: %d\n",
        msg.Value, msg.Offset)
    }
}
```

6. Create a file called `main.go` in a directory named `producer` with the following content:

```go
package main

import (

    "fmt"
    "log"

    sarama "github.com/Shopify/sarama"
```

```
    )

    func sendMessage(producer sarama.SyncProducer, value string) {
        msg := &sarama.ProducerMessage{Topic: "example", Value:
        sarama.StringEncoder(value)}
        partition, offset, err := producer.SendMessage(msg)
        if err != nil {

            log.Printf("FAILED to send message: %s\n", err)
             return
        }
        log.Printf("> message sent to partition %d at offset %d\n",
        partition, offset)
    }

    func main() {
        producer, err :=
        sarama.NewSyncProducer([]string{"localhost:9092"}, nil)
        if err != nil {
            panic(err)
        }
        defer producer.Close()

        for i := 0; i < 10; i++ {
            sendMessage(producer, fmt.Sprintf("Message %d", i))
        }
    }
```

7. Navigate up a directory.

8. Run `go run ./consumer`.

9. In a separate Terminal from the same directory, run `go run ./producer`.

10. In the producer Terminal, you should see the following:

```
$ go run ./producer
2017/05/07 11:50:38 > message sent to partition 0 at offset 0
2017/05/07 11:50:38 > message sent to partition 0 at offset 1
2017/05/07 11:50:38 > message sent to partition 0 at offset 2
2017/05/07 11:50:38 > message sent to partition 0 at offset 3
2017/05/07 11:50:38 > message sent to partition 0 at offset 4
2017/05/07 11:50:38 > message sent to partition 0 at offset 5
2017/05/07 11:50:38 > message sent to partition 0 at offset 6
2017/05/07 11:50:38 > message sent to partition 0 at offset 7
2017/05/07 11:50:38 > message sent to partition 0 at offset 8
2017/05/07 11:50:38 > message sent to partition 0 at offset 9
```

In the consumer Terminal, you should see this:

```
$ go run ./consumer
2017/05/07 11:50:38 Consumed message: "Message 0" at offset: 0
2017/05/07 11:50:38 Consumed message: "Message 1" at offset: 1
2017/05/07 11:50:38 Consumed message: "Message 2" at offset: 2
2017/05/07 11:50:38 Consumed message: "Message 3" at offset: 3
2017/05/07 11:50:38 Consumed message: "Message 4" at offset: 4
2017/05/07 11:50:38 Consumed message: "Message 5" at offset: 5
2017/05/07 11:50:38 Consumed message: "Message 6" at offset: 6
2017/05/07 11:50:38 Consumed message: "Message 7" at offset: 7
2017/05/07 11:50:38 Consumed message: "Message 8" at offset: 8
2017/05/07 11:50:38 Consumed message: "Message 9" at offset: 9
```

11. The `go.mod` file may be updated and the `go.sum` file should now be present in the top-level recipe directory.

12. If you have copied or written your own tests, go up one directory and run `go test`. Ensure all tests pass.

How it works...

This recipe demonstrates passing simple messages via Kafka. More complex methods should use a serialization format such as `json`, `gob`, `protobuf`, or others. The producer can send a message to Kafka synchronously through `sendMessage`. This does not handle cases well where the Kafka cluster is down, and may result in a hung process for these cases. This is important to consider for applications such as web handlers, as it may result in timeouts and hard dependencies on the Kafka cluster.

Assuming the message queues correctly, our consumer will observe the Kafka stream and do something with the results. Previous recipes in this chapter might make use of this stream to do some additional processing.

Using async producers with Kafka

It's often useful not to wait for a Kafka producer to complete before moving on to the next task. In cases like this, you can use an asynchronous producer. These producers take Sarama messages on a channel and have methods to return a success/error channel that can be checked separately.

In this recipe, we'll create a Go routine that will handle success and failure messages while we allow a handler to queue messages to send, regardless of the result.

Getting ready

Refer to the *Getting ready* section of the *Using Kafka with Sarama* recipe.

How to do it...

These steps cover writing and running your application:

1. From your Terminal or console application, create a new directory called `~/projects/go-programming-cookbook/chapter12/asynckafka` and navigate to this directory.

2. Run this command:

   ```
   $ go mod init github.com/PacktPublishing/Go-Programming-Cookbook-
   Second-Edition/chapter12/asynckafka
   ```

   You should see a file called `go.mod` that contains the following:

   ```
   module github.com/PacktPublishing/Go-Programming-Cookbook-Second-
   Edition/chapter12/asynckafka
   ```

3. Copy the tests from `~/projects/go-programming-cookbook-original/chapter12/asynckafka`, or use this as an exercise to write some of your own code!

4. Ensure that Kafka is up and running on `localhost:9092`.

5. Copy the consumer directory from the previous recipe.

6. Create a directory named `producer` and navigate to it.

7. Create a file called `producer.go` with the following content:

   ```go
   package main

   import (
       "log"

       sarama "github.com/Shopify/sarama"
   )

   // Process response grabs results and errors from a producer
   // asynchronously
   func ProcessResponse(producer sarama.AsyncProducer) {
       for {
           select {
               case result := <-producer.Successes():
   ```

```
            log.Printf("> message: \"%s\" sent to partition
            %d at offset %d\n", result.Value,
            result.Partition, result.Offset)
            case err := <-producer.Errors():
            log.Println("Failed to produce message", err)
        }
    }
}
```

8. Create a file called `handler.go` with the following content:

```
package main

import (
    "net/http"

    sarama "github.com/Shopify/sarama"
)

// KafkaController allows us to attach a producer
// to our handlers
type KafkaController struct {
    producer sarama.AsyncProducer
}

// Handler grabs a message from a GET parama and
// send it to the kafka queue asynchronously
func (c *KafkaController) Handler(w http.ResponseWriter, r
*http.Request) {
    if err := r.ParseForm(); err != nil {
        w.WriteHeader(http.StatusBadRequest)
        return
    }

    msg := r.FormValue("msg")
    if msg == "" {
        w.WriteHeader(http.StatusBadRequest)
        w.Write([]byte("msg must be set"))
        return
    }
    c.producer.Input() <- &sarama.ProducerMessage{Topic:
    "example", Key: nil, Value:
    sarama.StringEncoder(msg)}
    w.WriteHeader(http.StatusOK)
}
```

9. Create a file called `main.go` with the following content:

```go
package main

import (
    "fmt"
    "net/http"

    sarama "github.com/Shopify/sarama"
)

func main() {
    config := sarama.NewConfig()
    config.Producer.Return.Successes = true
    config.Producer.Return.Errors = true
    producer, err :=
    sarama.NewAsyncProducer([]string{"localhost:9092"}, config)
    if err != nil {
        panic(err)
    }
    defer producer.AsyncClose()

    go ProcessResponse(producer)

    c := KafkaController{producer}
    http.HandleFunc("/", c.Handler)
    fmt.Println("Listening on port :3333")
    panic(http.ListenAndServe(":3333", nil))
}
```

10. Navigate up a directory.

11. Run `go run ./consumer`.

12. In a separate Terminal from the same directory, run `go run ./producer`.

13. In a third Terminal, run the following commands:

```
$ curl "http://localhost:3333/?msg=this"
$ curl "http://localhost:3333/?msg=is"
$ curl "http://localhost:3333/?msg=an"
$ curl "http://localhost:3333/?msg=example"
```

In the producer Terminal, you should see the following:

```
$ go run ./producer
Listening on port :3333
2017/05/07 13:52:54 > message: "this" sent to partition 0 at offset
0
2017/05/07 13:53:25 > message: "is" sent to partition 0 at offset 1
```

```
2017/05/07 13:53:27 > message: "an" sent to partition 0 at offset 2
2017/05/07 13:53:29 > message: "example" sent to partition 0 at
offset 3
```

14. In the consumer Terminal, you should see this:

```
$ go run ./consumer
2017/05/07 13:52:54 Consumed message: "this" at offset: 0
2017/05/07 13:53:25 Consumed message: "is" at offset: 1
2017/05/07 13:53:27 Consumed message: "an" at offset: 2
2017/05/07 13:53:29 Consumed message: "example" at offset: 3
```

15. The go.mod file may be updated, and the go.sum file should now be present in the top-level recipe directory.
16. If you have copied or written your own tests, go up one directory and run go test. Ensure that all tests pass.

How it works...

Our modifications in this chapter were all made to the producer. This time, we created a separate Go routine to handle successes and errors. If these are left unhandled, your application will deadlock. Next, we attached our producer to a handler and we emit messages on it whenever a message is received, via a GET call to the handler.

The handler will immediately return success upon sending the message, regardless of its response. If this is not acceptable, a synchronous approach should be used instead. In our case, we're okay with later processing successes and errors separately.

Lastly, we curl our endpoint with a few different messages, and you can see them flow from the handler to where they're eventually printed by the Kafka consumer we wrote in the previous section.

Connecting Kafka to Goflow

This recipe will combine a Kafka consumer with a Goflow pipeline. As our consumer receives messages from Kafka, it will run strings.ToUpper() on them and then print the results. These naturally pair, as Goflow is designed to operate on an incoming stream, which is exactly what Kafka provides us.

Getting ready

Refer to the *Getting ready* section of the *Using Kafka with Sarama* recipe.

How to do it...

These steps cover writing and running your application:

1. From your Terminal or console application, create a new directory called `~/projects/go-programming-cookbook/chapter12/kafkaflow` and navigate to this directory.
2. Run this command:

```
$ go mod init github.com/PacktPublishing/Go-Programming-Cookbook-
Second-Edition/chapter12/kafkaflow
```

You should see a file called `go.mod` that contains the following:

```
module github.com/PacktPublishing/Go-Programming-Cookbook-Second-
Edition/chapter12/kafkaflow
```

3. Copy the tests from `~/projects/go-programming-cookbook-original/chapter12/kafkaflow`, or use this as an exercise to write some of your own code!
4. Ensure that Kafka is up and running on `localhost:9092`.
5. Create a file called `components.go` with the following content:

```go
package kafkaflow

import (
  "fmt"
  "strings"

  flow "github.com/trustmaster/goflow"
)

// Upper upper cases the incoming
// stream
type Upper struct {
  Val <-chan string
  Res chan<- string
}

// Process loops over the input values and writes the upper
```

```
// case string version of them to Res
func (e *Upper) Process() {
  for val := range e.Val {
    e.Res <- strings.ToUpper(val)
  }
}

// Printer is a component for printing to stdout
type Printer struct {
  flow.Component
  Line <-chan string
}

// Process Prints the current line received
func (p *Printer) Process() {
  for line := range p.Line {
    fmt.Println(line)
  }
}
```

6. Create a file called network.go with the following content:

```
package kafkaflow

import "github.com/trustmaster/goflow"

// NewUpperApp wires together the components
func NewUpperApp() *goflow.Graph {
  u := goflow.NewGraph()

  u.Add("upper", new(Upper))
  u.Add("printer", new(Printer))

  u.Connect("upper", "Res", "printer", "Line")
  u.MapInPort("In", "upper", "Val")

  return u
}
```

7. Create a file called main.go in a directory named consumer with the following content:

```
package main

import (
  "github.com/PacktPublishing/Go-Programming-Cookbook-Second-
Edition/chapter12/kafkaflow"
  sarama "github.com/Shopify/sarama"
```

```
    flow "github.com/trustmaster/goflow"
)

func main() {
  consumer, err := sarama.NewConsumer([]string{"localhost:9092"},
nil)
  if err != nil {
    panic(err)
  }
  defer consumer.Close()

  partitionConsumer, err := consumer.ConsumePartition("example", 0,
sarama.OffsetNewest)
  if err != nil {
    panic(err)
  }
  defer partitionConsumer.Close()

  net := kafkaflow.NewUpperApp()

  in := make(chan string)
  net.SetInPort("In", in)

  wait := flow.Run(net)
  defer func() {
    close(in)
    <-wait
  }()

  for {
    msg := <-partitionConsumer.Messages()
    in <- string(msg.Value)
  }

}
```

8. Copy the `producer` directory from the *Using Kafka with Saram* recipe.
9. Run `go run ./consumer`.
10. In a separate Terminal from the same directory, run `go run ./producer`.
11. In the producer Terminal, you should now see the following:

```
$ go run ./producer
2017/05/07 18:24:12 > message "Message 0" sent to partition 0 at
offset 0
2017/05/07 18:24:12 > message "Message 1" sent to partition 0 at
offset 1
2017/05/07 18:24:12 > message "Message 2" sent to partition 0 at
```

```
offset 2
2017/05/07 18:24:12 > message "Message 3" sent to partition 0 at
offset 3
2017/05/07 18:24:12 > message "Message 4" sent to partition 0 at
offset 4
2017/05/07 18:24:12 > message "Message 5" sent to partition 0 at
offset 5
2017/05/07 18:24:12 > message "Message 6" sent to partition 0 at
offset 6
2017/05/07 18:24:12 > message "Message 7" sent to partition 0 at
offset 7
2017/05/07 18:24:12 > message "Message 8" sent to partition 0 at
offset 8
2017/05/07 18:24:12 > message "Message 9" sent to partition 0 at
offset 9
```

In the consumer Terminal, you should see the following:

```
$ go run ./consumer
MESSAGE 0
MESSAGE 1
MESSAGE 2
MESSAGE 3
MESSAGE 4
MESSAGE 5
MESSAGE 6
MESSAGE 7
MESSAGE 8
MESSAGE 9
```

12. The `go.mod` file may be updated, and the `go.sum` file should now be present in the top-level recipe directory.
13. If you have copied or written your own tests, go up one directory and run `go test`. Ensure that all the tests pass.

How it works...

This recipe combines ideas from previous recipes in this chapter. As in previous recipes, we set up a Kafka consumer and producer. This recipe uses the synchronous producer from the *Using Kafka with Sarama* recipe, but could have also used an asynchronous producer instead. Once a message is received, we enqueue it on an in channel just as we did in the *Goflow for dataflow programming* recipe. We modify the components from this recipe to convert our incoming string to uppercase, rather than Base64-encoding it. We reuse the print components and the resultant network configuration is similar.

The end result is that all messages received through the Kafka consumer are transported into our flow-based work pipeline to be operated on. This allows us to instrument our pipeline components to be modular and reusable, and we can use the same component multiple times in different configurations. Similarly, we'll receive traffic from any producer that writes to Kafka, so we can multiplex producers into a single data stream.

Writing a GraphQL server in Go

GraphQL is an alternative to REST, created by Facebook (`http://graphql.org/`). This technology allows a server to implement and publish a schema, and the clients then can ask for the information they need, rather than understanding and making use of various API endpoints.

For this recipe, we'll create a `Graphql` schema that represents a deck of playing cards. We'll expose one resource card, which can be filtered by suit and value. Alternatively, this schema can return all the cards in the deck if no arguments are specified.

How to do it...

These steps cover writing and running your application:

1. From your Terminal or console application, create a new directory called `~/projects/go-programming-cookbook/chapter12/graphql` and navigate to this directory.
2. Run this command:

   ```
   $ go mod init github.com/PacktPublishing/Go-Programming-Cookbook-
   Second-Edition/chapter12/graphql
   ```

   You should see a file called `go.mod` that contains the following:

   ```
   module github.com/PacktPublishing/Go-Programming-Cookbook-Second-
   Edition/chapter12/graphql
   ```

3. Copy the tests from `~/projects/go-programming-cookbook-original/chapter12/graphql`, or use this as an exercise to write some of your own code!

4. Create and navigate to the `cards` directory.
5. Create a file called `card.go` with the following content:

```go
package cards

// Card represents a standard playing
// card
type Card struct {
    Value string
    Suit string
}

var cards []Card

func init() {
    cards = []Card{
        {"A", "Spades"}, {"2", "Spades"}, {"3", "Spades"},
        {"4", "Spades"}, {"5", "Spades"}, {"6", "Spades"},
        {"7", "Spades"}, {"8", "Spades"}, {"9", "Spades"},
        {"10", "Spades"}, {"J", "Spades"}, {"Q", "Spades"},
        {"K", "Spades"},
        {"A", "Hearts"}, {"2", "Hearts"}, {"3", "Hearts"},
        {"4", "Hearts"}, {"5", "Hearts"}, {"6", "Hearts"},
        {"7", "Hearts"}, {"8", "Hearts"}, {"9", "Hearts"},
        {"10", "Hearts"}, {"J", "Hearts"}, {"Q", "Hearts"},
        {"K", "Hearts"},
        {"A", "Clubs"}, {"2", "Clubs"}, {"3", "Clubs"},
        {"4", "Clubs"}, {"5", "Clubs"}, {"6", "Clubs"},
        {"7", "Clubs"}, {"8", "Clubs"}, {"9", "Clubs"},
        {"10", "Clubs"}, {"J", "Clubs"}, {"Q", "Clubs"},
        {"K", "Clubs"},
        {"A", "Diamonds"}, {"2", "Diamonds"}, {"3",
        "Diamonds"},
        {"4", "Diamonds"}, {"5", "Diamonds"}, {"6",
        "Diamonds"},
        {"7", "Diamonds"}, {"8", "Diamonds"}, {"9",
        "Diamonds"},
        {"10", "Diamonds"}, {"J", "Diamonds"}, {"Q",
        "Diamonds"},
        {"K", "Diamonds"},
    }
}
```

6. Create a file called `type.go` with the following content:

```go
package cards

import "github.com/graphql-go/graphql"

// CardType returns our card graphql object
func CardType() *graphql.Object {
    cardType := graphql.NewObject(graphql.ObjectConfig{
        Name: "Card",
        Description: "A Playing Card",
        Fields: graphql.Fields{
            "value": &graphql.Field{
                Type: graphql.String,
                Description: "Ace through King",
                Resolve: func(p graphql.ResolveParams)
                (interface{}, error) {
                    if card, ok := p.Source.(Card); ok {
                        return card.Value, nil
                    }
                    return nil, nil
                },
            },
            "suit": &graphql.Field{
                Type: graphql.String,
                Description: "Hearts, Diamonds, Clubs, Spades",
                Resolve: func(p graphql.ResolveParams)
                (interface{}, error) {
                    if card, ok := p.Source.(Card); ok {
                        return card.Suit, nil
                    }
                    return nil, nil
                },
            },
        },
    })
    return cardType
}
```

7. Create a file called `resolve.go` with the following content:

```go
package cards

import (
    "strings"

    "github.com/graphql-go/graphql"
)
```

```
// Resolve handles filtering cards
// by suit and value
func Resolve(p graphql.ResolveParams) (interface{}, error) {
    finalCards := []Card{}
    suit, suitOK := p.Args["suit"].(string)
    suit = strings.ToLower(suit)

    value, valueOK := p.Args["value"].(string)
    value = strings.ToLower(value)

    for _, card := range cards {
        if suitOK && suit != strings.ToLower(card.Suit) {
            continue
        }
        if valueOK && value != strings.ToLower(card.Value) {
            continue
        }

        finalCards = append(finalCards, card)
    }
    return finalCards, nil
}
```

8. Create a file called `schema.go` with the following content:

```
package cards

import "github.com/graphql-go/graphql"

// Setup prepares and returns our card
// schema
func Setup() (graphql.Schema, error) {
    cardType := CardType()

    // Schema
    fields := graphql.Fields{
        "cards": &graphql.Field{
            Type: graphql.NewList(cardType),
            Args: graphql.FieldConfigArgument{
                "suit": &graphql.ArgumentConfig{
                    Description: "Filter cards by card suit
                    (hearts, clubs, diamonds, spades)",
                    Type: graphql.String,
                },
                "value": &graphql.ArgumentConfig{
                    Description: "Filter cards by card
                    value (A-K)",
                    Type: graphql.String,
```

```
                },
            },
            Resolve: Resolve,
        },
    }

    rootQuery := graphql.ObjectConfig{Name: "RootQuery",
    Fields: fields}
    schemaConfig := graphql.SchemaConfig{Query:
    graphql.NewObject(rootQuery)}
    schema, err := graphql.NewSchema(schemaConfig)

    return schema, err
}
```

9. Navigate back to the `graphql` directory.
10. Create a new directory named `example` and navigate to it.
11. Create a file named `main.go` with the following content:

```
package main

import (
    "encoding/json"
    "fmt"
    "log"

    "github.com/PacktPublishing/
     Go-Programming-Cookbook-Second-Edition/
     chapter12/graphql/cards"
    "github.com/graphql-go/graphql"
)

func main() {
    // grab our schema
    schema, err := cards.Setup()
    if err != nil {
        panic(err)
    }

    // Query
    query := `
    {
        cards(value: "A"){
            value
            suit
        }
    }`
```

```
params := graphql.Params{Schema: schema, RequestString:
query}
r := graphql.Do(params)
if len(r.Errors) > 0 {
    log.Fatalf("failed to execute graphql operation,
    errors: %+v", r.Errors)
}
rJSON, err := json.MarshalIndent(r, "", " ")
if err != nil {
    panic(err)
}
fmt.Printf("%s \n", rJSON)
}
```

12. Run `go run main.go`.

13. You may also run the following command:

```
$ go build
$ ./example
```

You should see the following output:

```
$ go run main.go
{
    "data": {
        "cards": [
            {
                "suit": "Spades",
                "value": "A"
            },
            {
                "suit": "Hearts",
                "value": "A"
            },
            {
                "suit": "Clubs",
                "value": "A"
            },
            {
                "suit": "Diamonds",
                "value": "A"
            }
        ]
    }
}
```

14. Test some additional queries, such as the following:
    - `cards(suit: "Spades")`
    - `cards(value: "3", suit:"Diamonds")`

15. The `go.mod` file may be updated, and the `go.sum` file should now be present in the top-level recipe directory.

16. If you have copied or written your own tests, go up one directory and run `go test`. Ensure that all the tests pass.

How it works...

The `cards.go` file defines a `card` object and initializes the base deck in a global variable called `cards`. This state could also be held in long-term storage, such as a database. We then define `CardType` in `types.go`, which allows `graphql` to resolve card objects to responses. Next, we jump into `resolve.go`, where we define how to filter cards by value and type. This `Resolve` function will be used by the final schema, which is defined in `schema.go`.

For example, you would modify the `Resolve` function in this recipe in order to retrieve data from a database. Lastly, we load the schema and run a query against it. It's a small modification to mount our schema onto a REST endpoint, but for brevity, this recipe just runs a hardcoded query. For more information about `GraphQL` queries, visit `http://graphql.org/learn/queries/`.

13
Serverless Programming

This chapter will focus on serverless architectures and using them with the Go language. Serverless architectures are one where the developer does not manage the backend server. This includes services such as Amazon Lambda, Google App Engine and Firebase. These services allow you to quickly deploy applications and store data on the web.

All of the recipes in this chapter deal with third-party services that bill for use; ensure that you clean up when you're done using them. Otherwise, think of these recipes as kick-starters for spinning up larger applications on these platforms.

In this chapter, we will cover the following recipes:

- Go programming on Lambda with Apex
- Apex serverless logging and metrics
- Google App Engine with Go
- Working with Firebase using `firebase.google.com/go`

Go programming on Lambda with Apex

Apex is a tool for building, deploying, and managing AWS Lambda functions. It used to provide a Go `shim` for managing Lambda functions in code, but this is now done using the native AWS library (`https://github.com/aws/aws-lambda-go`). This recipe will explore creating Go Lambda functions and deploying them with Apex.

Getting ready

Configure your environment according to these steps:

1. Download and install Go 1.12.6 or greater on your operating system from `https://golang.org/doc/install`.
2. Install Apex from `http://apex.run/#installation`.
3. Open Terminal or console application and create and navigate to a project directory such as `~/projects/go-programming-cookbook`. All the code we will cover in this recipe will be run and modified from this directory.
4. Clone the latest code into `~/projects/go-programming-cookbook-original`. Here, you have the option to work from that directory rather than typing in the examples manually:

   ```
   $ git clone git@github.com:PacktPublishing/Go-Programming-Cookbook-
   Second-Edition.git go-programming-cookbook-original
   ```

How to do it...

These steps cover writing and running your application:

1. From your Terminal or console application, create a new directory called `~/projects/go-programming-cookbook/chapter13/lambda` and navigate to it.
2. Run the following command:

   ```
   $ go mod init github.com/PacktPublishing/Go-Programming-Cookbook-
   Second-Edition/chapter13/lambda
   ```

   You should see a file called `go.mod` that contains the following content:

   ```
   module github.com/PacktPublishing/Go-Programming-Cookbook-Second-
   Edition/chapter13/lambda
   ```

3. Create an Amazon account and an IAM role that can edit Lambda functions, which can be done from `https://aws.amazon.com/lambda/`.
4. Create a file called `~/.aws/credentials` with the following content, copying your credentials from what you set up in the Amazon console:

   ```
   [default]
   aws_access_key_id = xxxxxxxx
   aws_secret_access_key = xxxxxxxxxxxxxxxxxxxxxxxxx
   ```

5. Create an environment variable to hold your desired region:

```
export AWS_REGION=us-west-2
```

6. Run the `apex init` command and follow the onscreen instructions:

```
$ apex init

Enter the name of your project. It should be machine-friendly, as
this is used to prefix your functions in Lambda.

Project name: go-cookbook

Enter an optional description of your project.

Project description: Demonstrating Apex with the Go Cookbook

[+] creating IAM go-cookbook_lambda_function role
[+] creating IAM go-cookbook_lambda_logs policy
[+] attaching policy to lambda_function role.
[+] creating ./project.json
[+] creating ./functions

Setup complete, deploy those functions!

$ apex deploy
```

7. Remove the `lambda/functions/hello` directory.

8. Create a new `lambda/functions/greeter1/main.go` file with the following content:

```go
package main

import (
  "context"
  "fmt"

  "github.com/aws/aws-lambda-go/lambda"
)

// Message is the input to the function and
// includes a Name
type Message struct {
  Name string `json:"name"`
}

// Response is sent back and contains a greeting
```

```
  // string
  type Response struct {
    Greeting string `json:"greeting"`
  }

  // HandleRequest will be called when the lambda function is invoked
  // it takes a Message and returns a Response that contains a
  greeting
  func HandleRequest(ctx context.Context, m Message) (Response,
  error) {
    return Response{Greeting: fmt.Sprintf("Hello, %s", m.Name)}, nil
  }

  func main() {
    lambda.Start(HandleRequest)
  }
```

9. Create a new `lambda/functions/greeter/main.go` file with the following content:

```
package main

import (
  "context"
  "fmt"

  "github.com/aws/aws-lambda-go/lambda"
)

// Message is the input to the function and
// includes a FirstName and LastName
type Message struct {
  FirstName string `json:"first_name"`
  LastName string `json:"last_name"`
}

// Response is sent back and contains a greeting
// string
type Response struct {
  Greeting string `json:"greeting"`
}

// HandleRequest will be called when the lambda function is invoked
// it takes a Message and returns a Response that contains a
greeting
// this greeting contains the first and last name specified
func HandleRequest(ctx context.Context, m Message) (Response,
error) {
```

```
    return Response{Greeting: fmt.Sprintf("Hello, %s %s",
m.FirstName, m.LastName)}, nil
}

func main() {
  lambda.Start(HandleRequest)
}
```

10. Deploy them:

```
$ apex deploy
• creating function env= function=greeter2
• creating function env= function=greeter1
• created alias current env= function=greeter2 version=4
• function created env= function=greeter2 name=go-cookbook_greeter2
version=1
• created alias current env= function=greeter1 version=5
• function created env= function=greeter1 name=go-cookbook_greeter1
version=1
```

11. Invoke the newly deployed functions:

```
$ echo '{"name": "Reader"}' | apex invoke greeter1
{"greeting":"Hello, Reader"}

$ echo '{"first_name": "Go", "last_name": "Coders"}' | apex invoke
greeter2 {"greeting":"Hello, Go Coders"}
```

12. Take a look at the logs:

```
$ apex logs greeter2
apex logs greeter2
/aws/lambda/go-cookbook_greeter2 START RequestId:
7c0f9129-3830-11e7-8755-75aeb52a51b9 Version: 1
/aws/lambda/go-cookbook_greeter2 END RequestId:
7c0f9129-3830-11e7-8755-75aeb52a51b9
/aws/lambda/go-cookbook_greeter2 REPORT RequestId:
7c0f9129-3830-11e7-8755-75aeb52a51b9 Duration: 93.84 ms Billed
Duration: 100 ms
Memory Size: 128 MB Max Memory Used: 19 MB
```

13. Clean up the deployed services:

```
$ apex delete
The following will be deleted:

- greeter1
- greeter2
```

```
Are you sure? (yes/no) yes
• deleting env= function=greeter
• function deleted env= function=greeter
```

How it works...

AWS Lambda makes it easy to run functions on demand without maintaining a server. Apex provides facilities for deploying, versioning, and testing functions as you ship them to Lambda.

The Go library (`https://github.com/aws/aws-lambda-go`) provides native Go compilation in Lambda and allows us to deploy Go code as Lambda functions. This is accomplished by defining a handler, processing incoming request payloads, and returning a response. Currently, the functions you define must follow these rules:

- The handler must be a function.
- The handler may take between zero and two arguments.
- If there are two arguments, the first argument must satisfy the `context.Context` interface.
- The handler may return between zero and two arguments.
- If there are two return values, the second argument must be an error.
- If there is one return value, it must be an error.

In this recipe, we defined two greeter functions, one that took a full name and one where we split the name into a first name and last name. If we modified a single function, `greeter`, instead of creating two, Apex would have deployed the new version instead and called in `v2` rather than `v1` in all the preceding examples. It would be possible to roll back with `apex rollback greeter` as well.

Apex serverless logging and metrics

When working with serverless functions such as Lambda, it is valuable to have portable, structured logs. In addition, you can combine the earlier recipes that dealt with logging with this recipe. The recipes that we covered in `Chapter 4`, *Error Handling in Go*, are just as relevant. Because we're using Apex to manage our Lambda functions, we chose to use the Apex logger for this recipe. We'll also rely on metrics provided by Apex, as well as the AWS console. The earlier recipes explored more complex logging and metrics examples, and those still apply—the Apex logger can easily be configured to aggregate logs using, for example, Amazon Kinesis or Elasticsearch.

Getting ready

Refer to the *Getting ready* section of the *Go programming on Lambda with Apex* recipe in this chapter.

How to do it...

These steps cover writing and running your application:

1. From your Terminal or console application, create a new directory called `~/projects/go-programming-cookbook/chapter13/logging` and navigate to it.

2. Run the following command:

   ```
   $ go mod init github.com/PacktPublishing/Go-Programming-Cookbook-
   Second-Edition/chapter13/logging
   ```

   You should see a file called `go.mod` that contains the following content:

   ```
   module github.com/PacktPublishing/Go-Programming-Cookbook-Second-
   Edition/chapter13/logging
   ```

3. Create an Amazon account and an IAM role that can edit Lambda functions, which can be done at `https://aws.amazon.com/lambda/`.

4. Create a `~/.aws/credentials` file with the following content, copying your credentials from what you set up in the Amazon console:

   ```
   [default]
   aws_access_key_id = xxxxxxxx
   aws_secret_access_key = xxxxxxxxxxxxxxxxxxxxxxxxx
   ```

5. Create an environment variable to hold your desired region:

   ```
   export AWS_REGION=us-west-2
   ```

6. Run the `apex init` command and follow the onscreen instructions:

   ```
   $ apex init

   Enter the name of your project. It should be machine-friendly, as
   this is used to prefix your functions in Lambda.

   Project name: logging

   Enter an optional description of your project.
   ```

```
Project description: An example of apex logging and metrics

[+] creating IAM logging_lambda_function role
[+] creating IAM logging_lambda_logs policy
[+] attaching policy to lambda_function role.
[+] creating ./project.json
[+] creating ./functions

Setup complete, deploy those functions!

$ apex deploy
```

7. Remove the `lambda/functions/hello` directory.

8. Create a new `lambda/functions/secret/main.go` file with the following content:

```go
package main

import (
  "context"
  "os"

  "github.com/apex/log"
  "github.com/apex/log/handlers/text"
  "github.com/aws/aws-lambda-go/lambda"
)

// Input takes in a secret
type Input struct {
  Secret string `json:"secret"`
}

// HandleRequest will be called when the Lambda function is invoked
// it takes an input and checks if it matches our super secret
value
func HandleRequest(ctx context.Context, input Input) (string,
error) {
  log.SetHandler(text.New(os.Stderr))

  log.WithField("secret", input.Secret).Info("secret guessed")

  if input.Secret == "klaatu barada nikto" {
    return "secret guessed!", nil
  }
  return "try again", nil
}
```

```
func main() {
  lambda.Start(HandleRequest)
}
```

9. Deploy it to your specified region:

    ```
    $ apex deploy
    • creating function env= function=secret
    • created alias current env= function=secret version=1
    • function created env= function=secret name=logging_secret
    version=1
    ```

10. To invoke it, run the following command:

    ```
    $ echo '{"secret": "open sesame"}' | apex invoke secret
    "try again"

    $ echo '{"secret": "klaatu barada nikto"}' | apex invoke secret
    "secret guessed!"
    ```

11. Check the logs:

    ```
    $ apex logs secret
    /aws/lambda/logging_secret START RequestId: cfa6f655-3834-11e7-
    b99d-89998a7f39dd Version: 1
    /aws/lambda/logging_secret INFO[0000] secret guessed secret=open
    sesame
    /aws/lambda/logging_secret END RequestId: cfa6f655-3834-11e7-
    b99d-89998a7f39dd
    /aws/lambda/logging_secret REPORT RequestId: cfa6f655-3834-11e7-
    b99d-89998a7f39dd Duration: 52.23 ms Billed Duration: 100 ms Memory
    Size: 128 MB Max Memory Used: 19 MB
    /aws/lambda/logging_secret START RequestId: d74ea688-3834-11e7-
    aa4e-d592c1fbc35f Version: 1
    /aws/lambda/logging_secret INFO[0012] secret guessed secret=klaatu
    barada nikto
    /aws/lambda/logging_secret END RequestId: d74ea688-3834-11e7-aa4e-
    d592c1fbc35f
    /aws/lambda/logging_secret REPORT RequestId: d74ea688-3834-11e7-
    aa4e-d592c1fbc35f Duration: 7.43 ms Billed Duration: 100 ms
    Memory Size: 128 MB Max Memory Used: 19 MB
    ```

12. Check your metrics:

    ```
    $ apex metrics secret

    secret
    total cost: $0.00
    ```

```
invocations: 0 ($0.00)
duration: 0s ($0.00)
throttles: 0
errors: 0
memory: 128
```

13. Clean up the deployed services:

```
$ apex delete
Are you sure? (yes/no) yes
• deleting env= function=secret
• function deleted env= function=secret
```

How it works...

In this recipe, we created a new Lambda function called secret that will respond with whether or not you guessed a secret phrase. The function parses an incoming JSON request, performs some logging using `Stderr`, and returns a response.

After using the function a few times, we can see that our logs are visible using the `apex logs` command. This command can be run on a single Lambda function or across all of our managed functions. This is especially useful if you are chaining Apex commands together and want to watch logs across many services.

In addition, we have shown you how to use the `apex metrics` command to collect general metrics about your application, including cost and invocations. You can also see a lot of this information directly in the AWS console in the Lambda section. Like the other recipes, we tried to clean up after ourselves at the end.

Google App Engine with Go

App Engine is a Google service that facilitates the quick deployment of web applications. These applications have access to cloud storage and various other Google APIs. The general idea is that App Engine will scale easily with the load and simplify any operations management associated with hosting an app. This recipe will show how to create and optionally deploy a basic App Engine application. This recipe won't get into the details of setting up a Google Cloud account, setting up billing, or the specifics on cleaning up your instance. As a minimum requirement, access to Google Cloud Datastore (`https://cloud.google.com/datastore/docs/concepts/overview`) is required for this recipe to work.

Getting ready

Configure your environment according to these steps:

1. Download and install Go 1.11.1 or greater on your operating system from `https://golang.org/doc/install`.
2. Download the Google Cloud SDK from `https://cloud.google.com/appengine/docs/flexible/go/quickstart`.
3. Create an app that allows you to perform datastore access and record the app name. For this recipe, we'll use `go-cookbook`.
4. Install the `gcloud components install app-engine-go` Go app engine component.
5. Open Terminal or console application and create and navigate to a project directory such as `~/projects/go-programming-cookbook`. All the code we will cover in this recipe will be run and modified from this directory.
6. Clone the latest code into `~/projects/go-programming-cookbook-original`. Here, you have the option of working from that directory rather than typing in the examples manually:

```
$ git clone git@github.com:PacktPublishing/Go-Programming-Cookbook-
Second-Edition.git go-programming-cookbook-original
```

How to do it...

These steps cover writing and running your application:

1. From your Terminal or console application, create a new directory called `~/projects/go-programming-cookbook/chapter13/appengine` and navigate to it.
2. Run the following command:

```
$ go mod init github.com/PacktPublishing/Go-Programming-Cookbook-
Second-Edition/chapter13/appengine
```

You should see a file called `go.mod` that contains the following content:

```
module github.com/PacktPublishing/Go-Programming-Cookbook-Second-
Edition/chapter13/appengine
```

3. Create a file called `app.yml` with the following content, replacing `go-cookbook` with the name of the app you created in the *Getting ready* section:

```
runtime: go112

manual_scaling:
  instances: 1

#[START env_variables]
env_variables:
  GCLOUD_DATASET_ID: go-cookbook
#[END env_variables]
```

4. Create a file called `message.go` with the following content:

```
package main

import (
    "context"
    "time"

    "cloud.google.com/go/datastore"
)

// Message is the object we store
type Message struct {
    Timestamp time.Time
    Message string
}

func (c *Controller) storeMessage(ctx context.Context, message string) error {
    m := &amp;amp;Message{
        Timestamp: time.Now(),
        Message: message,
    }

    k := datastore.IncompleteKey("Message", nil)
    _, err := c.store.Put(ctx, k, m)
    return err
}

func (c *Controller) queryMessages(ctx context.Context, limit int) ([]*Message, error) {
    q := datastore.NewQuery("Message").
    Order("-Timestamp").
    Limit(limit)
```

```
        messages := make([]*Message, 0)
        _, err := c.store.GetAll(ctx, q, &amp;amp;messages)
        return messages, err
    }
```

5. Create a file called `controller.go` with the following content:

```go
package main

import (
    "context"
    "fmt"
    "log"
    "net/http"

    "cloud.google.com/go/datastore"
)

// Controller holds our storage and other
// state
type Controller struct {
    store *datastore.Client
}

func (c *Controller) handle(w http.ResponseWriter, r
*http.Request) {
    if r.Method != http.MethodGet {
        http.Error(w, "invalid method",
        http.StatusMethodNotAllowed)
        return
    }

    ctx := context.Background()

    // store the new message
    r.ParseForm()
    if message := r.FormValue("message"); message != "" {
        if err := c.storeMessage(ctx, message); err != nil {
            log.Printf("could not store message: %v", err)
            http.Error(w, "could not store
            message",
            http.StatusInternalServerError)
            return
        }
    }

    // get the current messages and display them
    fmt.Fprintln(w, "Messages:")
```

```
        messages, err := c.queryMessages(ctx, 10)
        if err != nil {
            log.Printf("could not get messages: %v", err)
            http.Error(w, "could not get messages",
            http.StatusInternalServerError)
            return
        }

        for _, message := range messages {
            fmt.Fprintln(w, message.Message)
        }
    }
}
```

6. Create a file called `main.go` with the following content:

```
package main

import (
    "log"
    "net/http"
    "os"

    "cloud.google.com/go/datastore"
    "golang.org/x/net/context"
    "google.golang.org/appengine"
)

func main() {
    ctx := context.Background()
    log.SetOutput(os.Stderr)

    // Set this in app.yaml when running in production.
    projectID := os.Getenv("GCLOUD_DATASET_ID")

    datastoreClient, err := datastore.NewClient(ctx, projectID)
    if err != nil {
        log.Fatal(err)
    }

    c := Controller{datastoreClient}

    http.HandleFunc("/", c.handle)
    port := os.Getenv("PORT")
    if port == "" {
        port = "8080"
        log.Printf("Defaulting to port %s", port)
    }
```

```
log.Printf("Listening on port %s", port)
log.Fatal(http.ListenAndServe(fmt.Sprintf(":%s", port), nil))
}
```

7. Run the `gcloud config set project go-cookbook` command, where `go-cookbook` is the project you created in the *Getting ready* section.

8. Run the `gcloud auth application-default login` command and follow the instructions.

9. Run the `export PORT=8080` command.

10. Run the `export GCLOUD_DATASET_ID=go-cookbook` command, where `go-cookbook` is the project you created in the *Getting ready* section.

11. Run the `go build` command.

12. Run the `./appengine` command.

13. Navigate to `http://localhost:8080/?message=hello%20there`.

14. Try a few more messages (`?message=other`).

15. Optionally, deploy the app to your instance with `gcloud app deploy`.

16. Navigate to the deployed app with `gcloud app browse`.

17. Optionally clean up your `appengine` instance and datastore at the following URLs:
    - `https://console.cloud.google.com/datastore`
    - `https://console.cloud.google.com/appengine`

18. The `go.mod` file may be updated and the `go.sum` file should now be present in the top-level recipe directory.

19. If you copied or wrote your own tests, run the `go test` command. Ensure that all the tests pass.

How it works...

Once the cloud SDK is configured to point at your application and has been authenticated, the GCloud tool allows quick deployment and configuration, allowing local applications to access Google services.

After authenticating and setting the port, we run the application on `localhost`, and we can begin working with the code. The application defines a message object that can be stored and retrieved from the datastore. This demonstrates how you might isolate this sort of code. You may also use a storage/database interface, as shown in previous chapters.

Next, we set up a handler that attempts to insert a message into the datastore, then retrieves all the messages, displaying them in a browser. This creates something resembling a basic guestbook. You may notice that the message doesn't always appear immediately. If you navigate without a message parameter or send another message, it should appear on a reload.

Lastly, ensure that you clean up the instances if you're no longer using them.

Working with Firebase using firebase.google.com/go

Firebase is another Google Cloud service that creates a scalable, easy-to-manage database that can support authentication and works especially well with mobile applications. For this recipe, we'll use the latest Firestore as our database backend. The Firebase service provides significantly more than what will be covered in this recipe, but we will just be looking at storing and retrieving data. We'll also look into how to set up authentication for your application and wrap the Firebase client with our own custom client.

Getting ready

Configure your environment according to these steps:

1. Download and install Go 1.11.1 or greater on your operating system from `https://golang.org/doc/install`.
2. Create a Firebase account, project, and database at `https://console.firebase.google.com/`.

 This recipe runs in test mode, which is not secure by default.

3. Generate a service admin token by going to `https://console.firebase.google.com/project/go-cookbook/settings/serviceaccounts/adminsdk`. Here, `go-cookbook` is replaced with your project name.
4. Move the downloaded token to `/tmp/service_account.json`.

5. Open Terminal or console application and create and navigate to a project directory such as `~/projects/go-programming-cookbook`. All the code we will cover in this recipe will be run and modified from this directory.

6. Clone the latest code into `~/projects/go-programming-cookbook-original`. Here, you have the option to work from that directory rather than typing in the examples manually:

```
$ git clone git@github.com:PacktPublishing/Go-Programming-Cookbook-
Second-Edition.git go-programming-cookbook-original
```

How to do it...

These steps cover writing and running your application:

1. From your Terminal or console application, create a new directory called `~/projects/go-programming-cookbook/chapter13/firebase` and navigate to it.

2. Run the following command:

```
$ go mod init github.com/PacktPublishing/Go-Programming-Cookbook-
Second-Edition/chapter13/firebase
```

You should see a file called `go.mod` that contains the following content:

```
module github.com/PacktPublishing/Go-Programming-Cookbook-Second-
Edition/chapter13/firebase
```

3. Create a file called `client.go` with the following content:

```go
package firebase

import (
  "context"

  "cloud.google.com/go/firestore"
  "github.com/pkg/errors"
)

// Client Interface for mocking
type Client interface {
  Get(ctx context.Context, key string) (interface{}, error)
  Set(ctx context.Context, key string, value interface{}) error
  Close() error
}
```

```
// firestore.Client implements Close()
// we create Get and Set
type firebaseClient struct {
  *firestore.Client
  collection string
}

func (f *firebaseClient) Get(ctx context.Context, key string)
(interface{}, error) {
  data, err := f.Collection(f.collection).Doc(key).Get(ctx)
  if err != nil {
    return nil, errors.Wrap(err, "get failed")
  }
  return data.Data(), nil
}

func (f *firebaseClient) Set(ctx context.Context, key string, value
interface{}) error {
  set := make(map[string]interface{})
  set[key] = value
  _, err := f.Collection(f.collection).Doc(key).Set(ctx, set)
  return errors.Wrap(err, "set failed")
}
```

4. Create a file called `auth.go` with the following content:

```
package firebase

import (
  "context"

  firebase "firebase.google.com/go"
  "github.com/pkg/errors"
  "google.golang.org/api/option"
)

// Authenticate grabs oauth scopes using a generated
// service_account.json file from
//
https://console.firebase.google.com/project/go-cookbook/settings/se
rviceaccounts/adminsdk
func Authenticate(ctx context.Context, collection string) (Client,
error) {

  opt := option.WithCredentialsFile("/tmp/service_account.json")
  app, err := firebase.NewApp(ctx, nil, opt)
  if err != nil {
    return nil, errors.Wrap(err, "error initializing app")
```

```
  }

  client, err := app.Firestore(ctx)
  if err != nil {
    return nil, errors.Wrap(err, "failed to intialize filestore")
  }
  return &amp;amp;firebaseClient{Client: client, collection:
collection}, nil
}
```

5. Create a new directory named `example` and navigate to it.
6. Create a file named `main.go` with the following content:

```go
package main

import (
  "context"
  "fmt"
  "log"

  "github.com/PacktPublishing/Go-Programming-Cookbook-Second-
Edition/chapter13/firebase"
)

func main() {
  ctx := context.Background()
  c, err := firebase.Authenticate(ctx, "collection")
  if err != nil {
    log.Fatalf("error initializing client: %v", err)
  }
  defer c.Close()

  if err := c.Set(ctx, "key", []string{"val1", "val2"}); err != nil
{
    log.Fatalf(err.Error())
  }

  res, err := c.Get(ctx, "key")
  if err != nil {
    log.Fatalf(err.Error())
  }
  fmt.Println(res)

  if err := c.Set(ctx, "key2", []string{"val3", "val4"}); err !=
nil {
    log.Fatalf(err.Error())
  }
```

```
     res, err = c.Get(ctx, "key2")
     if err != nil {
       log.Fatalf(err.Error())
     }
     fmt.Println(res)
   }
```

7. Run `go run main.go`.

8. You may also run `go build ./example`. You should see the following output:

```
$ go run main.go
[val1 val2]
[val3 val4]
```

9. The `go.mod` file may be updated and the `go.sum` file should now be present in the top-level recipe directory.

10. If you copied or wrote your own tests, go up one directory and run `go test`. Ensure that all the tests pass.

How it works...

Firebase provides convenient functions so that you can log in with a credentials file. After we're logged in, we can store any sort of structured, map-like object. In this case, we are storing `map[string]interface{}`. This data is accessible by a number of clients, including on the web and via mobile devices.

The client code wraps all the operations in an interface for ease of testing. This is a common pattern when writing client code and is also used in other recipes. In our case, we create a `Get` and `Set` function that stores and retrieves a value by a key. We also expose `Close()` so that code that's using the client can defer `close()` and clean up our connection at the end.

14
Performance Improvements, Tips, and Tricks

In this chapter, we will focus on optimizing an application and discovering bottlenecks. These are some tips and tricks that can be used immediately by existing applications. Many of these recipes are necessary if you or your organization requires fully reproducible builds. They're also useful when you want to benchmark an application's performance. The final recipe focuses on increasing the speed of HTTP; however, it's always important to remember that the web world moves quickly, and it's important to refresh yourself on the best practices. For example, if you require HTTP/2, it has been available using the built-in Go `net/http` package since version 1.6.

In this chapter, we will cover the following recipes:

- Using the pprof tool
- Benchmarking and finding bottlenecks
- Memory allocation and heap management
- Using fasthttprouter and fasthttp

Technical requirements

In order to proceed with all the recipes in this chapter, configure your environment according to these steps:

1. Download and install Go 1.12.6 or greater on your operating system from `https://golang.org/doc/install`.
2. Open a Terminal or console application and create and navigate to a project directory such as `~/projects/go-programming-cookbook`. All code will be run and modified from this directory.

3. Clone the latest code into `~/projects/go-programming-cookbook-original` and optionally work from that directory rather than typing the examples manually:

```
$ git clone git@github.com:PacktPublishing/Go-Programming-Cookbook-Second-Edition.git go-programming-cookbook-original
```

4. Optionally, install Graphviz from `http://www.graphviz.org/Home.php`.

Using the pprof tool

The `pprof` tool allows Go applications to collect and export runtime profiling data. It also provides webhooks to access the tool from a web interface. This recipe will create a basic application that verifies a `bcrypt`-hashed password against a plaintext one, then it will profile the application.

You might have expected the `pprof` tool to be covered in `Chapter 11`, *Distributed Systems*, with other metrics and monitoring recipes. It was instead put in this chapter because it will be used to analyze and improve a program much in the same way that benchmarking can be used. As a result, this recipe will largely focus on `pprof` for analyzing and improving the memory usage of an application.

How to do it...

These steps cover writing and running your application:

1. From your Terminal or console application, create a new directory called `~/projects/go-programming-cookbook/chapter14/pprof` and navigate to this directory.

2. Run this command:

```
$ go mod init github.com/PacktPublishing/Go-Programming-Cookbook-Second-Edition/chapter14/pprof
```

You should see a file called `go.mod` that contains the following:

```
module github.com/PacktPublishing/Go-Programming-Cookbook-Second-Edition/chapter14/pprof
```

3. Copy tests from `~/projects/go-programming-cookbook-original/chapter14/pprof`, or use this as an exercise to write some of your own code!

4. Create a directory named `crypto` and navigate to it.

5. Create a file called `handler.go` with the following content:

```go
package crypto

import (
    "net/http"

    "golang.org/x/crypto/bcrypt"
)

// GuessHandler checks if ?message=password
func GuessHandler(w http.ResponseWriter, r *http.Request) {
    if err := r.ParseForm(); err != nil{
        // if we can't parse the form
        // we'll assume it is malformed
        w.WriteHeader(http.StatusBadRequest)
        w.Write([]byte("error reading guess"))
        return
    }

    msg := r.FormValue("message")

    // "password"
    real :=
    []byte("$2a$10$2ovnPWuIjMx2S0HvCxP/mutzdsGhyt8rq/
JqnJg/6OyC3B0APMGlK")

    if err := bcrypt.CompareHashAndPassword(real, []byte(msg));
    err != nil {
        w.WriteHeader(http.StatusBadRequest)
        w.Write([]byte("try again"))
        return
    }

    w.WriteHeader(http.StatusOK)
    w.Write([]byte("you got it"))
    return
}
```

6. Navigate up a directory.
7. Create a new directory named `example` and navigate to it.
8. Create a `main.go` file with the following content:

```
package main

import (
    "fmt"
    "log"
    "net/http"
    _ "net/http/pprof"

    "github.com/PacktPublishing/
    Go-Programming-Cookbook-Second-Edition/
    chapter14/pprof/crypto"
)

func main() {

    http.HandleFunc("/guess", crypto.GuessHandler)
    fmt.Println("server started at localhost:8080")
    log.Panic(http.ListenAndServe("localhost:8080", nil))
}
```

9. Run `go run main.go`.
10. You may also run the following command:

```
$ go build
$ ./example
```

You should now see the following output:

```
$ go run main.go
server started at localhost:8080
```

11. In a separate Terminal, run the following:

```
$ go tool pprof http://localhost:8080/debug/pprof/profile
```

12. This will start a 30-second timer.

13. Run several `curl` commands while `pprof` runs:

```
$ curl "http://localhost:8080/guess?message=test"
try again

$curl "http://localhost:8080/guess?message=password"
you got it


    .
    .
    .
    .


$curl "http://localhost:8080/guess?message=password"
you got it
```

14. Return to the `pprof` command and wait for it to complete.

15. Run the `top10` command from the `pprof` prompt:

```
(pprof) top 10
930ms of 930ms total ( 100%)
Showing top 10 nodes out of 15 (cum >= 930ms)
flat flat% sum% cum cum%
870ms 93.55% 93.55% 870ms 93.55%
golang.org/x/crypto/blowfish.encryptBlock
30ms 3.23% 96.77% 900ms 96.77%
golang.org/x/crypto/blowfish.ExpandKey
30ms 3.23% 100% 30ms 3.23% runtime.memclrNoHeapPointers
0 0% 100% 930ms 100% github.com/agtorre/go-
cookbook/chapter13/pprof/crypto.GuessHandler
0 0% 100% 930ms 100%
golang.org/x/crypto/bcrypt.CompareHashAndPassword
0 0% 100% 30ms 3.23% golang.org/x/crypto/bcrypt.base64Encode
0 0% 100% 930ms 100% golang.org/x/crypto/bcrypt.bcrypt
0 0% 100% 900ms 96.77%
golang.org/x/crypto/bcrypt.expensiveBlowfishSetup
0 0% 100% 930ms 100% net/http.(*ServeMux).ServeHTTP
0 0% 100% 930ms 100% net/http.(*conn).serve
```

16. If you installed Graphviz or a supported browser, run the `web` command from the `pprof` prompt. You should see something like this with a much longer chain of red boxes on the right side:

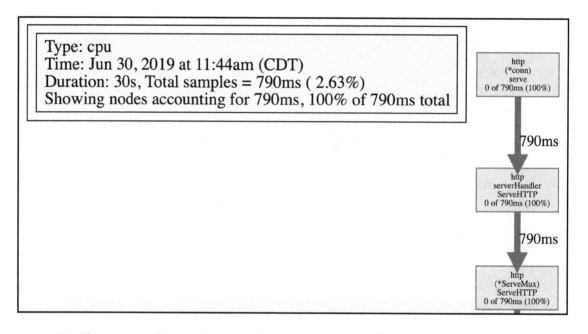

17. The `go.mod` file may be updated and the `go.sum` file should now be present in the top-level recipe directory.
18. If you have copied or written your own tests, go up one directory and run `go test`. Ensure that all the tests pass.

How it works...

The `pprof` tool provides a lot of runtime information about your application. Using the `net/pprof` package is usually the most simple to configure—all that's required is listening on a port and doing an import.

In our case, we wrote a handler that uses a very compute-heavy application (`bcrypt`) so that we can demonstrate how they pop up when profiling with `pprof`. This will quickly isolate chunks of code that are creating bottlenecks in your application.

We chose to collect a general profile that causes `pprof` to poll our application endpoint for 30 seconds. We then generated traffic against the endpoint to help produce results. This can be helpful when you're attempting to check a single handler or branch of code.

Lastly, we looked at the top 10 functions in terms of CPU utilization. It's also possible to look at memory/heap management with the `pprof` `http://localhost:8080/debug/pprof/heap` command. The `web` command in the `pprof` console can be used to look at a visualization of your CPU/memory profile and helps highlight more active code.

Benchmarking and finding bottlenecks

Another method for determining slow parts of code is to use benchmarks. Benchmarks can be used to test functions for average performance and can also run benchmarks in parallel. This can be useful when comparing functions or doing micro-optimizations for certain code, especially to see how a function implementation might perform when using it concurrently. For this recipe, we'll create two structures that both implement an atomic counter. The first will use the `sync` package, and the other will use `sync/atomic`. We'll then benchmark both the solutions.

How to do it...

These steps cover writing and running your application:

1. From your Terminal or console application, create a new directory called `~/projects/go-programming-cookbook/chapter14/bench` and navigate to this directory.

2. Run this command:

```
$ go mod init github.com/PacktPublishing/Go-Programming-Cookbook-
Second-Edition/chapter14/bench
```

You should see a file called `go.mod` that contains the following:

```
module github.com/PacktPublishing/Go-Programming-Cookbook-Second-
Edition/chapter14/bench
```

3. Copy tests from `~/projects/go-programming-cookbook-original/chapter14/bench`, or use this as an exercise to write some of your own code!

 Note that copied tests also include benchmarks written later in this recipe.

4. Create a file called `lock.go` with the following content:

```
package bench

import "sync"

// Counter uses a sync.RWMutex to safely
// modify a value
type Counter struct {
    value int64
    mu *sync.RWMutex
}

// Add increments the counter
func (c *Counter) Add(amount int64) {
    c.mu.Lock()
    c.value += amount
    c.mu.Unlock()
}

// Read returns the current counter amount
func (c *Counter) Read() int64 {
    c.mu.RLock()
    defer c.mu.RUnlock()
    return c.value
}
```

5. Create a file called `atomic.go` with the following content:

```
package bench

import "sync/atomic"

// AtomicCounter implements an atmoic lock
// using the atomic package
type AtomicCounter struct {
    value int64
}
```

```
// Add increments the counter
func (c *AtomicCounter) Add(amount int64) {
    atomic.AddInt64(&c.value, amount)
}

// Read returns the current counter amount
func (c *AtomicCounter) Read() int64 {
    var result int64
    result = atomic.LoadInt64(&c.value)
    return result
}
```

6. Create a file called `lock_test.go` with the following content:

```
package bench

import "testing"

func BenchmarkCounterAdd(b *testing.B) {
    c := Counter{0, &sync.RWMutex{}}
    for n := 0; n < b.N; n++ {
        c.Add(1)
    }
}

func BenchmarkCounterRead(b *testing.B) {
    c := Counter{0, &sync.RWMutex{}}
    for n := 0; n < b.N; n++ {
        c.Read()
    }
}

func BenchmarkCounterAddRead(b *testing.B) {
    c := Counter{0, &sync.RWMutex{}}
    b.RunParallel(func(pb *testing.PB) {
        for pb.Next() {
            c.Add(1)
            c.Read()
        }
    })
}
```

7. Create a file called `atomic_test.go` with the following content:

```
package bench

import "testing"

func BenchmarkAtomicCounterAdd(b *testing.B) {
    c := AtomicCounter{0}
    for n := 0; n < b.N; n++ {
        c.Add(1)
    }
}

func BenchmarkAtomicCounterRead(b *testing.B) {
    c := AtomicCounter{0}
    for n := 0; n < b.N; n++ {
        c.Read()
    }
}

func BenchmarkAtomicCounterAddRead(b *testing.B) {
    c := AtomicCounter{0}
    b.RunParallel(func(pb *testing.PB) {
        for pb.Next() {
            c.Add(1)
            c.Read()
        }
    })
}
```

8. Run the `go test -bench .` command, and you will see the following output:

```
$ go test -bench .
BenchmarkAtomicCounterAdd-4 200000000 8.38 ns/op
BenchmarkAtomicCounterRead-4 1000000000 2.09 ns/op
BenchmarkAtomicCounterAddRead-4 50000000 24.5 ns/op
BenchmarkCounterAdd-4 50000000 34.8 ns/op
BenchmarkCounterRead-4 20000000 66.0 ns/op
BenchmarkCounterAddRead-4 10000000 146 ns/op
PASS
ok github.com/PacktPublishing/Go-Programming-Cookbook-Second-
Edition/chapter14/bench 10.919s
```

9. If you have copied or written your own tests, go up one directory and run `go test`. Ensure that all the tests pass.

How it works...

This recipe is an example of comparing a critical path of code. For example, sometimes your application must execute certain functionality often, maybe every call. In this case, we've written an atomic counter that can add or read values from multiple go routines.

The first solution uses `RWMutex` and `Lock` or `RLock` objects to write and read, respectively. The second uses the `atomic` package, which provides the same functionality out of the box. We make the signatures of our functions the same, so benchmarks can be reused with minor modifications and so that either can satisfy the same `atomic` integer interface.

Lastly, we write standard benchmarks for adding values and reading them. Then, we write a parallel benchmark that calls the add and read functions. The parallel benchmark will create lot of lock contention, so we expect a slowdown. Perhaps unexpectedly, the atomic package significantly outperforms `RWMutex`.

Memory allocation and heap management

Some applications can benefit a lot from optimization. Consider routers, for example, which we'll look at in a later recipe. Fortunately, the tool benchmark suite provides flags to collect a number of memory allocations as well as memory allocation size. It can be helpful to tune certain critical code paths to minimize these two attributes.

This recipe will show two approaches to writing a function that glues together strings with a space, similar to `strings.Join("a", "b", "c")`. One approach will use concatenation, while the other will use the `strings` package. We'll then compare performance and memory allocations between the two.

How to do it...

These steps cover writing and running your application:

1. From your Terminal or console application, create a new directory called `~/projects/go-programming-cookbook/chapter14/tuning` and navigate to this directory.
2. Run this command:

```
$ go mod init github.com/PacktPublishing/Go-Programming-Cookbook-
Second-Edition/chapter14/tuning
```

You should see a file called `go.mod` that contains the following:

```
module github.com/PacktPublishing/Go-Programming-Cookbook-Second-
Edition/chapter14/tuning
```

3. Copy tests from `~/projects/go-programming-cookbook-original/chapter14/tuning`, or use this as an exercise to write some of your own code!

 Note that copied tests also include benchmarks written later in this recipe.

4. Create a file called `concat.go` with the following content:

```go
package tuning

func concat(vals ...string) string {
    finalVal := ""
    for i := 0; i < len(vals); i++ {
        finalVal += vals[i]
        if i != len(vals)-1 {
            finalVal += " "
        }
    }
    return finalVal
}
```

5. Create a file called `join.go` with the following content:

```go
package tuning

import "strings"

func join(vals ...string) string {
    c := strings.Join(vals, " ")
    return c
}
```

6. Create a file called `concat_test.go` with the following content:

```go
package tuning

import "testing"

func Benchmark_concat(b *testing.B) {
```

```
        b.Run("one", func(b *testing.B) {
            one := []string{"1"}
            for i := 0; i < b.N; i++ {
                concat(one...)
            }
        })
        b.Run("five", func(b *testing.B) {
            five := []string{"1", "2", "3", "4", "5"}
            for i := 0; i < b.N; i++ {
                concat(five...)
            }
        })

        b.Run("ten", func(b *testing.B) {
            ten := []string{"1", "2", "3", "4", "5",
            "6", "7", "8", "9", "10"}
            for i := 0; i < b.N; i++ {
                concat(ten...)
            }
        })
    }
```

7. Create a file called `join_test.go` with the following content:

```
package tuning

import "testing"

func Benchmark_join(b *testing.B) {
    b.Run("one", func(b *testing.B) {
        one := []string{"1"}
        for i := 0; i < b.N; i++ {
            join(one...)
        }
    })
    b.Run("five", func(b *testing.B) {
        five := []string{"1", "2", "3", "4", "5"}
        for i := 0; i < b.N; i++ {
            join(five...)
        }
    })

    b.Run("ten", func(b *testing.B) {
        ten := []string{"1", "2", "3", "4", "5",
        "6", "7", "8", "9", "10"}
        for i := 0; i < b.N; i++ {
            join(ten...)
        }
    })
```

```
      })
   }
```

8. Run the `GOMAXPROCS=1 go test -bench=. -benchmem -benchtime=1s` command and you will see the following output:

```
$ GOMAXPROCS=1 go test -bench=. -benchmem -benchtime=1s
Benchmark_concat/one 100000000 13.6 ns/op 0 B/op 0 allocs/op
Benchmark_concat/five 5000000 386 ns/op 48 B/op 8 allocs/op
Benchmark_concat/ten 2000000 992 ns/op 256 B/op 18 allocs/op
Benchmark_join/one 200000000 6.30 ns/op 0 B/op 0 allocs/op
Benchmark_join/five 10000000 124 ns/op 32 B/op 2 allocs/op
Benchmark_join/ten 10000000 183 ns/op 64 B/op 2 allocs/op
PASS
ok github.com/PacktPublishing/Go-Programming-Cookbook-Second-
Edition/chapter14/tuning 12.003s
```

9. If you have copied or written your own tests run `go test`. Ensure that all the tests pass.

How it works...

Benchmarking helps us tune applications and do certain micro-optimizations for things such as memory allocations. When benchmarking allocations for applications with input, it's important to try a variety of input sizes to determine whether it affects allocations. We wrote two functions, `concat` and `join`. Both join together a `variadic` string parameter with spaces, so the arguments (*a, b, c*) will return the string *a b c*.

The `concat` approach accomplishes this solely through string concatenation. We create a string and append the strings in the list and spaces in a `for` loop. We omit adding a space on the last loop. The `join` function uses the internal `Strings.Join` function to accomplish this far more efficiently in most cases. It can be helpful to benchmark standard library compared to your own functions to help better understand trade-offs in performance, simplicity, and functionality.

We used sub-benchmarks to test all of our parameters, which also work excellently with table-driven benchmarks. We can see how `concat` approach results in a lot more allocations than `join`, at least for single length inputs. A good exercise would be to try this with variable-length input strings as well as a number of arguments.

Using fasthttprouter and fasthttp

Although the Go standard library provides everything you need to run an HTTP server, sometimes you need to further optimize for things such as routing and request time. This recipe will explore a library that speeds up request handling, called `fasthttp` (https://github.com/valyala/fasthttp), and a router that dramatically speeds up routing performance, called `fasthttprouter` (https://github.com/buaazp/fasthttprouter). Although `fasthttp` is quick, it's important to note that it doesn't support HTTP/2 (https://github.com/valyala/fasthttp/issues/45).

How to do it...

These steps cover writing and running your application:

1. From your Terminal or console application, create a new directory called `~/projects/go-programming-cookbook/chapter14/fastweb` and navigate to this directory.

2. Run this command:

   ```
   $ go mod init github.com/PacktPublishing/Go-Programming-Cookbook-
   Second-Edition/chapter14/fastweb
   ```

   You should see a file called `go.mod` that contains the following:

   ```
   module github.com/PacktPublishing/Go-Programming-Cookbook-Second-
   Edition/chapter14/fastweb
   ```

3. Copy tests from `~/projects/go-programming-cookbook-original/chapter14/fastweb`, or use this as an exercise to write some of your own code!

4. Create a file called `items.go` with the following content:

   ```go
   package main

   import (
       "sync"
   )

   var items []string
   var mu *sync.RWMutex

   func init() {
       mu = &sync.RWMutex{}
   ```

```
    }

    // AddItem adds an item to our list
    // in a thread-safe way
    func AddItem(item string) {
        mu.Lock()
        items = append(items, item)
        mu.Unlock()
    }

    // ReadItems returns our list of items
    // in a thread-safe way
    func ReadItems() []string {
        mu.RLock()
        defer mu.RUnlock()
        return items
    }
```

5. Create a file called `handlers.go` with the following content:

```
    package main

    import (
        "encoding/json"

        "github.com/valyala/fasthttp"
    )

    // GetItems will return our items object
    func GetItems(ctx *fasthttp.RequestCtx) {
        enc := json.NewEncoder(ctx)
        items := ReadItems()
        enc.Encode(&items)
        ctx.SetStatusCode(fasthttp.StatusOK)
    }

    // AddItems modifies our array
    func AddItems(ctx *fasthttp.RequestCtx) {
        item, ok := ctx.UserValue("item").(string)
        if !ok {
            ctx.SetStatusCode(fasthttp.StatusBadRequest)
            return
        }

        AddItem(item)
        ctx.SetStatusCode(fasthttp.StatusOK)
    }
```

6. Create a file called `main.go` with the following content:

```
package main

import (
    "fmt"
    "log"

    "github.com/buaazp/fasthttprouter"
    "github.com/valyala/fasthttp"
)

func main() {
    router := fasthttprouter.New()
    router.GET("/item", GetItems)
    router.POST("/item/:item", AddItems)

    fmt.Println("server starting on localhost:8080")
    log.Fatal(fasthttp.ListenAndServe("localhost:8080",
    router.Handler))
}
```

7. Run the `go build` command.
8. Run the `./fastweb` command:

```
$ ./fastweb
server starting on localhost:8080
```

9. From a separate Terminal, test it our with some `curl` commands:

```
$ curl "http://localhost:8080/item/hi" -X POST

$ curl "http://localhost:8080/item/how" -X POST

$ curl "http://localhost:8080/item/are" -X POST

$ curl "http://localhost:8080/item/you" -X POST

$ curl "http://localhost:8080/item" -X GET
["hi","how", "are", "you"]
```

10. The `go.mod` file may be updated and the `go.sum` file should now be present in the top-level recipe directory.
11. If you have copied or written your own tests, run `go test`. Ensure that all the tests pass.

How it works...

The `fasthttp` and `fasthttprouter` packages can do a lot to speed up the life cycle of a web request. Both packages do a lot of optimization on the hot path of code, but with the unfortunate caveat of rewriting your handlers to use a new context object rather than traditional requests and response writer.

There are a number of frameworks that have taken a similar approach to routing, and some have directly incorporated `fasthttp`. These projects keep up-to-date information in their `README` files.

Our recipe implemented a simple `list` object that we can append to with one endpoint and that will be returned by the other. The primary purpose of this recipe is to demonstrate working with parameters, setting up a router that now explicitly defines the supported methods instead of the generic `Handle` and `HandleFunc`, and to show how similar they are to standard handlers, but with many other benefits.

Other Books You May Enjoy

If you enjoyed this book, you may be interested in these other books by Packt:

Learn Data Structures and Algorithms with Golang
Bhagvan Kommadi

ISBN: 978-1-78961-850-1

- Improve application performance using the most suitable data structure and algorithm
- Explore the wide range of classic algorithms such as recursion and hashing algorithms
- Work with algorithms such as garbage collection for efficient memory management
- Analyze the cost and benefit trade-off to identify algorithms and data structures for problem solving
- Explore techniques for writing pseudocode algorithm and ace whiteboard coding in interviews
- Discover the pitfalls in selecting data structures and algorithms by predicting their speed and efficiency

Machine Learning With Go
Daniel Whitenack

ISBN: 978-1-78588-210-4

- Learn about data gathering, organization, parsing, and cleaning.
- Explore matrices, linear algebra, statistics, and probability.
- See how to evaluate and validate models.
- Look at regression, classification, clustering.
- Learn about neural networks and deep learning
- Utilize times series models and anomaly detection.
- Get to grip with techniques for deploying and distributing analyses and models.
- Optimize machine learning workflow techniques

Leave a review - let other readers know what you think

Please share your thoughts on this book with others by leaving a review on the site that you bought it from. If you purchased the book from Amazon, please leave us an honest review on this book's Amazon page. This is vital so that other potential readers can see and use your unbiased opinion to make purchasing decisions, we can understand what our customers think about our products, and our authors can see your feedback on the title that they have worked with Packt to create. It will only take a few minutes of your time, but is valuable to other potential customers, our authors, and Packt. Thank you!

Index

CPSIA information can be obtained
at www.ICGtesting.com
Printed in the USA
LVHW021723310719
626020LV00012B/391/P